MW00996668

AMERICA'S FORGOTTEN TERRORISTS

America's Forgotten Terrorists

THE RISE *and* FALL *of the* GALLEANISTS

Jeffrey D. Simon

POTOMAC BOOKS
AN IMPRINT OF THE UNIVERSITY OF NEBRASKA PRESS

Potomac Books is an imprint of the University of Nebraska Press.
Manufactured in the United States of America.

Library of Congress Cataloging-in-Publication Data
Names: Simon, Jeffrey D. (Jeffrey David), 1949– author.
Title: America's forgotten terrorists: the rise and fall of the Galleanists / Jeffrey D. Simon.
Description: Lincoln: Potomac Books, an imprint of the University of Nebraska Press, [2022] | Includes bibliographical references and index.
Identifiers: LCCN 2021037029
ISBN 9781640124042 (hardback)
ISBN 9781640125308 (epub)
ISBN 9781640125315 (pdf)
Subjects: LCSH: Galleani, Luigi, 1861–1931. | Anarchists—United States—History—20th century. | Anarchism—United States—History—20th century. | Terrorism—United States—History—20th century. | BISAC: HISTORY / United States / 20th Century | POLITICAL SCIENCE / Terrorism
Classification: LCC HX843 .S56 2022 | DDC 335/.830973—dc23
LC record available at https://lccn.loc.gov/2021037029

Set in Sabon Next by Mikala R. Kolander.
Designed by N. Putens.

CONTENTS

ILLUSTRATIONS

ACKNOWLEDGMENTS

As any author knows, writing a book is a long journey. It begins with an idea for what might be a compelling story and then continues with the research and writing. There are many people I would like to thank for making this journey exciting, fun, and gratifying.

First, I am indebted to the incredible and dedicated people who work at archives and libraries around the United States. They were indispensable in helping with the research that went into telling the story of the Galleanists. These include the following: Haley Maynard and Cate Brennan (National Archives in College Park, Maryland); William Creech (National Archives in Washington DC); Melissa Lindberg, Kelly Dyson, Frederick Plummer, Alexis Valentine, Courtney Matthews, and DeCarlos Boyd (Library of Congress); Lee Aura Bonamico (Aldrich Public Library in Barre, Vermont); Paul Carnahan and Margorie Strong (Vermont Historical Society); Andrew Rais (Vermont State Archives and Records Administration); Ruth Ruttenberg (Barre Historical Society in Barre, Vermont); Prudence Doherty and Chris Burns (Silver Special Collections Library, University of Vermont); Maria Avery (David W. Howe Memorial Library, University of Vermont); Tom McMurdo (Vermont Department of Libraries); Sue Walker, Elena Hirshman-Seidel, and Joe Coffill (Lynn Museum in Lynn, Massachusetts); Jessy Wheeler, Kim Reynolds, and Aaron Schmidt (Boston Public Library); Judith Maas (Massachusetts Historical Society); Christopher Carter and Elizabeth Bouvier (Massachusetts Supreme Judicial Court Archives); Gina Modero (New-York Historical Society); Joseph Scelsa (Italian American Museum in New York); Patrick Byrnes (Passaic County Historical Society in Paterson, New Jersey); Katie Levi and Ellen Keith (Chicago History Museum); Luke Meagher (Sandor Teszler Library Archives and Special Collections, Wofford College); Thomas White (Gumberg Library,

Duquesne University); and Diane Mizrachi (Charles E. Young Research Library, UCLA). The staff in the FBI's Freedom of Information Act division were also very helpful and provided the relevant documents and files I requested for this book.

My colleague Bennett Ramberg was an early and enthusiastic supporter of this project and offered valuable feedback and encouragement during our many discussions about the Galleanists, as did Martin Balaban, Phil Rothenberg, and Ted Zwicker. Nicholas Connizzo provided excellent research assistance regarding the years Luigi Galleani lived in Barre, Vermont. I am also indebted to Beverly Gage, J. Reid Meloy, Dennis Pluchinsky, and David Rapoport for reading the entire manuscript.

I would also like to thank the following colleagues, friends, and others who helped in many different ways: Annie Abbot, Athena Angelos, Eric Baldwin, John Barry, Theresa Hart Barry, Kamran Behnam, Mark Cacciatore, Eddie Chan, Shirley Chan, Ken Chin, Sandra Chin, Joe Cirillo, Gary Citrenbaum, MaryAnne Cliff, Reese Cuevas, Bob Cullum, Drew Cuthbertson, Mike Dash, Paul Heller, Mark Jacob, Steven Kafka, Eddie Kamiya, Janet Kamiya, Ken Karmiole, Ed Kobak, Rosanne Levin, James Lynch, Anthony McGinty, Sue Moran, John Mueller, Amy Goldberg Palacio, Niko Pfund, Adam Quinn, Silka Quintero, Margo Raines, Robin Hazard Ray, Alice Richter, Randy Roberts, Ed Rosato, Ken Ryan, William Flynn Sanders, Cyndy Foerstel Snell, Lorron Snell, Warren Spencer, Bill Teachworth, Kevin Terpstra, Griff Thomas, Donna Wald, Carole Wood, and Kenyon Zimmer.

Catherine L. Hensley of CLH Editing provided superb editing skills for the manuscript and, as usual, was a joy to work with. I would also like to thank everybody at Potomac Books and the University of Nebraska Press, especially editor Tom Swanson, for their enthusiasm for a book about the Galleanists. Thank you, as well, to copyeditor Joseph Webb and indexer Judy Staigmiller.

My incredible agent, Jill Marsal, championed this book from the beginning, and I am in her debt once again for her unwavering support. Nobody could ask for a better agent.

Finally, special thanks go to Ellen, Richard, Julie, Penya, Jack, Eric, Caleb, Oscar, Elijah, and Justine for being a very special part of my life.

AMERICA'S FORGOTTEN TERRORISTS

Introduction

It was all about the soup.

That is what the more than two hundred distinguished guests would remember from the banquet dinner on February 10, 1916, at the elegant University Club in Chicago. The occasion was to honor George Mundelein, the newly appointed archbishop of the city. Among the guests were the governor and former governor of Illinois, the former mayor of Chicago, bank presidents, judges, and Roman Catholic priests from around the country.

It wasn't long after everybody sat down that the chicken soup was served. That's when the trouble began. Many guests became violently ill, clutching their stomachs and falling to the ground. Mundelein did not eat the soup and was thus not affected. But those that were, approximately one hundred diners, began throwing up. Unbeknownst to everyone, a chef at the club had put arsenic in the soup in an attempt to kill each person at the event. But he'd miscalculated and put in too much, causing the diners to vomit it up, thereby preventing the poison from taking its full effect.[1]

A nationwide search began for the chef, Jean Crones, a German immigrant, who didn't report for work on February 11. Police searched his boardinghouse room and found six bottles of poison, a quantity of nitroglycerin, an unloaded rifle, and other weapons. They also found volumes of anarchist literature.[2]

Crones taunted the authorities while on the run, writing a letter to the *New York Times* shortly after the poison plot, which claimed he was living in a small town in New York and had dyed his dark hair white and then red. The police would never catch him, Crones said in the letter. The authorities determined it was Crones indeed who wrote the letter, as he'd provided facts only the perpetrator of the crime could have known, such as correcting the police who had said gun cotton in tin cans had been found in his room. According to Crones, it was shredded asbestos used as packing material for the vials of poison he had ordered through the mail. The signature on the letter also matched Crones's signature in the payroll receipt book at the University Club. Crones revealed that he had studied chemistry from a correspondence school, writing "I love science [and] hathe [*sic*] religion." In the most ominous passage in the letter, he threatened more killings: "I am sorry that not all or at least a 100 got killed for the world will be more happy without them. I have a good portion of energy left and some intelligence and the next time I am going to use them so my next work in that line will be a full success."[3]

There would be more letters from Crones, or by others posing as him, to the *New York Times*. In a second letter that the authorities also verified as the work of Crones, the fugitive wrote that he'd wanted to kill all those at the banquet because while "thousands of men and women are tramping the streets without food and shelter . . . the Church holds diners [*sic*] with Beluga Caviar and Champagne." He added that "those conditions are an [*sic*] scandal" and that "Christianity [is] an insult toward honesty and a Challenge to Humanity."[4]

Fears that Crones, or somebody like him, would strike again gripped the nation. Police in Chicago warned all churches to establish security measures against a possible attack. The Irish Fellowship Club used an official food taster for its annual St. Patrick's Day banquet. He tasted each dish an hour before guests were served. In New York detectives kept close watch on Catholic churches and also all entrances to police headquarters, since Crones had boasted that he'd actually visited the headquarters building after escaping from Chicago. Police feared he might try to set off a bomb there.[5]

Sightings of Crones came pouring in to police and newspapers from all over the country. He became "a sort of comedic bogeyman, stalking America from sea to shining sea." He was reportedly spotted in rural North Carolina, a mining town in Colorado, and locations in Nebraska, Missouri, and Ohio, to name just a few. He was even believed to be a cook with the American Expeditionary Forces in France during World War I. The most bizarre sighting, however, occurred in Pittsburgh in May 1916, with Crones supposedly disguised as a nun.[6]

By 1919 a frustrated Chicago Police Department had had enough of chasing down false leads and officially called off its search for Crones. The indictments against him for assault with intent to kill and murder were dropped, the authorities reserving the right to reopen the case should Crones ever be captured. He wasn't and died on a farm in Connecticut in 1932. It turned out the name "Jean Crones" was an alias. His real name was Nestor Dondoglio. And he was a member of one of the most innovative, creative, and dangerous terrorist groups in history: the Galleanists.[7]

Dondoglio's soup poisoning attempt was in line with the out-of-the-box Galleanist thinking on strategies and tactics. The group thought up and initiated attacks that nobody had done before in the United States. It was the first group to send package bombs across the country and to set off near-simultaneous bombings one night in seven cities, including Washington DC, where a member of the Galleanists was killed when the dynamite bomb he was carrying up the front steps of the home of Attorney General A. Mitchell Palmer went off prematurely. And it set off the first vehicle bombing in the United States, when a Galleanist was suspected of detonating a bomb in a horse-drawn wagon on Wall Street, killing thirty-eight people and injuring hundreds of others. This remained the worst domestic terrorist attack in America until the 1995 Oklahoma City bombing that killed 168 people.

Who, then, were the Galleanists? The group's leader, Luigi Galleani, was a charismatic Italian immigrant who arrived in America in 1901 at the age of forty after living a life of anarchist agitation in Italy, France, and Switzerland. He spent more than five years in prison and exile in Italy before escaping in 1900 from Pantelleria, an island off the coast of Sicily. Once he was in the United States, his voluminous writings and spellbinding speeches won him a loyal following among many Italian immigrants who were experiencing discrimination, low wages, and long working hours (for those able to find jobs) instead of the better life they'd hoped for when they came to America.[8]

Those who heard Galleani speak described him as a "forceful orator," a "most effective debater," and the "soul of the movement." One anarchist recalled that "you hung on every word when he spoke," while another said that "he spoke directly to my heart." Still others said that "he expressed what I wanted to say but couldn't because I didn't have the words" and "you heard Galleani speak and you were ready to shoot the first policeman you saw." William J. Flynn, chief of the U.S. Secret Service during Galleani's time in America and then the director of the Bureau of Investigation (the predecessor to the Federal Bureau of Investigation), described him as "one of the most difficult individuals the United States Secret Service has ever had to deal with because he was the brainiest."[9]

Like many terrorist groups today, the Galleanists were decentralized, with several autonomous cells scattered throughout the country. There were probably never more than fifty or sixty hard-core members, but Galleani's supporters, who worked in construction, mining, factories, and other manual labor jobs, numbered in the thousands. It was not, however, a unified movement. There were rivalries and disputes over doctrines, tactics, and other matters. The different cells had names such as "Autonomy," "Demolition," "The Insurgents," "The Eleventh of November" (named after the date in 1887 when four anarchists were executed for the Haymarket Square affair of May 4, 1886, an incident in which a bomb was tossed into a column of policemen in Chicago, killing seven officers), "The Twenty-Ninth of July" (named after the date in 1900 when an anarchist, Gaetano Bresci, assassinated King Umberto I of Italy), and "The Bresci Group."[10]

Galleani did not view his movement as an organization. He wrote that "we are opposed to those anarchists who call themselves organizationalists, whether they wish to organize an anarchist party politically, or whether, in order to strengthen it, they aim to base it on labour organizations as they exist now, or on other ones they might organize that correspond more to their aims." Yet as one observer remarked about the Galleanists, "The so-called anti-organizationalists were the best organized group." Another noted that the Galleanist "mini-war against American capitalism and government was probably the most extensive, best organized, and carefully planned operation of its type ever undertaken by Italian anarchists anywhere."[11]

Although Galleani did not necessarily direct or order the numerous terrorist attacks his group committed, he certainly inspired them. Just like the Islamic State of Iraq and Syria (ISIS) used the internet and social media to urge individuals anywhere to take violent action against the "infidels," Galleani used his speeches and writings in his newspaper *Cronaca Sovversiva* (Subversive chronicle) to inspire others to engage in "propaganda by deed." He even published a bomb manual for his followers to use in their war against the government, capitalists, religious institutions, and other perceived enemies.[12]

From the time Galleani arrived in the United States until he was deported in 1919, America was undergoing fundamental changes. It was a period of "profound discontent, in which many Americans began to decry the economic system as a perversion of justice, run for the benefit of the few." These years also "saw the rise of . . . militant groups as well: socialists, anarchists, and other revolutionaries dedicated not to the reform of capitalism but to its abolition." The Galleanists were at the forefront of the insurrectionary anarchist movement in the United States during this period. Galleani viewed anarchism as "the struggle for a condition of society where the only link among individuals is solidarity, basically the solidarity of material and moral interests, which leads to the elimination of vicious daily competitions between individuals and among peoples." He wrote that "whereas the bourgeois regime is the domination of a majority over the minority, we aspire to realize *the autonomy of the individual within the freedom of association*, the independence of his thought, of his life, of his development, of his destiny. [Emphasis in the original.]"[13]

The Galleanists became the prime targets of the Department of Justice, and the DOJ named Galleani "the leading anarchist in the United States" and *Cronaca Sovversiva* "the most rabid, seditious and anarchistic sheet ever published in this country." The bombings in seven cities on the night of June 2, 1919, including at the home of Attorney General Palmer, eventually led the government to retaliate with the Palmer Raids, a roundup of alien radicals throughout the country with the aim of deportation. Historian Paul Avrich notes that at "no time in living memory had there been such a ruthless invasion of civil rights. Roundups of innocent people, detention without warrant, denial of counsel, secret testimony of undercover informants, seizure of property, extortion of confessions—such practices were not easily tolerated by those who cherished American traditions of personal liberty and fair play."[14]

Galleani, along with several of his close aides, had already been deported to Italy by the time the Palmer Raids began in November 1919. Many Galleanists fled the country before they could be arrested. By the summer of 1920 it appeared that the Galleanists were finished. The government believed it had finally won this early "war on terrorism." Yet while the group was no longer the force and threat it had been the year before, in the world of terrorism it does not take many extremists to make an impact. That was demonstrated on September 16, 1920, when one of the last remaining members of the group, Mario Buda, was suspected of perpetrating the Wall Street bombing. The motive appeared to be retaliation for the murder indictment of Nicola Sacco and Bartolomeo Vanzetti, two members of the Galleanists, that had been issued less than a week earlier. Buda fled the country before he could be identified and arrested.[15]

Despite the prominence of the Galleanists in the history of violence in America, they are a forgotten group. With a few notable exceptions, there is hardly a mention of them in most books on terrorism. Yet they foreshadowed much of what is seen today: alienation and frustration among segments of a community being transformed into the birth of a militant extremist movement; the planning and implementation of simultaneous, innovative attacks, the level of violence continually increasing; use of the media to their advantage; the taunting of the authorities with publicized threats and subsequent attacks; and the governmental labeling of terrorist violence as an "act of war."[16]

Galleani once wrote, "No act of rebellion is useless: no act of rebellion is harmful." He and his followers believed they were on a mission to change not only America but also the world. They chose violence as the means to achieve this. The rise and fall of the Galleanists is a journey into a turbulent time in U.S. history but one that is still relevant today as we deal with the never-ending threat of terrorism.[17]

1 The Soul of the Movement

Pantelleria is a remote, volcanic Italian island located sixty miles south of Sicily and forty miles east of Tunisia. It's known as "the black pearl of the Mediterranean" for its black lava rocks and deep blue seas. Truman Capote once described it as "a chilling beauty." Fashion designer Giorgio Armani has a villa there, and Madonna, Sting, Julia Roberts, and Martin Scorsese are among the celebrities who've stayed there or have homes on the island. A five-star luxury hotel with twenty suites opened in 2016. Pantelleria has become a favorite place for the jet-setters.[1]

In the late 1880s, however, Pantelleria was the last place on earth you'd want to be. Those who went there had no choice; they'd been banished by the Italian government. The island was a penal colony where many anarchists and other agitators who had completed prison sentences on mainland Italy were sent. This policy was known as *domicilio coatto*, or internal exile. Being exiled to Pantelleria was considered one of the harshest punishments one could receive. At the time the island was sparsely populated, poor, and isolated.[2]

It is not surprising that Luigi Galleani eventually wound up in Pantelleria. Born on August 12, 1861, to a middle-class family in Vercelli, a city in the Piedmont region of northern Italy, Galleani was first drawn to anarchism in his late teens. His father, an elementary school teacher, pressured him to study law at the University of Turin, something Galleani did not want to do. He would later describe his father as the "son of a soldier who has the cult of authority in his blood." He never graduated, instead becoming an outspoken militant railing against capitalism and government. He began writing articles in the early 1880s for democratic, Socialist, and anarchist publications in Piedmont and Tuscany. By the late 1880s he was also active in the Italian labor movement, participating in several national congresses of the Italian Workers' Party and leading a number of strikes. He fled to Paris in 1889 to avoid arrest by the Italian authorities, but he soon ran into trouble there too. He was imprisoned for four months and then expelled from France for participating in the 1890 May Day demonstration in Paris.[3]

Galleani's next stop was Switzerland, where he first worked as a railroad laborer in Geneva and then assisted the exiled French geographer and anarchist Elisée Reclus in the preparation of his classic, nineteen-volume *Nouvelle géographie universelle* (New universal geography) by compiling statistics on Central America. Galleani greatly admired and was influenced by Reclus, who was a proponent of revolutionary violence. Reclus once wrote, "Against injustice we call for revolution. But justice is only a word, they tell us. What exists is the right of force! . . . Either justice is the human ideal in which case we demand it for all; or it is only force that governs society and therefore we will use force against our enemies. Either freedom of equals or the law of retaliation." Galleani benefited from being exposed to the extensive network of anarchists and scientists Reclus knew around the world. This "provided a great source of enrichment and knowledge for Galleani."[4]

Galleani also worked with students at the University of Geneva to arrange a celebration in honor of the Haymarket prisoners. Four had been hanged in Chicago in 1887 for conspiracy to commit murder after a bomb had been thrown into a group of policemen, killing seven officers and four bystanders, on May 4, 1886. The policemen had been trying to break up a protest by thousands of people in Haymarket Square upset with them for firing into a crowd of striking workers the day before at the McCormick harvester plant. Galleani's participation in the memorial celebration resulted in him being expelled from Switzerland as a dangerous agitator.[5]

Galleani then returned to Italy and continued to get in trouble with the authorities. He made propaganda tours of northern and central Italy early in 1891, delivering spellbinding speeches that mesmerized audiences. Police reports about Galleani highlighted his charisma and leadership abilities, one stating that "he is always the mind that thinks, that advises, that organizes; his comrades are his limbs." His anarchist philosophy was also described by the police as follows: "He is a very ardent advocate of that anti-social existence in which each person has a law of their own. According to him there should be no restrictions of any kind, collective and private property should be eliminated, family and morality should be abolished, each person should be free to think and act as they wish." In one speech Galleani exhorted the audience to "get hold of a rifle, a dagger, a revolver, by means of theft if you have no money." In late March 1892 he was arrested and after a trial sentenced to three months in prison for, in a public lecture, encouraging the unemployed to rebel.[6]

Despite all the trouble Galleani got into during his years of activism throughout Europe, he managed to avoid incurring long prison sentences. That changed in June 1894. He had been arrested the previous December in Genoa, Italy, along with thirty-four other men, and charged with conspiracy to commit crimes "against the administration of justice, or public trust, or public safety, or good customs and family order or against people or property." The Genoa police viewed the men as a dangerous group encouraged by Galleani to be "ready to rise up at the opportune moment." This was a particularly apprehensive time for the Italian authorities, as peasants throughout Sicily had attacked private and public property in December 1893, an event known as the Fasci Siciliani uprising. Italian radicals had earlier that year organized workers and peasants into several *fasci*, or primitive trade unions and mutual-benefit societies dedicated to workers' rights and helping villagers protect their land from enclosure. The Italian government declared a state of siege and sent forty thousand troops to Sicily in early January 1894, eventually leading to the dissolution of all *fasci*.[7]

Galleani's trial did not begin until May, when he and the other accused men were brought from prison to the courthouse in police wagons, handcuffed and accompanied by a platoon of soldiers and military police. That show of force didn't intimidate the crowd that had gathered outside—the crowd applauded the prisoners. Inside, Galleani denounced the court when interrogated, stating it was biased and only interested in defending the bourgeoisie. He said he was a revolutionary anarchist and that the real wrongdoers were those conducting the trial. This naturally angered the prosecutor, who stopped the proceedings and ordered Galleani and the other men back to prison. A scuffle then broke out among the accused, the attorneys, the military police, and family members and sympathizers.[8]

The trial resumed in June, with Galleani and the other prisoners locked in cages and guarded by military police with fixed bayonets. He and twenty of the accused were convicted, but whereas the others were sentenced to prison terms ranging from six to sixteen months, Galleani received the harshest sentence: three years of imprisonment. Then, at the end of this term, he was sent to Pantelleria to serve two more years under police supervision. This *domicilio coatto*, a punishment given to many anarchists, sometimes had the opposite effect from what the authorities may have been hoping for. As scholar Nunzio Pernicone writes, "*Domicilio coatto* was the hammer and the anvil that forged a stronger generation of anarchists, intensifying their hatred of the state and deepening their belief in the righteousness of their cause. No amount of suffering, it seemed, could sway their convictions."[9]

Galleani arrived in Pantelleria in late November 1896 and was first placed in one of the shared dormitories of the dark, hot, and damp-walled Barbacane Castle. His only possessions were a bed frame consisting of two wooden planks, a straw mattress, and a blanket, along with a small allowance to enable him to purchase bread and beans. All prisoners were required to be in the dormitories from 6:30 p.m. until 6:00 a.m., at which time they were allowed to walk around the island. Always the activist, Galleani spoke to the island's residents during his daytime walks. They were poor and receptive to his anarchist philosophy. This alarmed the authorities, who transferred him in early 1897 to another small penal colony, on Favignana, off the coast of Sicily. There Galleani tried to organize the workers of the island, who were mainly quarrymen. This led to him being transferred to yet another island prison. Galleani would continue over the next year to be shuffled from one island prison to another, including Pantelleria a few more times, as the authorities worried about his ability to influence those he came in contact with.[10]

In August 1898 Galleani was once again returned to Pantelleria, this time for health reasons. He had developed stomach problems caused by the impurity of the water on the other islands. Pantelleria, by contrast, had good spring water. The prisoners had also earlier won the right to have their own lodgings, something Galleani had taken advantage of during one of his previous periods of confinement there. Galleani's house was a three-room dwelling situated at the top of a hill overlooking the sea. He enjoyed working as a private teacher, instructing many of the island's children, providing lessons in politics, sociology, sciences, and language. The inhabitants referred to him as "the professor." The father of one of his pupils eventually provided Galleani with an even more spacious house.[11]

Meanwhile, a Socialist deputy proposed that Galleani and other anarchists in internal exile be put up as candidates for Parliament on the Socialist Party ticket as a way to publicize their plight and at least enable some of them to leave their confinement. They all declined the offer, "asserting once and for all their firm refusal to compromise, or in any way distort, their opposition to the State—a fundamental tenet of their convictions as anarchists." The prisoners published on November 2, 1899, a special newspaper they called *I Morti* (The dead), in which Galleani eloquently explained the anarchists' position in a front-page editorial titled "Faith Remains Unchanged":

> If in order to leave here we must submit before a banner that is not ours, if our liberation must be the result of a compromise, if we must leave these shoals counting among our days here even one of which we must be ashamed, if we must return as apostates, diminished, stunted, transfigured, after having burned incense of false adoration before idols which we repudiate—better to remain! . . . Alone, with the truth, against all the world, even in a garret, that is a sweet and consoling solitude.[12]

It was Pantelleria where Galleani met the love of his life. Maria Rallo was married with two children, a son and an infant daughter, when they met and fell in love in the fall of 1899. "We were under the surveillance of ferocious guards," Galleani would later write to a friend. "She was beautiful and kind and we loved each other despite [this] terrible surveillance. . . . I love her with all of my strength." She and Galleani would have four more children, two daughters and two sons, together in the ensuing years.[13]

Even though he was nearing the end of his sentence, Galleani decided to escape from Pantelleria in February 1900 in a boat captained by the father of one of his students. He knew that he would be placed under continual surveillance and not allowed to engage in political activity if he returned to mainland Italy after serving his sentence. He first landed in Tunis, used a fake passport to enter Malta, and then traveled to Alexandria in Egypt. Maria, several months pregnant with their first child, remained in Pantelleria and joined him with her two children a few months later. But soon after their first child was born in June, health and financial problems plagued the family. Galleani contracted malaria and required three months of extensive treatment, including large doses of quinine that aggravated previous stomach problems and left him exhausted. It also caused damage to his eyesight. For a long time he was unable to walk and also suffered from heart problems. Maria was hospitalized due to health issues soon after giving birth. The family had little money and lacked food and clothing. They went into debt and had to sell their personal possessions. "We are in a mess up to our necks," a dejected Galleani wrote to a friend. "We have nothing, nothing, nothing."[14]

To make matters worse, Galleani was arrested in Egypt during the summer of 1900 following the assassination of King Umberto I of Italy by an anarchist. Even though Galleani had not been involved in the assassination, he was still arrested, probably due to his fame and reputation as an anarchist. Italy requested his extradition, but after protests from the Italian expatriate community in Egypt, as well as the local press, the Egyptian authorities released him.[15]

Galleani eventually found a temporary job in Alexandria working at a legal firm. He also helped create a free university in the city and then another one in Cairo when he moved there from Alexandria. The idea was not to have these institutions be exclusively anarchist but rather "open to the progressive world in general, over which anarchist content and methods could exert a certain influence."[16]

While these creative endeavors gave Galleani satisfaction, he was still worried about his financial future. He wanted to provide economic stability for his family and did not see that happening in Egypt. When he was offered the editor's job at the leading Italian anarchist periodical in the United States at that time, *La Questione Sociale* (The social question), in Paterson, New Jersey, he accepted. After first stopping to visit fellow anarchists in Britain, Galleani and his family set sail for the United States, arriving on October 10, 1901.[17]

Galleani was now forty years old and showing no signs of slowing down. The "soul of the movement," as some described him, was ready for new challenges. It would not take long for him to make his presence felt in his new country.[18]

Welcome to America

When Galleani arrived in the United States, the country was still reeling from the assassination on September 6, 1901, of President William McKinley. The assassin, Leon Czolgosz, had wanted to join anarchist movements but had been rebuffed by other anarchists who viewed him suspiciously as a possible government agent. He asked too many questions and wanted to be introduced to other anarchists around the country. He also advocated violence that not all the anarchists in the United States prescribed.[19]

Czolgosz, who may have been mentally ill, was tried and convicted in a two-day trial that began on September 23. He was sentenced to death and executed by electric chair one month later. The assassination of McKinley by an anarchist was exploited by the new president, Theodore Roosevelt, to justify a war on anarchism. He denounced anarchism as "a crime against the whole human race" in his first State of the Union address in December 1901. He urged "all mankind . . . to band against the anarchist" and further stated that an anarchist

> is not the victim of social or political injustice. There are no wrongs to remedy in his case. The cause of his criminality is to be found in his

> own evil passions and in the evil conduct of those who urge him on, not in any failure by others or by the state to do justice to him or his. He is a malefactor and nothing else. He is in no sense, in no shape or way, a product of social conditions. . . . Anarchist speeches, writings, and meetings are essentially seditious and treasonable.[20]

Congress contributed to the antianarchist sentiment in the country by passing an immigration law in March 1903 that excluded from American shores "anarchists, or persons who believe in or advocate the overthrow by force or violence of the Government of the United States, or of all government, or of all forms of law, or the assassination of public officials." Galleani would likely have been prevented from entering the United States had the law been in effect when he emigrated from London in 1901.[21]

Italian immigration to America grew rapidly from the end of the nineteenth century to the beginning of the twentieth. Between 1820 and 1870, fewer than twenty-five thousand Italian immigrants came to America. By the 1880s, however, there were three hundred thousand Italian immigrants in the country. This rose to six hundred thousand during the 1890s and to more than two million in the next decade. By 1920, when immigration from Italy began to decline, there were more than four million Italian immigrants in the United States, representing more than 10 percent of America's foreign-born population.[22]

Discrimination against Italians was rampant. They were portrayed in the media as "ignorant, insular, superstitious, prone to crime, ignorant of the law, ignorant of democracy and prone to righting wrongs with personal vendettas and acts of violence." Galleani believed that Italian immigrants in many countries were scorned in part due to the way they looked. "Americans and English, Polish and Slavs, Germans and French are *whites*," Galleani wrote, "the blacks—there is no possible doubt—are *negroes*. The *Italians*? . . . The Italians are not more black, but they are still not white, they are *Italians*, something between the white and the black." Galleani further argued that Italians were viewed as less than human by others: "The *dago* is not only the foreigner or the barbarian, he is . . . in the anthropological classification, the bottom rung; something of a hybrid between a man and a gorilla. [Emphasis in the original.]"[23]

Italians were also victims of violence in America, with approximately fifty lynchings targeting Italians taking place from 1890 to 1920. The largest one occurred in New Orleans on March 14, 1891, when eleven Italians were murdered by a mob seeking revenge for the killing of the city's chief of police, David Hennessey, several months earlier. As he lay dying, Hennessey reportedly said it was "dagoes" who had gunned him down. Nine Italians were tried for the crime, with the jury acquitting six of them and unable to reach a verdict on the other three. All the men were then returned to the city's prison because of outstanding charges against them. The next day a mob, after hearing fiery speeches by angry public officials and others, stormed the prison and shot nine Italian prisoners and dragged two others outside, where they hanged them from lampposts. Not all of the Italians killed were the ones acquitted or deadlocked by the jury.[24]

The media approved of the mob violence. An editorial in the *New York Times* stated the following: "These sneaking and cowardly Sicilians, the descendants of bandits and assassins, who have transported to this country the lawless passions, the cut-throat practices, and the oath-bound societies of their native country, are to us a pest without mitigations. Our own rattlesnakes are as good citizens as they. . . . Lynch law was the only course open to the people of New Orleans to stay the issue of a new license to the Mafia to continue its bloody practices."[25]

There were no lynchings in Paterson, New Jersey, where Galleani settled after immigrating to the United States. That city had become a center for Italian anarchists who owned private libraries, where they distributed pamphlets and, as noted, published the influential anarchist periodical *La Questione Sociale*. There were also anarchist taverns and clubs that hosted distinguished speakers from around the world.[26]

Paterson gained worldwide notoriety on July 29, 1900. A young Italian immigrant working there, Gaetano Bresci, had returned to Italy and assassinated King Umberto I. Bresci had been employed as a weaver in one of Paterson's numerous silk mills, where many Italian immigrants worked because they'd gotten experience in that industry back home. Many of them also, like Bresci, were either already anarchists before they came to the United States or had been exposed to anarchist ideology in their home country.[27]

Bresci's path to anarchism began, like Galleani's, during his teenage years in Italy. Unlike Galleani, however, who grew up in a middle-class family and was university-educated, Bresci, born on November 11, 1869, in the small village of Coiano on the periphery of Prato in the region of Tuscany, started working as a factory apprentice when he was only eleven years old to help his family make ends meet. His parents owned a small piece of land where they grew grain, olives, and grapes, but their economic condition worsened around 1880, when the import of cheaper grain from the United States greatly reduced the incomes of peasant landowners. The prices for their crops declined, and the family lived in relative poverty for several years afterward.[28]

By the age of fifteen, Bresci was a fully qualified silk weaver. He also became active in an anarchist group in Prato; his attraction to anarchism stemmed from the economic hard times he and his family experienced. For that he blamed Italy's social order and the exploitation he observed and experienced as a factory worker. He served a brief prison sentence, only fifteen days, in 1892 for contempt and insubordination to the police. That got him labeled a "dangerous anarchist" by the Italian authorities. He served a longer sentence in *domicilio coatto* on an island prison in 1895 after helping to organize a strike of textile workers in Prato. He was released, however, along with other prisoners one year later following a royal amnesty in May 1896.[29]

Bresci remained in Italy for a few more years before deciding to immigrate to the United States. He first settled in West Hoboken in 1898 and began working at a local silk factory. He found a better-paying job at another silk factory in nearby Paterson one year later. Meanwhile, he had met and married an Irish-American seamstress, Sophie Knieland, who gave birth to their daughter. They lived in West Hoboken, but Bresci stayed at a hotel in Paterson during the workweek and returned to his family on the weekends.[30]

Shortly after his arrival in the United States, Bresci joined an anarchist group in Paterson, Gruppo Diritto all'Esistenza (Right to an Existence Group); regularly attended its meetings; and read *La Questione Sociale*. When he learned of a massacre of protesters in Milan that had occurred on May 7, 1898, he vowed to take revenge. Italian troops under the command of General Fiorenzo Bava-Beccaris had fired on demonstrators who were protesting rising food prices. At least 118 people were killed, and hundreds more were wounded. King Umberto I approved of Bava-Beccaris's actions and even awarded him Italy's highest decoration, the Great Cross of the Order of Savoy. He also praised him for "the great service you have rendered to our institutions and to civilization" in a personal telegram he sent to the general. "When in Paterson I read of the events in Milan, where they even used cannons, I wept with rage and prepared myself for vengeance," Bresci would later say at his trial in Italy. "I thought of the king who awarded a prize to those who carried out the massacres, and I became convinced that he deserved death."[31]

Bresci put his plan for revenge into action two years later, purchasing a revolver at a Paterson hardware store for $7 and a tourist discount ticket to France, where the Paris Exposition was being held, for $27. He sailed for Le Havre in May 1900 and eventually made his way to Italy, telling nobody about his plans. He stayed with his brother in Coiano and then with his sister in Castel San Pietro Terme near Bologna before traveling to Milan, where he learned that Umberto I was scheduled to attend a gymnastics exhibition in nearby Monza.[32]

At the event, after distributing prizes to the athletes and making a short speech to the crowd, the king returned to his carriage. The enthusiastic crowd, however, rushed from their seats to the carriage, preventing its departure. When the carriage finally began to move, Bresci stood on his seat about twelve feet away from Umberto I and fired three shots, fatally wounding the king. Enraged spectators descended on Bresci, kicking and beating him with canes. The Carabinieri (national police force) and the Fire Brigade intervened and arrested Bresci, who told them, "I did not kill Umberto. I have killed a king. I have killed a Head of State."[33]

In a one-day trial held a month later, Bresci was convicted and sentenced to life imprisonment, as there was no death penalty in Italy. He was first held for a short time in a Milan prison but was then transferred to a fortress prison on the island of Elba. There he was held in a subterranean cell below the water level in the prison tower, despite that type of confinement having been banned by prison reforms legislated a few years earlier. Prison authorities decided to transfer Bresci to another prison, though, before news of his irregular treatment became public, something that could lead to protests.[34]

He did not fare much better at his new prison on Santo Stefano, located among the remote Pontine Islands. He was held with his feet shackled in a ten-by-ten-foot cell isolated in the highest tier of the prison. There were two adjacent rooms, where guards watched him twenty-four hours a day. Despite this surveillance, prison authorities announced on May 22, 1901, that Bresci had committed suicide by hanging himself with a towel tied to the bars of his cell window. Many people, however, believed he was killed by his jailors. The new king of Italy, Victor Emmanuel III, son of the slain Umberto I, responded when informed of Bresci's death, "It is perhaps the best thing that could have happened to the unhappy man."[35]

Shortly after Umberto I's assassination, Paterson was labeled the "capital of world anarchism" by police and newspapers. Authorities believed there had been a conspiracy hatched in Paterson among anarchists to assassinate Umberto, and many people were arrested. No evidence of such a conspiracy was ever uncovered. The New Jersey Supreme Court launched an inquiry into the assassination and found that "no anarchist plot existed in Paterson or West Hoboken for the assassination of the late King Humbert [Umberto] of Italy."[36]

One person who felt the brunt of the postassassination crackdown on anarchists was Bresci's wife, Sophie. She was not an anarchist, and Bresci had never tried to recruit her to become one. Though she knew that her husband was an anarchist, she did not understand what that meant. She told investigators after the assassination that he was an anarchist "in the same way that one is a Catholic or a Protestant." Sophie also did not know about his plans to assassinate Umberto I. He had told her that he had to go back to Italy in order to sell the house and land that his recently deceased parents had left to him and his siblings. He also told her that it would not be a good idea for her and their daughter to come along since Sophie was pregnant with their second child and their daughter was too young to travel.[37]

Despite the fact that there was no evidence linking Sophie to the assassination or to any type of anarchist activity, the mayor of Cliffside Park, New Jersey, where she had moved after the assassination and opened a boardinghouse, asked her to leave in order "to prevent future trouble." The house was placed under police surveillance. She refused to leave at first, but the hostility from the city and the community, as well as the continual police surveillance, became too much for her, and she eventually moved to Chicago. "I suppose that I will be hounded in every place I go, and branded as an Anarchist," she said. "People would like to see me driven to the poorhouse and left there to die."[38]

Bresci's assassination of Umberto I was met with criticism in some anarchist circles. Errico Malatesta, a leading anarchist of the time, did not see the value in killing the king. "We do not believe in the right to punish; we reject the idea of revenge as a barbarous sentiment," he wrote. "We have no intention of being either executioners or avengers. It seems to us that the role of liberators and peacemakers is more noble and positive." Malatesta was also concerned that assassinations by anarchists could "harm the very cause they were intended to serve."[39]

Others, however, enthusiastically approved of Bresci's actions. "In the flash of Bresci's pistol shot," wrote another prominent anarchist, Voltairine de Cleyre, "the whole world for a moment saw the tragic figure of the Italian people, starved, stunted, crippled, huddled, degraded, murdered; and at the same moment that their teeth chattered with fear, they came and asked the Anarchists to explain themselves. And hundreds of thousands of people read more in those few days than they had ever read of the idea before."[40]

Galleani also gave his stamp of approval to the assassination, writing years later that "the humble weaver from Prato rose alone above the general indolence, and alone faced the symbols of so much infamy. With a stroke he put back history, wayward and arrested, back on the path of its future, towards its destiny. That gesture spoke to the confused masses."[41]

Speaking to and writing for the masses was something that Galleani relished doing. Already having a reputation as one of the leading European anarchists, Galleani appealed to the large Italian population in Paterson once he arrived in the fall of 1901, with his articles in *La Questione Sociale* and his speeches (always in Italian). The population then of Paterson was about one hundred thousand, with ten thousand being Italian immigrants. Of that population about a thousand people subscribed to *La Questione*

Sociale. Had Galleani stuck to just writing, he probably could have stayed a long time in Paterson. He had a job, a family, and supporters.[42]

Events in 1902, however, forced Galleani to go on the run yet again. That year was a particularly brutal one for Paterson. First there was a massive fire in February that destroyed five hundred buildings, including city hall and the entire business district. One of the buildings burnt out by the fire contained the printing office of *La Questione Sociale*. Then in March the Passaic River flooded parts of the city, destroying bridges, homes, and buildings and causing about $1 million in damages.[43]

It was a strike by silk workers, though, that proved to be the most significant event for Galleani that year. Paterson was known as "Silk City" because it was the largest producer of silk in the United States. In late April silk dyers went on strike for better wages, shorter hours, and better working conditions. This included a workweek of no more than fifty-five hours, five-minute wash periods before lunch and the end of the day, and a five-year employment contract. They formed a union they named the United Dyers, Helpers, and Finishers of America. The number of silk dyers on strike reached 3,700.[44]

Galleani became involved with the Italian-speaking branch of the movement, even though he was supposedly opposed to organizations, including labor unions, believing that power in such a group would be held by a minority serving its own interests and not that of its members. He saw organizations of any kind as "the antithesis of anarchism." Nevertheless, one observer later noted that Galleani was "the soul of the famous silk strike of 1902." Two anarchists from New York, William McQueen and Rudolf Grossmann, were brought to Paterson to work with the English- and German-speaking strikers, respectively.[45]

The goal of the anarchist leaders was to wrest control of the movement from the more moderate elements and "to escalate the strike, which presently sought limited gains . . . into a full-fledged general strike which would generate a revolutionary opportunity." But things weren't going well for the strikers. Efforts to establish solidarity with Pennsylvania dyers failed. As it turned out, Pennsylvania mills were subcontracted to dye the silk from Paterson. Workers began to trickle back to their mills. Something needed to be done to galvanize the workers once again and keep them unified. A mass meeting to boost morale was held on the morning of June 18 at Belmont Park in Haledon, a close suburb of Paterson.[46]

The two main speakers were McQueen and Galleani. A local newspaper reported that McQueen's speech was "rather mild." Galleani's speech in Italian, however, was electric: "A clique, a thirst for gold and human blood, has been exploiting your labor for many years, comrades. For them: wealth, luxury; for you: misery, shame. And while your veins are drained, the coffers of your bosses fill with money. With that hoard, your masters build other fortunes; and if it transpired, alas! They buy the consciences of these miserable (scabs) whom they pay to slit your throats. Will you let them slit your throats? [Parentheses in original translation.]"[47]

Galleani was just warming up: "Look at your wives; they were pretty, brimming with health. The work to which the bosses have condemned them has made them pale, emaciated, anemic. Look at your children; you dream of seeing them grow up handsome, affectionate, intelligent: the factory is there to brutalize them. Look at yourselves. Weren't you full of hope as you left a homeland crushed beneath a medieval tyranny? Alas! In this country of so-called progress, you are equally foresworn to another tyranny equally crushing."[48]

A vote was taken on extending the dye workers' strike to a general strike by all branches of the silk industry. "Nobody voted in the negative: no one dared to do so," the *New York Times* reported. The strike leaders, including Galleani, then huddled together to decide on a course of action to report back to the crowd. But Galleani soon emerged from the impromptu meeting, waving his cane in the air and urging the crowd to follow him out of the park and toward the silk mills. The crowd of several thousand people did just that, rushing down the streets, with Galleani at the lead. They were joined by scores of other workers and supporters as they headed to Paterson's silk mills.[49]

The first mill they reached was the Columbia Mill, only a quarter mile from the park. The striking workers battered down the locked doors and shattered the windows with stones. Twenty young women who were on the first floor of the mill stood firm and threatened to fight the strikers who had now entered the mill. The silk weavers who worked on the second floor ran down to assist the women. One of the mill workers took command and, while denouncing the anarchists, directed his coworkers to leave the mill.[50]

The strikers' next target was the Cedar Cliff Mill a half mile away. Word of the approaching crowd had reached the mill, and some of the workers had begun to leave. Once the crowd arrived, Galleani and others stood at the door and ordered those who were leaving to hurry up. One young woman passed Galleani on the way out and slapped him across the face after he pushed her. Galleani's supporters leapt forward toward the woman, but the men from the mill ran to her aid and took her away.[51]

Many more mills were attacked that day, and a shooting occurred between the police and the crowd at the J. A. Hall and Company factory. Galleani was wounded in the face. Around this time the mayor of Paterson, John Hinchcliffe, called upon firemen to aid the police. The rioting tapered off by the end of the day. Hinchcliffe criticized the chief of police, Frederick Graul, for not preventing the violence. He said the anarchist leaders should never have been allowed to address the meeting in Belmont Park, to which Graul replied that "hindsight is better than foresight." The mayor suspended Graul the next day.[52]

Ten people were reported wounded in the rioting. The moderate leader of the strike committee, James McGrath, was seen in tears over the day's events. He denounced the anarchists and said he would resign from the committee. The National Guard was called out and kept Paterson under martial law until July 2. Galleani's hope that the silk dyers' strike would expand to a general strike was dashed. "The dyers' helpers' strike is lost now," the *New York Times* reported. "There was a disposition on the part of the other branches of the silk trade to help them in a pinch if the strike became desperate; but to-day the strikers attacked those who might have helped them, and none were more bitter in their denunciations this evening than the leaders of the weavers, twisters, and other branches of the silk trade. The American dyers' helpers also say privately that they are through and that they will go back to work even at the terms of the company, rather than be associated longer with the element that broke loose to-day." All the mills soon resumed operations, and the strike was declared over a week later.[53]

Galleani, McQueen, and Grossmann were all indicted for inciting to riot, rioting, atrocious assault, and malicious mischief. McQueen and

Grossmann were eventually tried and convicted. Each was sentenced to five years of hard labor, despite the fact that there was evidence that Grossmann had not even been present at the rally in Belmont Park and that McQueen had tried to stop the crowd from becoming violent. Nevertheless, the *Paterson Daily Press* gloated about the verdicts, writing that "the chief regret felt in Paterson is that Galleani was not here to have a dose of Jersey justice administered to him also."[54]

Galleani had no intention of taking his chances with "Jersey justice." He fled to Canada and stayed with a friend in Montreal. "Once again I've been outlawed," he wrote in July 1902 to Jacques Gross, a close friend in Europe. He described the situation in Paterson after the riots: "The bourgeoisie and the city are furious, they want our heads and the application of new laws against anarchists. . . . They consider me the person responsible for the movement and the riots, particularly as several thousand Italians took part in the demonstration. Luckily I have escaped and I can wait in the hope that the brutal impulsiveness of the moment will fade somewhat over time."[55]

That "brutal impulsiveness of the moment," however, was still there a year later. The *Paterson Evening News* conjectured in July 1903 that Galleani would probably never voluntarily return to Paterson to stand trial since he "left behind him some very unpleasant memories. It is not likely he will come back, even if the chance were offered him, for the vengeance of the courts is not all which awaits him."[56]

Galleani continued to edit and write articles for *La Questione Sociale* but was not happy in his new country. "I've been here for three days," he wrote to Gross shortly after arriving in Montreal, "and I detest this city. . . . I'd like to leave, but to where?" The separation from his family was difficult for him. Maria and the children remained in Paterson until December 1902, when he'd earned enough money working in a cigar factory to finally send for them. He was also getting bored. The only reading materials he could find in Montreal were religious publications. For the restless, energetic, and passionate Galleani, continuing to live there must have seemed like a prison sentence.[57]

He decided to risk reentry into the United States in early 1903, sneaking across the border and settling in a Vermont town nestled in the Green Mountains. It would be from there that he would launch a nationwide anarchist movement unlike any America had seen before.

2 Green Mountain Boys—Anarchist Style

When your city is named after the man who coined the term "Sons of Liberty," it's not surprising that it could become a center for freethinking, antiauthority individuals. Such was the case for Barre, Vermont, named after Isaac Barré, a member of the British Parliament who in 1765 defended the American colonists in a speech after another member of Parliament referred to the colonists as "children planted by our care." Barré angrily exclaimed, "They planted by your Care? No! your Oppressions planted em in America." He further said that the behavior of the British rulers over the Americans "has caused the Blood of those Sons of Liberty to recoil within them. . . . They are a people jealous of their liberties and who will vindicate them if ever they should be violated."[1]

Barré became a hero in the colonies after his speech was published in American newspapers. He introduced "Sons of Liberty" months before groups that took that name sprung into action, becoming instrumental in preparing the colonists to eventually rise up in rebellion against the British. In 1793 the city of Wildersburgh, Vermont, changed its name to Barre.[2]

The town, nestled in the Green Mountains, would see enormous growth, mainly due to immigration, between the end of the nineteenth and the beginning of the twentieth centuries. From 1882 to 1914 Barre's population increased from two thousand to over ten thousand, with about 25 percent of the new immigrants being Italian. The town's anarchist group, formed in 1894, was one of the earliest such groups in New England, its members mostly stone and marble cutters who had emigrated from Carrara and other towns in northern Italy. Many had fled to avoid arrest after an anarchist insurrection in Carrara failed early in 1894. Anarchism and radicalism were such big parts of the heritage of the stone carvers in Carrara that a popular slogan of the time was "Even the stones are anarchists." Barre was a popular destination point for the immigrants due to its granite quarries and potential for work for the new arrivals. Barre's granite industry had benefited from the expansion of the railroad in the late 1800s, which allowed the granite to be more easily transported from the quarries into town for carving.[3]

The opportunities for employment, however, came with serious health risks. Many granite workers died young from silicosis, a lung disease. In Italy they worked with marble and granite in open sheds, but in Vermont they had to work through the much colder winters in enclosed sheds with a different type of granite that had a higher concentration of silica. The introduction of pneumatic stonework tools in the late nineteenth century, making granite-carving faster, also meant that high levels of microscopic granite dust were produced and lodged in the workers' lungs. Calls for better ventilation in the sheds went unheeded. "The winter will soon be upon us," wrote an observer in 1906, "and the dust boxes, called sheds, closed up again for the [winter] season; each ready to produce its quota of candidates for the premature inheritance of six feet of earth."[4]

The Italian immigrants in Barre and the surrounding towns were a close-knit community that did not let go of their customs and traditions from the old country. Many of them opened up shops that sold Italian products, and most kitchens were filled with rice, polenta, pasta, wine, and grappa. They were also strongly politicized, hosting lectures by distinguished anarchists such as Pietro Gori in 1895, Emma Goldman in 1898, and Errico Malatesta in 1899. They formed the Circolo di Studi Sociali di Barre (Social

Studies Circle of Barre), with members gathering in each other's homes and businesses, meeting halls, and parks. They also created libraries, schools, food cooperatives, theater troupes, and independent presses.[5]

The police in Barre were naturally concerned with the growing anarchist presence in their city. And they had good reason to be, given the anarchists' contempt for all authority, including the police. For the most part, there were no major incidents of violence attributed to the anarchists until the winter of 1900, when an assassination attempt on the chief of police would give Barre the type of national publicity that city officials and others had been hoping to avoid.

During the early morning hours of December 27, Patrick Brown, the chief of police, was patrolling the streets of Barre when he was shot several times by Italian anarchists and believed to be mortally wounded. (He survived.) He had earlier broken up a disturbance at a dance attended by anarchists. The shooting was reported by newspapers across the country, with one in Texas publishing the following headline: "In Pious Old Vermont: Even in That Sterile Country a Breed of Redhanded Anarchists Show Themselves; Shoot Down an Officer." The *New York Times* publicized the incident on its front page under the story heading "Shoot a Chief of Police. Italian Anarchists in Barre, Vt., Probably Fatally Wound Their Victim—Six Under Arrest."[6]

If people around the country had not heard of Barre before the shooting, they certainly were familiar with it after the incident. An editorial in a Vermont newspaper expressed the anger and frustration of some of the state's citizens:

> Vermont is not the place to foster the feverish theories and criminal practice of the Italian Mafia. We of the Green Mountain State will not meekly tolerate the inoculation of our social frame with the poisonous virus of . . . anarchy. We shall demand, at the hands of our prosperous young city, a drastic purging of her system. Not even a fibre of this alien and unhealthy growth must be tolerated. Root and branch, tendril and filament, it must be torn out. . . . We shall expect from Barre such an action on this outrage as will forever terminate the existence of old-world anarchy in our midst.[7]

Rather than be wiped out, however, the ideology of "old-world anarchy" would grow to new heights, not just in Barre but throughout the country. A new arrival in Barre would make sure of that.

The Birth of a Newspaper

When he came to Barre in 1903 using the alias "G. Pimpino," Luigi Galleani found an enthusiastic and welcoming Italian anarchist community there. The Cìrcolo di Studi Sociali, apparently aware of him hiding in Montreal, had invited him to move to Barre, located less than 140 miles across the border. He was well known and respected among the Italian immigrants in the town, having met some of them when he was making speeches and encouraging anarchist activity in Italy.[8]

Galleani was confident enough that his identity would be protected by the Italian immigrants in Barre to make the risky move from Canada back to the United States. There was always the danger that he could be extradited to New Jersey to face charges for the Paterson riots if the authorities learned of his true identity. While in Barre, at least initially, he took precautions to conceal his identity, including going out only in the evenings and continuing to use an alias.[9]

Galleani did not, of course, plan to live a quiet life in the Vermont town. Within a few months he started an Italian-language weekly newspaper, *Cronaca Sovversiva* (Subversive chronicle), that would eventually grow to become the most influential Italian anarchist paper in the country. To raise the funds to launch it, Cìrcolo di Studi Sociali held a bicycle raffle and obtained a little over $70. Raffles, donations, and other creative forms of fundraising, more so than subscriptions, helped keep the newspaper running for many years, although it was nearly always at a deficit. The paper never printed paid advertisements, though it did advertise anarchist books and other anarchist literature.[10]

The first issue of *Cronaca Sovversiva* was published on June 6, 1903. Its initial weekly run was three thousand copies, eventually rising to five thousand in subsequent years. Special issues had a circulation of ten thousand. The primary audience for the newspaper was Italian-language working communities in the United States, but the paper also reached readers in Italy, Australia, Canada, and several other countries in Europe,

North Africa, and South America. While there were many individuals who wrote articles for *Cronaca Sovversiva* and worked in different capacities on the publication, the "movement that was created with *Cronaca* certainly revolved around Galleani. It could not be separated from him." He exerted a "huge influence over large groups of workers. His presence was essential for written and oral propaganda, and, using his charisma, he was able to maintain unity among groups and places."[11]

The newspaper was beautifully designed, with local artist and anarchist Carlo Abate creating many of the illustrations that adorned its pages. One that was used often within the *Cronaca Sovversiva* nameplate at the top of the paper was of a muscular man with outstretched arms and chained wrists, two torches behind him. On one side of him was printed in Italian the subtitle of the newspaper, *Ebdomadario anarchico di propaganda rivoluzionaria* (Anarchist weekly of revolutionary propaganda), while on the other side was a Latin quote of the ancient Roman poet Horace, "*Ut redeat miseria abeat fortuna superbis!*" ("That fortune may leave the proud and return to the wretched!").[12]

The illustration of a chained man lifting his arms was used to convey "a general state of oppression alongside a struggle for liberation." Many other illustrations would appear several times in *Cronaca Sovversiva*, some created by Abate and some by other artists. These included a drawing of three women under trees reaching out into a shining light, evoking the dawn of a utopia. Another one was of workers reading a copy of *Cronaca Sovversiva* with a woman flying in the background over an industrial cityscape, carrying a torch and an axe, symbolic of the workers' revolution the anarchists were hoping for. The artwork and imagery were aimed at having the newspaper connect visually as well as ideologically with its readers.[13]

The inaugural issue urged readers to forsake "passive Buddhist contemplation" and instead contribute energetically to propaganda and action. Everyone was encouraged to "give to the cause of the revolution and emancipation . . . [all their] strength." The newspaper was clear on what needed to be overcome—namely, "the glaring inequality of economic conditions [by which] we, the great laboring majority, are at the mercy of a handful of parasites." It also let readers know that *Cronaca Sovversiva* "is not a particular organ of individuals, of groups, of churches or academies, [but rather] it yearns to be the faithful voice of truth, the proud voice of the working proletariat."[14]

For the first issue, Galleani was able to elicit a welcoming letter and column from Emma Goldman, the Russian-born anarchist who had been to Barre and was well known throughout the United States. "To the comrades and readers of the Subversive Chronicle," she wrote, "greetings and best wishes for a good fight." Goldman and other notable anarchists would contribute articles to *Cronaca Sovversiva* over the years.[15]

Each edition of the newspaper was typically four pages, although some special issues were eight pages long. The first two to three pages of the regular edition usually contained feature articles, oftentimes beginning with international news, history, and analysis. Readers learned about the latest developments regarding revolutionary movements around the world and anarchist perspectives on current events. The back page consisted of letters to the editor, reports from affiliated groups, announcements, calls to action, and a library section, where one could order anarchist and radical literature by mail. As one observer noted, *Cronaca Sovversiva* was more than just a newspaper; it was "a literary space where radical counterculture, Italian immigrant culture, anarchist philosophy, and insurrectionary propaganda became interconnected and mutually reinforcing."[16]

Connecting with local workers and others in Barre was an important part of Galleani and his fellow anarchists' strategy to build bonds of trust and loyalty. They accomplished this by relentlessly attacking in *Cronaca Sovversiva* corrupt police, union leaders, store owners, and others that they believed were exploiting the immigrant workers of Barre. But they also organized fun activities such as picnics, dances, and theater performances. When the weather was good, there were gatherings and picnics in an area known as Thousand Wood, located in the countryside near the city, where a stage had been built for musicals and plays. Amateur dramatic groups with names like the Transatlantic Band and the Stone Cutters Band performed for the crowds. There were also fruit and flower festivals and masquerade balls held at Pavilion Hall in Barre. Participants wore anarchist-related masks and costumes, dressing up as injured workers, Russian revolutionaries, and evil capitalists.[17]

The idea of anarchists holding a dance was derided by some. A planned dance in New York in 1896 featuring Johann Most, a German anarchist who advocated the use of violence, as the floor manager was sarcastically written about in the *Chicago Tribune*:

> It is difficult to realize that Anarchists can forget their grievance against the world long enough to indulge in the levity of a dance, and it staggers the imagination to attempt to picture the unspeakable Most in the act of calling for "two more side couples this way" or otherwise performing the functions usually pertaining to the position he will assume. It is not announced where this ball will be held, but it will be probably in some armory or in some of the forts near New York. Probably the managers will take the precaution to make the rule that all patrons must leave their bombs in the cloakroom, but there can be no assurance that in the rush of guests this rule will not be extensively violated. It is to be expected, therefore, that at intervals during the evening stray bombs will be shaken from pockets, and to guard against any widespread destruction of property, the entertainment must be held in some such bomb-proof structure.[18]

Still, the hundreds of social events that the anarchists in Vermont organized and that were announced and promoted in *Cronaca Sovversiva* earned them respect and admiration from the wider community and helped foster interpersonal relationships. The events became an important part of social life in Barre and provided Galleani and his fellow anarchists with opportunities, in addition to the articles and columns they wrote, "to insert anarchist ideas and transnational anarchist solidarity into what would have been otherwise a much more provincial world." Dances, picnics, theater presentations, and other activities connected the anarchists to different immigrant communities in the region and also helped them raise funds for future endeavors.[19]

Galleani and his fellow anarchists also ingratiated themselves with the community by providing educational services and making books available for loan at the Cìrcolo di Studi Sociali library. The Italian anarchists believed that in order to raise or reawaken the consciousness of the people as a first step in bringing about a social revolution, they needed to manage education themselves and not let only the state or other entities mold the minds of young people.[20]

There were also, however, altruistic motives for the educational efforts. Carlo Abate, the beloved artist in Barre and main illustrator for *Cronaca Sovversiva* who also wrote articles for the paper and for a time was listed as its publisher (although that may have been to hide Galleani's role, because he was a fugitive from the law), established a drawing school that was initially free. Instructors at the school taught young men new skills, including architecture and the sculpting of plaster models. This was done to assist them in obtaining jobs that weren't as dangerous to their health as working in the granite quarries, where many people were exposed to deadly granite dust and eventually died from that exposure. The fact that Abate, Galleani (an active participant in the school), and other anarchists were providing technical training to the young people of the town endeared them to the parents, who appreciated that this might help their children lead healthier lives. Efforts by Galleani and Abate to get the parents more involved with the school by contributing funds and time were not successful. Nevertheless, it was able to survive for many years.[21]

Abate would remain in Barre for the rest of his life. Born in Milan in 1860, the same year as Galleani, Abate had established a reputation as a skilled sculptor and received an honorary degree from the Milan School of Fine Arts. After his wife and three of their five children died during an epidemic in 1894, he immigrated two years later to the United States with his two other children, first living in Quincy, Massachusetts, and then settling in Barre in 1899. Abate was not the serious, fiery orator and prolific writer that Galleani was, but he was still a dedicated anarchist. Whereas "Galleani was a classic example of a political exile and a transnational revolutionary . . . Abate was a textbook case of the transatlantic labor migrant." He was generous and fearless, entering the homes of those who were sick to provide whatever assistance he could. He also purchased groceries and shoes for poor families.[22]

Yet for all the social and educational activities organized by the anarchists in Barre, it was still the written word, and Galleani's eloquent and electric speeches, that really attracted followers to the cause. *Cronaca*

Sovversiva got off to a controversial start, something Galleani probably didn't mind since it was good for publicity. The *Barre Daily Times* described the paper as "a neatly printed publication" with a subscription price of one dollar a year. The *Orwell Citizen* in Vergennes, Vermont, however, took a more skeptical stance: "The Socialists of Barre have a new newspaper, printed in Italian, which is designed to voice the peculiar sentiments of that class. The Barre Socialist is pretty close to anarchism, and 'Cronaca Sovversiva' will bear watching."[23]

One agency that indeed began watching the newspaper with alarm was the U.S. State Department. "Sir: I have the honor to invite your attention to the revolutionary and anarchistical character of a sheet which has been brought to the notice of this Department," wrote Alvey Adee, acting secretary of state, in August 1903 to the governor of Vermont, John G. McCullough. Adee said it was "called the Cronaca Sovversiva, and purporting to be printed and published at Barre, Vermont . . . for the 'Circola [*sic*] Studi Sociali' of that town." McCullough then wrote to the state's attorney, Frank A. Bailey, for Washington County, where Barre is located: "You will please give the subject matter of this communication [from the State Department] your most careful consideration and take such measures and adopt such means in the premises as the laws warrant, to investigate the character of the sheet and if the laws justify to suppress the same."[24]

Bailey began an investigation but found no state laws that specifically covered this case. *Cronaca Sovversiva* was allowed to continue publishing. The local newspaper, the *Barre Daily Times*, offered a vigorous defense of *Cronaca Sovversiva* and the Italian anarchists in the city:

> While the Times has no sympathy with the principles advocated by those engaged in the publication of "Cronaca Sovversiva" and believes that if they have transgressed any of the laws of the country they should be punished, it knows them to be good citizens in that they are peaceable, honest men who mind their own affairs, pay their bills, and have no desire to trouble anyone, and whose children are among the brightest scholars in our public schools. . . . Large numbers of Italians have come from northern Italy to Barre in the past few years and the

> work of assimilation and of making them American citizens with a right understanding of what American liberty means is making steady progress and in years to come they will be counted among the best blood of Vermont.[25]

Although Galleani and *Cronaca Sovversiva* survived this first attempt at suppression, it was a harbinger of what would unfold in later years. For now, though, the paper was off and running, and Galleani had a platform to spread his anarchist beliefs.

Trouble with the Socialists

When *Cronaca Sovversiva* was launched in June 1903, another radical newspaper, *Il Proletario* (The proletarian), was already established as a major periodical for Italian Socialists in the United States. Its editor, Giacinto Menotti Serrati, had clashed with Galleani many times in the past, including when both were living in Italy and then in Paterson, New Jersey, in 1902 during the silk dyers' strike. Galleani had wanted the strikers to attack the factories, and succeeded, while Serrati had preached restraint. It was an acrimonious debate carried out by both men in public and through their respective newspapers. At that time Galleani was the editor of *La Questione Sociale*.[26]

As an antiorganizationalist anarchist, Galleani "viewed labor unions as an unnecessary evil that bred authoritarianism and perpetuated the capitalist system." He believed they were corrupt institutions. He favored strikes only as a means for a potential insurrection. When strikes occurred, Galleani wanted them to be "pushed to their furthest extremes in every instance." He also viewed "legalitarian" Socialists such as Serrati with disdain, believing they were not helping the masses by trying to work through the system to change laws, win concessions for workers, and so forth. "For direct pressure put against the ruling classes by the masses," Galleani wrote, "the Socialist Party has substituted representation and the rigid discipline of the parliamentary socialists who have always sacrificed the general interest of the proletariat to the advantage of their own political and parliamentarian function." He also wrote that "socialists need authoritarian organizations, centralized and disciplined, for their legal and parliamentarian activities. . . . Anarchism [on the other hand] rejects authority in any form."[27]

Socialists were attacked more often than any other group in the stories and editorials in *Cronaca Sovversiva* between 1903 and 1912, the period that Galleani lived in Barre and printed the newspaper from there. Serrati responded by referring to the Vermont anarchists as ruffians, counterfeiters, and liars. His most egregious action in the eyes of the Galleanists, however, was revealing in an article published in *Il Proletario* in August 1903 that Galleani was living in Barre. For unknown reasons, the authorities in New Jersey (where Galleani was wanted for his role in the 1902 Paterson riots) did not act on this information until a few years later, when they requested his extradition. Serrati claimed he had not intentionally revealed Galleani's whereabouts, that it was just a mistake. The Galleanists did not believe that, and Galleani vowed revenge. Serrati was depicted in *Cronaca Sovversiva* as a "provocateur," a "reptile," and a "*Pagnacca*," a word that became slang for spy or rat.[28]

It was no surprise, then, that trouble occurred at the newly built Socialist Labor Party Hall in Barre when Serrati was scheduled to deliver a lecture on the "Methods of Socialist Struggle" in October 1903. The radical element of town was divided between Socialists and anarchists, and if one did not know who was a Socialist and who was an anarchist, clothing would give them away. Much like in the recent past when gangs wore different colors to show their affiliations, such as the Bloods in red and the Crips in blue, the Socialists and anarchists of Barre had their own ways of showing off their colors. The Socialists wore red half bow ties while the anarchists wore black ones. "If you look at some of the family portraits in town," recalled one longtime resident of Barre, "you can get a clue as to some of the political leanings of some people's ancestors in town. A lot of people have really forgotten the significance of the different color of ties."[29]

Serrati was taunted by Galleani's supporters on the streets of Barre on his way to the labor hall, including by women and children who came out of their houses to yell "spy" and other names at him. At the scheduled start time for his lecture, he was not there, and a fight erupted between the anarchists, who had packed the hall intending to disrupt Serrati's speech, and the Socialists, who'd come to hear Serrati talk but were outnumbered. One of the Socialists, Alessandro Garretto, who later claimed that he'd acted in self-defense, fired into the crowd, killing Elia Corti, an anarchist who was one of Barre's most respected stone carvers.[30]

Garretto was convicted of manslaughter and sentenced to ten to twelve years in prison but was pardoned after serving only five and a half years. In his request for a pardon, Garretto claimed that he'd been convicted due to perjury and fabrication by the anarchist witnesses at his trial, and because of "that law-breaking psychologically sick crowd, my family has lost a bread winner and has been deprived of a husband and father." Galleani was apparently not at the labor hall on the night of the violence, but investigators noted that it was "believed by many that Galleani instigated the disturbance at this meeting for the purpose of breaking up the socialist circle and dominating the entire neighborhood with his anarchist group." Serrati also wasn't at the hall when the shooting occurred, but he was nevertheless tried for complicity in the incident. Galleani, of course, didn't miss the opportunity to continue his attacks on Serrati during the trial, writing a series of articles titled "Giacinto Menotti Serrati: Spy and Assassin." Though Serrati was acquitted, he was shaken by the experience, and shortly after the trial, he returned to Italy.[31]

Serrati was not the only prominent Socialist Galleani had disputes with. Francesco Saverio Merlino was a well-known Italian anarchist who visited the United States in 1892. A prolific writer, speaker, lawyer, and scholar, he founded one of the earliest anarchist journals in America, *Il Grido degli Oppressi* (The cry of the oppressed). Fluent in English, he also founded the English-language journal *Solidarity*. After returning to Europe in 1893, he continued his anarchist activity and defended Gaetano Bresci at his trial in Milan in 1901 for assassinating King Umberto I.[32]

But Merlino eventually lost faith in anarchism and joined the Socialist Party. In an interview with the Turin, Italy, newspaper *La Stampa* (The press) in 1907 titled "The End of Anarchism," he asserted that anarchism was a doomed movement, having become obsolete due to a lack of first-rate theorists and torn apart by internal debates between those in favor of organizations and those against them. "The *organizationalists* are unable to find a form of organization compatible with their anarchist principles,"

Merlino said. "The *individualists*, who are opposed to organization in any form, can't find a clear way to action. [Emphasis in the original.]"[33]

Merlino continued his critique of anarchism by stating, "*I believe that the anarchist party is bound to end*. It is my personal impression that the anarchist party hasn't any more men of high calibre. [Elisee] Reclus and [Peter] Kropotkin were the last. Furthermore the anarchist party is no longer intellectually productive; no scientific or political work of notable value has come from the anarchist party. In fact, it has not even proliferated." Merlino also believed that the best ideas of anarchism had already been absorbed by Socialism, "while the Utopian part has been recognized as such and has been dropped as useless. [Emphasis in the original.]"[34]

For the fiery and equally scholarly Galleani, this was the equivalent of a call to battle. His dispute with Merlino, though, did not evolve into the diatribe and name-calling that had occurred with Serrati. Galleani wrote that Merlino "is a formidable debater, wise, vested in dialectics, [and] learned." But Galleani probably took it as an insult that Merlino said, "The anarchist party hasn't any more men of high calibre." Galleani undoubtedly saw himself as a leading voice and theorist for antiorganizationalist anarchism. The idea that anarchism was dead was what really incensed him. He responded with a series of articles published in *Cronaca Sovversiva*, "The End of Anarchism?" The addition of the question mark to the title of Merlino's interview was meant to immediately convey Galleani's opposition to what Merlino had said. (Many years later the articles were published as a book with the same title.) In the series, Galleani offered a vigorous defense of anarchism: "Upon the ruins of his [Merlino's] unfortunate thesis would remain this victorious conclusion: that anarchism, as a doctrine and as a movement, has never had more than today its own good reason to exist, and it never has asserted itself more than at present with such intensity and such dimension; that far from being moribund, it lives, it develops and it goes forward."[35]

Galleani argued that "the enduring portion of anarchist principles has never been absorbed by socialism." Instead "the anarchist movement, compared to all other trends of socialism, is the slow but persistent forerunner of a different and more advanced society than has been conceived by any other doctrine and by any other political party." For Galleani that meant a society of autonomy, independence, self-determination, and direct action. He also extolled the virtues of aiming very high for change and not what he viewed as the piecemeal gains the Socialists sought:

> Anarchists believe that rather than short-range ineffectual conquests, tactics of corrosion and continuous attack should be preferred, which demand from strikes of an openly revolutionary character more than shorter hours or paltry wage increases; which demand, instead, the experience of a more extensive solidarity and an ever deeper awareness of an indispensable condition for the realization of the *general economic strike* of a whole trade, of all the trades, in order to obtain, through the inevitable use of force and violence, the unconditional surrender of the *ruling* classes. Merlino, himself, knows that they *yield only to force*. Thus, instead of the mere passive and polite resistance so fervently recommended by the socialists, the anarchists prefer boycott, sabotage, and, for the sake of struggle itself, the immediate attempts at partial expropriation, individual rebellion and insurrection—actions which usually reap so much socialist horror and cursing, but which exert the most spirited influence over the masses and resolve themselves in a moral advantage of the highest order. [Emphasis in the original.][36]

Galleani knew that words alone were not enough to achieve the "individual rebellion and insurrection" that he was hoping for. The use of "force and violence" to bring about "the unconditional surrender of the ruling classes" required weapons. How, though, could he get weapons into the hands of his followers? And how could he do it without getting caught?

It's a Cookbook!

In one of the most memorable episodes of the classic television series *The Twilight Zone*, aliens arrive claiming that they've come in peace and want to share their knowledge and technology with Earth people. One of the aliens addresses the United Nations, promising to help end famine, war, and suffering. He then accidently leaves a book behind whose title is deciphered as *To Serve Man*. Convinced of the benevolence of the aliens, thousands of people book trips to their planet, including one decoding expert who had tried, but failed, to decipher the entire book. As he is about to board the spaceship, his assistant, who has just completed deciphering all of the text, comes running up to warn him not to get on. "The rest of the book," she shouts, "*To Serve Man*—it's a cookbook!" But it's too late, and he can't escape. The episode ends with the scientist held prisoner on his way to the mysterious planet to become somebody's dinner.[37]

Galleani would have enjoyed this episode since he too used a deceptive title to hide the true content of one of his publications. In 1905 an ad appeared in the back pages of *Cronaca Sovversiva* for a pamphlet titled *La Salute è in Voi!* (Health is in you!). If anybody thought this was something to help lead a healthier life, that person, like the characters in *The Twilight Zone*, would have been mistaken. It was a bomb manual! The misleading title was likely used to prevent the authorities from becoming suspicious of the work. The forty-six-page pamphlet had been adapted from a guide to explosives compiled years earlier by an anarchist chemist, Ettore Molinari, for whom Galleani had worked in Paris.[38]

Galleani wrote in the beginning of *La Salute è in Voi!* that the purpose of the work was "to eliminate the vulgar objection that subversives who continually preach individual and collective revolt to the oppressed, neglect to give them the means and weapons for it." To that end he provided detailed instructions for manufacturing explosives, cautioning that before working with large explosives, "it is better to first test a quantity 15 or 20 times smaller until one has gained practice and the necessary assurance. Therefore for every explosive we will indicate the amounts for the small tests, and the amounts for the large ones. Before using an explosive it is best to go into the countryside to test the small quantity."[39]

One can only imagine Galleani's embarrassment, or perhaps horror, when he learned three years later that he had made a mistake when transcribing Molinari's formula for manufacturing nitroglycerine, a mistake that could result in users being blown up. *Cronaca Sovversiva* published a column titled "Correggete!" ("Correct!"), giving the correct amount of nitric acid required. Always the proud man and reluctant to admit mistakes, Galleani wrote in the column that the original error should have been apparent "to whomever reads with some attentiveness."[40]

Even before he published *La Salute è in Voi!*, Galleani urged his followers to use dynamite against government authorities. In an article in *Cronaca Sovversiva* in 1904, written under his alias, "G. Pimpino," he informed readers that "dynamite is found everywhere in North America at fifteen cents a pound." Indeed, the invention of dynamite in 1867 by the Swedish chemist Alfred Nobel had been hailed by anarchists and other radicals around the world as the great equalizer in their battle against more powerful government adversaries. Russian revolutionary groups such as Narodnaya Volya (The People's Will) used it in many operations, including the assassination of Tsar Alexander II in 1881. Nobel was horrified to see his invention become the weapon of choice for many terrorists, since he had intended it for peaceful purposes, like construction. (That was part of the reason why he left millions of dollars in his will to establish the annual Nobel Prizes, including the Nobel Peace Prize.) The excitement that the invention of dynamite generated among radicals can be seen in this letter to a newspaper editor by an anarchist in the United States in the 1880s:

> Dynamite! Of all the good stuff, this is the stuff. Stuff several pounds of this sublime stuff into an inch pipe (gas or water-pipe), plug up both ends, insert a cap with a fuse attached, place this in the immediate neighborhood of a lot of rich loafers who live by the sweat of other people's brows, and light the fuse. A most cheerful and gratifying result will follow. In giving dynamite to the downtrodden millions of the globe, science has done its best work. The dear stuff can be carried around in the pocket without danger, while it is a formidable weapon against any force of militia, police or detectives that may want to stifle the cry for justice that goes forth from the plundered slaves. . . . It brings terror only to the guilty.[41]

Having provided his followers with the knowledge—after an important correction—of how to make explosives, it would still be several years before Galleani would see that knowledge put to use through a series of terrorist attacks that would startle the country. In the meantime, he continued to build his base of support through his writings in *Cronaca Sovversiva*, his lecture tours throughout the country, and his involvement in the affairs of the Barre community. If he was concerned that Serrati's disclosure of his identity and whereabouts could result in his being brought back to

Paterson, New Jersey, to face charges, he didn't show it. Though he was still writing articles for *Cronaca Sovversiva* under a pseudonym, he no longer maintained the low profile he'd exhibited when he first moved to Barre, when he would only go out in the evenings.

It was at a daytime picnic during the summer of 1905, however, that Galleani got into trouble and risked attracting the attention of the Paterson authorities. On July 23 Galleani and other anarchists were enjoying one of their regular outings in Thousand Wood when police raided the gathering, looking for contraband liquor. The anarchists objected to what they thought was an unjustified interference with their picnic and quarreled with the police over possession of the liquor. When the police seized a rifle the anarchists had been using for target shooting at the picnic, Galleani struggled with them. He was arrested and charged with breach of the peace. Galleani was brought before a court and, according to the *Barre Daily Times*, "conducted his own case with a skill that might have resulted in acquittal, instead of conviction, as it did, had he been better versed in Vermont law." He was fined $10 for breach of peace and set free.[42]

Local newspapers identified him as "Louis Galleani," who is "supposed to be the real editor of the Cronaca Sovverina [*sic*]." In *Cronaca Sovversiva*, Galleani's real name was used in the reporting on the incident: "The lawsuit established on complaint by the policeman [Patrick] Brown against comrade Galleani for an alleged breach of peace that the same would have perpetrated on the occasion of the last raid of the police at Thousand Wood, had its obligatory epilogue in Court, last Monday 31 July. . . . Our companion was inexorably sentenced to a ten dollar fine and expenses!"[43]

Despite this publicizing of Galleani's identity and whereabouts, the authorities in Paterson did not follow up and seek his extradition to New Jersey. Perhaps they weren't aware of the stories about his arrest because they appeared in local Vermont newspapers and not national publications. They also may not have had people on staff who could translate Italian and were therefore not monitoring *Cronaca Sovversiva*. That might be the explanation for why nothing happened after Serrati exposed Galleani's whereabouts in *Il Proletario* two years earlier. It is surprising, though, because Italian anarchists were still active in Paterson and likely being watched by the police. Maybe the Paterson authorities just didn't care anymore about Galleani and did not want to spend time and resources trying to bring the fugitive to justice.

Whatever the reason, Galleani must have felt pretty good escaping his latest bout with the police with only a fine. A year that had not started off well for Galleani—a fire in January destroyed the building in Barre that housed the editorial and composing rooms for *Cronaca Sovversiva*—was now looking better. But if the arrest was a warning sign to be more careful and assume a lower profile in Barre, it went unheeded. He would become immersed in a bitterly fought election issue that would alienate powerful business interests and ultimately prove to be a watershed in his life and career.[44]

Whiskey and Widows

One of the saddest situations in Barre in the early 1900s was the plight of the many women who had lost husbands to silicosis, the deadly lung disease caused by working in the granite sheds. Left alone with children and no means of support, these women struggled to make ends meet. Most had little or no education or skills and did not speak English. Finding salaried jobs was very difficult. They had a lifeline, though, and it involved selling liquor.[45]

Vermont was among the first states to ban the sale and consumption of alcohol in 1853. The law, however, was never fully enforced, and by 1904, Vermont repealed its state ban on alcohol. (National prohibition went into effect in 1920.) For many widows, the opportunity to sell alcohol from their homes or other places gave them the possibility of being able to provide for their families. But there was one major problem. Only licensed taverns were allowed to sell liquor, and the cost of a license was a $3,000 bond plus a $1,000 annual fee, amounts way beyond the women's means. The license requirement ensured that the better-off merchants and other businessmen had a monopoly on the alcohol trade. The widows who skirted the law risked being arrested and, if they could not pay the $500 fine (most could not), sent to jail.[46]

In a referendum held in March 1906 where the choice was either "license only" or "no license," the voters in Barre (each town and city in Vermont held its own referenda) chose "no license." Galleani was one of the leaders of the movement for no license, having taken part in many meetings. He also authored resolutions urging all Italians to refrain from voting on the license question. (As an antiorganizationalist anarchist, he was opposed to elections.) This angered those who supported requiring a license because they wanted a large turnout in their favor. They felt that Galleani urging people not to vote, in addition to his attacks on the business community in his writings and speeches, was hurting their cause.[47]

Another referendum on the liquor issue was scheduled for 1907. Once again Galleani attacked the liquor-license side and urged people not to vote. But before that referendum could be held, Galleani's past activities in Paterson, New Jersey, finally caught up with him. On December 30, 1906, as he was sitting down at home with his partner, Maria, and their children for lunch, Barre police, working with the Paterson authorities, burst into the house and arrested him. Galleani, who had a revolver in his pocket that the police confiscated, did not offer any resistance. After kissing Maria and the children goodbye, he announced that he was ready to accompany the officers to the county jail in Montpelier. Once there, he was put in jail and eventually turned over to a Paterson policeman and a prosecutor who had come to bring Galleani back to their city to face charges for the 1902 Paterson riots.[48]

Galleani and his supporters believed that his arrest in Barre for the Paterson riots so many years after the actual incident took place was due to his activity during the liquor-license referendum. Galleani wrote in *Cronaca Sovversiva* in January 1907, when he was out on bail, that his arrest had been purely revenge orchestrated by the Barre business community. He argued that the Paterson police had not tried to arrest him even after his whereabouts became public, either in 1903 from Serrati's disclosure in *Il Proletario* or 1905 when he was arrested in Barre. He claimed that his name and addresses were published in the Barre directory as well as in several major newspapers throughout New England. He also said that since the 1902 riots, he had traveled and spoken in New Jersey approximately twenty times and the Paterson authorities had always ignored him. But now the "pirates," as he liked to call the business community, police, and corrupt local politicians in Barre, wanted to remove him from the scene so he would not be a factor in the next election campaign regarding liquor licenses, this one scheduled for March 1907.[49]

While these comments don't resolve the question of why the Paterson police didn't try to bring Galleani in earlier, they do explain how Galleani and his followers viewed the arrest. They saw the businessmen and politicians in Barre as having enough influence to persuade the Paterson authorities to act at long last and remove Galleani from their city. What the authorities and business community didn't realize, however, was that the arrest and subsequent trial in Paterson would elevate Galleani to rock-star status throughout the anarchist world.

The Trial

Galleani was held at the Montpelier jail while his lawyers considered fighting the extradition. But Galleani decided not to do so and only requested a couple of days to get his affairs in order. Word of his arrest had already spread throughout the region, and while in the county jail, Galleani was visited by an endless stream of supporters. When it was time to depart for Paterson on January 3, hundreds of people gathered at the train station in Montpelier. Just before the train pulled out, a photographer tried to take a picture of Galleani for a local newspaper and was attacked by the crowd, who thought he was working for the police.[50]

The tumult of the past few days had taken a toll on Galleani, who now only wanted some peace and quiet. On the trip to Paterson, he wrote a note in broken English to the police officer accompanying him: "When I get to Paterson jail will I be only?" He wanted to be left alone. He indicated that he did not even know many of the people who had visited him at the Montpelier jail.[51]

Galleani and the two Paterson officials were met at the train depot late that night by several more police officers who quickly took him to the station house. There an officer recognized Galleani but remembered him from the 1902 riots as a much heavier man and remarked that he seemed forty pounds lighter. A local newspaper described Galleani as "tall, well built, of commanding and intellectual appearance." It also depicted him as having "thin, black hair, mustache and a long, black chin whiskers.... [He] looks like the Italian count of melodrama."[52]

Galleani's arrest became national news, elevating the anarchist to a new heightened status. The *New York Times*, *Boston Globe*, and *Washington Herald*, among others, published stories about him. The *New York Times* indicated that there was concern in Paterson that his arrest might lead to new labor troubles with the silk workers. Meanwhile, protests against the arrest occurred in many cities, and benefits and fundraisers were held in Barre and other places, raising thousands of dollars for his legal defense.[53]

After a couple of weeks in jail, Galleani was released on $6,000 bail. The night of his release, he addressed a large gathering in Paterson, thanking everyone for their support. Also speaking there were two well-known anarchists, Emma Goldman and her partner, Alexander Berkman. A circular distributed earlier in the day in Paterson before Galleani's release illustrates how the anarchist community rallied to his cause. It was addressed "To All Honest Working People" and stated, "Every one of you know who Luigi Galleani is. He is now in jail for having advanced your interests. It is your duty now to show your solidarity to him. Therefore do not fail to attend the international mass meeting."[54]

While awaiting trial, Galleani returned to Barre, where meetings and benefits on his behalf continued to be held, including another joint appearance with Goldman, this time at the Barre Opera House. Through his newspaper, Galleani expressed his gratitude to his supporters: "Maria and Luigi Galleani send from the columns of the Chronicle a cordial thanks and an affectionate greeting to comrades from all over America and Europe who . . . [have sent] letters and telegrams of solidarity and sympathy. . . . Sorry for not being able, for now, to personally answer each one."[55]

The anarchist community displayed an impressive ability to mobilize support for Galleani. As one historian notes, "The anarchists were effective at prisoner solidarity work, using pressure from the police to radicalize those not already directly involved in anarchist propaganda projects, thus using the oppressive force of the state to expand their support base and energizing their movement." Galleani also benefited from his association with Goldman. Their appearances together at fundraisers and meetings held after Galleani's arrest helped to elevate his position among anarchists around the country.[56]

The trial began on April 24 in the Paterson Court of Assizes (also known as the Court of Quarter Sessions) and was followed closely by several American newspapers, raising Galleani's status even more. He was charged with inciting to riot, two counts of atrocious assault and battery, and three counts of malicious mischief related to the damage done to three silk dye mills by the crowd of demonstrators. He faced a maximum of twenty-two years in prison and $17,000 in fines. Money, it turned out, was never a problem, as his supporters and others had raised enough funds—$37,000—to pay for two lawyers who assured Galleani that they would get the charges dropped or reduced.[57]

On the first day of the trial, silk dyers' helpers at the Bamford Mill (one of the locations attacked by the rioters in 1902) went on strike to show solidarity with Galleani. Police went to the mill to protect it from any outbreaks of violence. The courthouse was also placed under heavy guard, with all "suspicious" people—in other words, anarchists or "those with anarchistic tendencies"—questioned by the police.[58]

Rumors had been circulating that Galleani would not appear in court but rather flee Paterson, as he had done in 1902. Galleani, however, was in no mood to go on the run again and instead walked into the courtroom "dressed in the immaculate manner and looking the same refined gentleman that are characteristic of him." During the questioning of prospective jurors, it was revealed that one of them had applied for a job with the local police. This alarmed Galleani, who told his lawyers, through his interpreter, "That's a cop, and I don't want him at all." That individual was excused, and after further questioning of potential jurors, a jury was empaneled.[59]

The prosecution presented several witnesses who testified that they had seen Galleani at Belmont Park, where the strikers gathered on the day of the riot (June 18, 1902) and then again afterward, leading the mob that attacked the silk mills and "urging them by words and gestures to commit the acts of violence." Galleani's defense was that this was a case of mistaken identity. His lawyers had not one but two aces up their sleeves in what one newspaper described as "a most extraordinary and unique defense." To the astonishment of everyone in the courtroom, they presented two men who were almost identical in appearance, each with a striking resemblance to Galleani. But when the defense lawyers asked the prosecution's witnesses if they could have easily mistaken either of the men for Galleani, they all said no and reiterated that Galleani was the person they saw that day.[60]

One witness for the defense testified that it was William McQueen, an anarchist serving a prison sentence for his part in the riots, and not Galleani who made the incendiary address to the strikers at Belmont Park and then led them in their attacks on the mills. Another defense witness claimed that while Galleani was still speaking at the park, a large majority of the crowd left for the mills, proving that Galleani could not have led the riot. The defense also read an affidavit taken before the U.S. vice consul general in Paris from a sociology professor at the University of Brussels, Paul Ghio. He had traveled to Paterson in 1902 and heard Galleani speak on the day of the riots. Ghio stated that Galleani did not express any anarchist sentiments in his speech. He also said that "Luigi Galleani, in my opinion, is not a dangerous man. He is an intellectual man, a generous dreamer, believing in an ideal betterment of individuals and society."[61]

A key witness for the defense was Galleani's partner, Maria, who testified that Galleani left their house at 11:00 a.m. on the day of the riots and returned shortly after 1:00 p.m. Since the riots occurred between 2:00 and 3:00 p.m., her testimony was aimed at convincing the jury that Galleani couldn't have taken part in the violence because he was home at the time. She also said that Galleani wore a light suit that day, contradicting the testimony of the prosecution's witnesses who said he was in a dark suit. One of the men who looked like Galleani, Anthony Ferris, a wine merchant from New York City, also testified for the defense, claiming he was with the mob on the day of the violence. An earlier witness had said that he didn't think the man he saw leading the rioters was Galleani but rather somebody with a greater resemblance to Ferris.[62]

The question on everybody's mind was whether Galleani would testify on his own behalf. Surely, his supporters must have thought, the gifted orator would mesmerize the courtroom with his verbal skills, impressing even those who didn't understand Italian, his spoken words communicated by his interpreter. On the third and final day of the trial, one of his lawyers did indeed call him to the stand. What followed was something that those present would not likely forget.

Galleani strode to the witness stand with confidence, purpose, and "the military bearing which characterizes him." A court constable offered him a Bible so that he could be sworn in. Galleani put his hands behind his back in a defiant manner and said through his interpreter that he would not take the oath. Both the judge and the prosecutor were startled and almost in unison asked, "Why not?" After Galleani replied in Italian, his interpreter told the court, "Because he says he does not believe in the Supreme Being, has no religion, and does not believe in taking such an oath."[63]

The judge tried to find a middle ground and told Galleani that he could testify if he would solemnly affirm that he would tell the truth. Galleani replied that he would not even do that but that he would agree to answer any questions on the witness stand. The judge naturally couldn't accept that and declared Galleani ineligible as a witness. But in his instructions to the jury before they began deliberations, the judge made it clear that they should not be influenced by the fact that Galleani did not believe in God.[64]

Galleani, Maria, and a few friends remained in the courtroom while the jury deliberated. He told his friends that the longer the jury was out, the better it was, for it probably meant that he would not be convicted. But he looked worried and nervously paced the corridor while awaiting the verdict. When the jury returned to the courtroom at nine that evening after about four hours of deliberations, Maria began to cry. She had been emotional throughout the trial, including swooning a couple of times and having to be helped from the courtroom. Most dramatically she rushed up to Galleani's side "with an almost inaudible cry of impending misfortune" when the constables who were to attend to the jury were being sworn in. She put her arm around his neck and had tears in her eyes. Galleani gently took her arm from his shoulder and patted her hand, trying to comfort her. This entire scene played out in front of the jury and, as one newspaper reported, "must have lingered in their minds."[65]

The twelve-man jury reported that they were deadlocked at seven for acquittal and five for conviction and that there was no possibility the tally would change with further deliberations. Galleani smiled as the jury was dismissed. He would never be tried again for the 1902 riots. When asked by reporters for his reaction to the nonverdict, he simply praised the work of his lawyers. After staying a few nights with friends in Paterson, Galleani returned triumphantly to Barre on May 1 and entered the city "like some Roman Consul from a war of conquest. He was from that day the acknowledged leader of the cult."[66]

Meanwhile, subscriptions and donations to Galleani's newspaper, *Cronaca Sovversiva*, soared as a result of the trial. He also became a much sought-after speaker, traveling even more so than he had done in the past to give lectures around the country, thereby becoming involved in various labor and other contentious issues. This served his objective to "radicalize the communities he visited and . . . incorporate them into the *Cronaca*'s ever expanding network." The 1907 trial, therefore, can be seen as a key event that thrusted Galleani and his newspaper into national and international prominence.[67]

Concern over Galleani's elevated status, however, and the growth of his anarchist network can be seen in the following editorial from a Vermont newspaper, which foreshadowed the Red Scare that would sweep the nation more than a decade later:

> In the opinion of this paper, there is a matter of grave concern in the steady growth of the little knot of Anarchists in Barre, who celebrate the anniversary of the Chicago Haymarket riots, who listen to inflammatory speeches and who hiss the name of the president. It is a startling thing to reflect on the existence and possible growth of this dangerous propaganda right in the heart of patriotic Vermont. It is alarming to observe the power of a magnetic persuasive orator like Galleani over his impulsive countrymen. The situation presents suggestions that are of sinister significance. . . . [The] authorities would do well to observe with some degree of attention the growth of this movement and to have it and its leaders under some sort of systematic oversight. If the Anarchists in Barre or any other Vermont town are getting strong enough to cause trouble in the future the matter should be investigated and the societies broken up if it is possible to do so, and the time to do it is before some outrage has been committed.[68]

Another local newspaper viewed Galleani as more dangerous than Emma Goldman, who had spoken several times in Barre. Following a talk she gave with Galleani, the paper wrote, "It is the local anarchist, with brains and education, steadily and regularly instilling his dangerous doctrines by speech, implication and printed words, that we have to fear. We should call Galleani a much more dangerous element to Barre and Montpelier than Goldman ever could be."[69]

Time to Move On

It wasn't just newspaper editorials that rang alarm bells regarding Galleani. Some within the anarchist community in Barre were also concerned about, and perhaps jealous of, his newfound stature and prominence. Fellow anarchists accused Galleani's supporters of improperly handling the money raised for Galleani's trial defense. There were also accusations that Galleani himself had embezzled from a different benefit fund that was used for the children of Gaetano Bresci, who had assassinated King Umberto I in 1900 and then died in his prison cell in 1901. Galleani vehemently denied this, pointing out that he'd never had personal access to those funds. *Cronaca Sovversiva* published a letter from Bresci's widow, Sophia, and from the person who ran the benefit fund for her, attesting to Galleani's honesty and selflessness.[70]

Financial irregularities regarding the operations of *Cronaca Sovversiva* were also asserted, all again denied by Galleani and his supporters. While they admitted to lax bookkeeping on the part of one of Galleani's top aides, who was the newspaper's treasurer, they insisted there was nothing sinister or deliberate about it. The divisions among the Barre anarchists became so bitter that on one occasion in July 1910, Galleani and one of the leaders of the anti-Galleani faction got into a brawl at the local post office, resulting in both men being arrested. Compared with his previous legal problems, however, this one was over quickly, as Galleani pleaded guilty to the charge of breach of the peace and paid a $10 fine and an additional court cost of $5.14.[71]

Galleani got into trouble once again later that year when a $5,000 slander suit was filed against him by a former associate. But before police could serve him the papers, he went into hiding and eventually left town to elude the authorities. As the drama between the anti-Galleani and Galleani factions continued to play out and be reported in the press, anarchists across the country were concerned and suggested that it was time for *Cronaca Sovversiva* to find a new home to avoid the trouble brewing in Barre. With Galleani a wanted man there, it was thought that it would be difficult to continue publishing the paper from that location.[72]

There was another reason, though, for the widespread calls for *Cronaca Sovversiva* to relocate—namely, that it had outgrown its purpose in the small Vermont town. It now needed to be closer to where the action was, the large urban centers of the country, where industry flourished and large Italian-speaking communities could support the paper financially. That was where Galleani and *Cronaca Sovversiva* could have a greater influence on the lives of manual workers. Anarchist groups in Pittsburgh, New York, Chicago, and Boston, among other cities, all offered to host the newspaper and cover the costs of transporting the printing presses.[73]

Discussions about where to relocate *Cronaca Sovversiva* continued until Lynn, Massachusetts, a small city on the outskirts of Boston, was chosen as the newspaper's new home. The first edition with "Lynn, Mass." instead of "Barre, Vermont" at the top of the paper appeared on February 10, 1912. With a large Italian immigrant population in the surrounding areas, easy access to communication and transportation lines with Europe via its proximity to the Atlantic Ocean, and an active network of anarchists already there, Lynn was a logical choice for *Cronaca Sovversiva* and Galleani to continue to expand their activities.[74]

Up to this point, despite Galleani's preaching of "propaganda by deed" and advocating direct action and confrontation, including the publishing of a bomb manual for his followers to use, the Galleanists had not launched any terrorist attacks. This would change dramatically, however, during the second decade of the twentieth century, when events both in the United States and overseas would propel the Galleanists to the forefront of anarchist terrorism in America.

3 Targeting the Galleanists

The women and children were huddled together in a pit that had been dug beneath their tent. They were terrified, hiding from the gunfire that had been going on all day between striking coal miners and the Colorado National Guard. For several months, more than a thousand strikers and their families, mostly immigrants from Italy, Greece, and Serbia, had been living in a tent city they constructed near the entrances to the coal mines after being evicted from their company-owned homes in Ludlow, Colorado. Industrialist John D. Rockefeller Jr. was determined to break the strike that had evolved around demands for improved working conditions, better wages, and union recognition at his Colorado Fuel and Iron Company. The United Mine Workers of America was trying to organize the eleven thousand coal miners at Rockefeller's company.[1]

Only a couple of weeks before the battle erupted between the strikers and the National Guard on April 20, 1914, Rockefeller testified before a congressional committee justifying his antiunion stance. "There is just one thing that can be done to settle this strike," he said, "and that is to unionize the camps [mines], and our interest in labor is so profound and we believe so sincerely that that interest demands that the camps shall be open camps, that we expect to stand by the officers at any cost." When the committee chairman asked him, "And you will do that if it costs all your property and kills all your employees?" Rockefeller replied, "It [open mines] is a great principle."[2]

That "principle" resulted in the National Guardsmen raiding the camp at nightfall on April 20, setting the tent city ablaze. The true horror of what would become known as the Ludlow Massacre was not evident until the next day, when a telephone linesman went to the camp and discovered the burned remains of eleven children and two women in the pit. The death toll from the massacre and the days of violent skirmishes that followed eventually reached at least sixty-six people. But it was the image of the burned children and women that inflamed passions throughout the country. "The Ludlow camp is a mass of charred debris, and buried beneath it is a story of horror unparalleled in the history of industrial warfare," wrote the *New York Times*. "In the holes which had been dug for their protection against the rifles' fire the women and children died like trapped rats when the flames swept over them."[3]

Among those incensed were the Galleanists, who along with other anarchists and radicals in the United States viewed Ludlow as "the ultimate symbol of capitalist brutality in a period of severe economic depression and rampant unemployment among workers." To them, Rockefeller was public enemy number one. He was labeled a "tormentor billionaire" in the pages of *Cronaca Sovversiva*.[4]

Protests were held in many cities, but the horrific nature of what had happened in Ludlow called for more than just street protests and rallies in the eyes of some anarchists. The more militant ones now believed they had the moral high ground to launch a violent war against capitalism, government, and all authority figures. The Galleanists would play a central role in that war.

Beginning the Revenge

The Ludlow Massacre was not the first time the public was shocked by violence surrounding a labor-management conflict. A few years earlier, one of the worst acts of domestic terrorism in America up to this point occurred during a strike at the *Los Angeles Times*. A long period of union-management disputes and strikes at the newspaper culminated with the dynamiting of the *Times* building on October 1, 1910. The bombing stunned the nation, as twenty-one nonunion workers were killed and an estimated $500,000 in damages resulted. Two other bombs were discovered that same day: one at the home of *Times* owner Harrison Otis and another at the home of the secretary of the Merchants and Manufacturers Association. Police were able to remove the bomb at Otis's home to an open area, where it exploded harmlessly, while the second bomb failed to explode due to a weak battery.[5]

An enraged Otis vented his anger in an editorial in his newspaper that called the bombers "anarchist scum," "cowardly murderers," and "midnight assassins . . . whose hands are dripping with the innocent blood of your victims." He lamented about "the wails of poor widows and the cries of fatherless children" and was relentless in trying to pin the bombing on organized labor. He hired William Burns, the country's most famous detective, to track down the bombers.

After many months of investigation, Burns and police detectives arrested John J. McNamara, the secretary-treasurer of the International Association of Bridge and Structural Iron Workers, and James B. McNamara, John's younger brother, in Indiana in April 1911 and brought them back to Los Angeles to stand trial for the *Times* bombing. Otis was thrilled with the arrest, rejoicing with a headline that implied that no trial was really necessary: "The Dynamiters of the Times Building Caught. Crime Traced Directly to High Union Labor Officials." Labor union leaders and workers around the country rallied to the McNamara brothers' defense, believing they'd been framed by big business as a way to destroy labor.

Just as Otis had hired the most skilled detective in the country to apprehend the bombers, labor hired one of the most prominent lawyers in America, Clarence Darrow, to handle the McNamara brothers' defense. However, as evidence against them mounted, they both confessed to the bombing in order to escape the death penalty. James admitted to placing a suitcase containing sixteen sticks of dynamite and a timing device in the *Times* building the night before the explosion, while John confessed to being an accessory to the act. James was sentenced to life imprisonment, while John was sentenced to fifteen years.

The confessions of the McNamara brothers were a major blow to the labor movement. Many Americans condemned the McNamaras in particular and the labor movement in general for the bombing. There were fears that the country might be facing a new wave of violence if striking workers increasingly turned to the use of dynamite in their disputes with management. Still, the episode illustrates how sometimes a terrorist incident can raise awareness of problems in society that need to be addressed. The presidential-appointed United States Industrial Commission conducted an inquiry a few years later into the causes of violence in labor-management relations. While the commission focused initially on the McNamara case, it also studied the plight of workers in America and, according to one historian, "played an important role in educating public opinion about the realities of the labor-capital conflict."[6]

After the Ludlow Massacre, however, the public didn't really need any more education about the realities of labor-capital conflicts. What happened in Ludlow was a clear-enough signal that workers were no match for wealthy, powerful families such as the Rockefellers. That it occurred when the country was in the midst of an economic depression, with many people out of work, highlighted the discrepancies between the rich and the poor. The public "threw its support behind the miners, and newspapers 'crucified' John D. Rockefeller, Jr., who launched the nation's first public relations campaign, hiring a former newspaper man to 'spin' the conflict."[7]

Among the "spin" efforts was the shifting of any blame away from the company, placing it squarely on the backs of the strikers and the National Guard. "The deplorable loss of life in Colorado," Rockefeller said in a statement to the *New York Times*, "especially that among the women and children, which has so much aroused public feeling, did not occur in conflicts between the owners of the mining properties and the strikers, but in conflicts between the strikers and the troops of the State of Colorado." In another statement, he explained that he was not opposed to unions in general, only to a union trying to impose its will on all of the workers: "We do not question the right of any workmen to freely associate themselves in unions for the furtherance of their common and legitimate interests, but we do assert the equal right of an individual to work independently of a union if he so chooses. We are contending against the right of unions to impose themselves upon an industry by force, by assault and murder, and not against the right of men to organize for their mutual benefit."[8]

Rockefeller's attempt to control the narrative of the events in Colorado did little to stem the tide of protests against him and his family. His offices in Manhattan were picketed by people wearing black armbands in memory of the strikers killed in Colorado and to symbolize their holding of Rockefeller responsible for the carnage. The idea for the black armband protest came from noted novelist and Socialist Upton Sinclair, who sent a note to Rockefeller stating, "I intend to indict you for murder before the people of this country. The charges will be pressed, and I think the verdict will be 'Guilty.'"[9]

Protesters, particularly those from New York City, also took the battle to Rockefeller's estate near Tarrytown, New York, about thirty miles north of Manhattan. The Rockefellers (John D. Rockefeller Jr. and his father, John D. Rockefeller, the founder of Standard Oil) were popular in Tarrytown, employing hundreds of people at their estate and staying involved in community affairs. It was also a very wealthy community, with many other millionaires residing there. The protesters, many of whom were anarchists and Socialists, received a harsh welcome from both the police and the citizens.[10]

On one occasion in May 1914, one of the anarchists from New York, Arthur Caron, a member of the Industrial Workers of the World (IWW, also known as the "Wobblies"), stood on a soapbox in the town square and started a diatribe against Rockefeller. "Did you ever hear the wail of a dying mother?" he asked the crowd. "They were murdered in Colorado while the American flag flew over the tents in which they lived and the murderer was John D. Rockefeller, Jr., who lives in this—." Before Caron could finish his sentence, he was pulled from the box by a policeman. Another person then took his place and tried to speak, but he too was seized and pulled to the ground by the police. This was repeated each time someone tried to speak. Police arrested eleven men and one woman that day, charging them with blocking traffic and holding a street meeting without a permit.[11]

Caron was at the center of another protest that took place in Tarrytown on June 22. He and other anarchists trying to address a crowd at an outdoor venue were pelted with rotten eggs and vegetables by irate townspeople, who also blared sirens and horns to drown out the speakers. At one point, Caron was struck in the head by a large stick thrown at him by somebody at the gathering. The crowd eventually rushed the area where the anarchists had gathered to talk, forcing them to retreat toward the railway station. Among the anarchists that day was Alexander Berkman, the partner of Emma Goldman and a well-known anarchist himself, having gained notoriety in America in 1892 by attempting to assassinate industrialist Henry Clay Frick during the Homestead steel strike. (He served fourteen years in prison in Pennsylvania for that crime.) Berkman became separated from his group on their way back to the railway station and had to be rescued by a policeman when he was attacked by a mob.[12]

Tensions were so high in Tarrytown that when a young man was arrested for trying to gain entry to the Rockefeller estate, unfounded rumors circulated among the townspeople that the intruder was one of the anarchists or Socialists from New York City. Police had to protect him from an angry crowd when he was escorted to the police station. It turned out he was just a local teenager who'd tried to penetrate the security at the estate as a prank. It wasn't a smart move on the young man's part, as the Rockefellers were taking no chances with all the threats and protests directed against them. By the end of June, there were sixty guards and twenty-four sheriff's deputies guarding the Rockefeller family and their estate. John D. Rockefeller Jr., nevertheless, thought it would be wise to leave the area and spend the rest of the summer in Maine. His father decided to remain at home and didn't seem too worried about the danger posed by the anti-Rockefeller groups. He spent his mornings playing golf and his afternoons listening to organ recitals at the estate, inviting neighbors, school teachers, and church people to join him.[13]

On July 1 one of John D. Rockefeller Jr.'s most vocal critics, Upton Sinclair, said it was time to end the protests and taunts of Rockefeller and that it would be best to just "let him alone." Not getting that memo, however, was a group of anarchists who, working with a faction of the Galleanists, had a special surprise planned for the Rockefeller estate on the Fourth of July.[14]

Still reeling from their rough treatment in Tarrytown, Caron, Berkman, and several other anarchists plotted their revenge. Their group included members of the Gruppo Gaetano Bresci of East Harlem, New York, devoted followers of Galleani also known as the Bresci Group. What better "propaganda by deed" to commit than setting off a bomb at the magnificent Rockefeller estate? It didn't matter that their main target, John D. Rockefeller Jr., would not be there, a fact they were probably aware of because it had been printed in newspapers that he was spending the summer in Maine. There would still be another Rockefeller there, John D. Rockefeller Sr., and even if the bomb went off in an empty house, the symbolic nature of penetrating the security at the estate and doing damage to the home would be invaluable publicity for their cause and energize their supporters.[15]

However, the bomb they created exploded prematurely on the morning of July 4. They had been storing it in a tenement apartment on Lexington Avenue. Perhaps they had used Galleani's inaccurate formula for making bombs and had not seen the correction he published afterward. Killed in the explosion were Caron and two other anarchists who lived there, along with another tenant not believed to have been associated with the militants. Several other people were also injured in the blast. Later that day, the police arrested a member of the Bresci Group, Frank Mandese, who was found "in uncomfortable proximity" to the Rockefeller estate. Although he was soon released due to a lack of evidence, the police suspected the Bresci Group of involvement in the bomb plot, raided its headquarters, and roughed up its members.[16]

The Bresci Group was one of the largest and most militant of all the Galleani factions. Named after Gaetano Bresci, who assassinated King Umberto I of Italy in 1900, the group met in the basement of a building in the Italian section of East Harlem, where Galleani, Emma Goldman, and other anarchists had delivered lectures. The members were faithful readers and supporters of *Cronaca Sovversiva*.[17]

One week after the Lexington Avenue bombing, a memorial was held in Union Square in Manhattan for the three anarchists killed in the blast. Five thousand anarchists and radicals filled the square as seven hundred policemen stood guard, ready to move in if necessary. The rally went peacefully, with Alexander Berkman finishing his speech by proposing that the crowd give three cheers for the men killed in the bombing. The crowd responded enthusiastically and threw their hats wildly into the air.[18]

The Lexington Avenue bombing was a wake-up call to the New York Police Department. Prior to the incident, their main dealings with militant anarchists had been monitoring speeches and protests, using physical force against various individuals, disrupting meetings, engaging in occasional skirmishes with demonstrators, making arrests, and so forth. Now, though, they had to worry about bombs going off in their city. The anarchists had demonstrated that they could build bombs, and even though the Lexington Avenue one had gone off prematurely, the next one might not, and scores of people could be killed. Because of this possibility, the NYPD decided to form a unit that could not just dismantle bombs but also ferret out anarchists and other militants who intended to use them.[19]

The Bomb Squad, as it was officially named, was thus created in August 1914 and served as a special undercover, antiradical unit for the police. It had to go to work quickly, as just a few months later the city was rocked by a series of bombings at churches and courthouses. First, on the afternoon of October 13, the five-year anniversary of the execution in Barcelona of Spanish anarchist Francisco Ferrer, a bomb exploded inside St. Patrick's Cathedral, causing minimal damage. Then, that evening, dynamite was found outside St. Alphonsus Church, and one week later another bomb exploded in that same church, causing slight damage. On November 11, the anniversary of the Haymarket executions of 1887, a bomb was set off in the Bronx Courthouse, once again causing minor damage. Three days later, on November 14, another bomb was found, this time near the seat of a magistrate in the Tombs Police Court, located in the Criminal Courts Building in Manhattan. The bomb was removed from the courtroom by a police officer just as the magistrate, John A. L. Campbell, who had sentenced many anarchists to jail, was about to take his seat.[20]

The manner in which that bomb was disposed of would probably make most bomb experts today cringe. However, the policeman who discovered it simply acted on instinct in order to save lives. Patrolman George O'Connor was in the courtroom waiting for the arraignment of a prisoner when he saw smoke coming from under a bench near where

Magistrate Campbell sat. He immediately dashed toward the area and picked up a package wrapped in newspaper. One end of a fuse was sizzling, and some of the sparks dropped on the newspaper, setting it on fire. O'Connor tore the fuse from the bomb, put out the fire, and then ran from the courtroom, clutching the bomb close to his body.[21]

After reaching the rotunda of the building, he dashed through the doors and down a long flight of stairs to the street. When he got to the curb, he simply let go of the bomb with enough of a push that it landed first on trolley tracks and then rolled across the street into the gutter, where it finally stopped. Crowds of people who had been in the rotunda, as well as several police officers, followed O'Connor to see what was going on. The police then blocked off the street where the bomb lay, but an elderly woman came out of a store across the sidewalk from the bomb and became confused when the crowd of onlookers shouted at her to get away from the object. She mistakenly walked closer to it, prompting another heroic action by O'Connor, who ran down the block, picked her up, and carried her to a safer area.[22]

Meanwhile, tenants in the buildings near where the bomb lay could see it in the gutter and were terrified that it might go off at any moment. O'Connor, who must have been going on adrenaline by this point, picked up the bomb and placed it in a bucket of water that an office worker had brought to the scene. He then carried the bucket to the pen of the police court, where it remained until the bomb experts arrived. The bomb turned out to be an oil can filled with two pounds of black and smokeless powder and thirty bullet cartridges ranging in caliber from .32 to .44, and a fuse had been attached. "There was enough powder in the can," said a bomb expert, "to have wrecked the courtroom. The effect would also have been to scatter bullets all over the courtroom."[23]

Although O'Connor's actions were heroic and received much praise in the press, the rash of bombings and attempted bombings was still very embarrassing for the newly formed Bomb Squad. It had been created to weed out anarchists and others who were planning terrorist attacks, and it had failed these first several tests. The bombing attempt at the Tombs particularly rattled the police, since they knew that had it not been discovered in time, it would have killed many people in the courtroom, including Magistrate Campbell. They could view the bombings and attempted bombings of the previous month as basically "protest bombs," or "scare bombs," not necessarily aimed at killing people. The Tombs one, though, was different. "The bomb which [the policeman] discovered under the bench in the courtroom today," said a police inspector, "was meant to kill; it was far deadlier than the others."[24]

All the bombs were seen as the work of an organized group and not "the sporadic outbursts of individuals." The police regarded the bombings as "part of a general plan of terrorists under the direction of an organization or a collection of agitators." They were also convinced "that the time has arrived for drastic police action." The main target of this action was going to be the Bresci Group, whom they believed to be responsible for the recent campaign of violence.[25]

Their plan was to infiltrate the group with an undercover agent. That task fell to a young Italian immigrant, Amedeo Polignani, who'd immigrated to the United States in 1901 and joined the NYPD in December 1913. He became a member of the Bomb Squad the same month as the incident at the Tombs Police Court. Captain Thomas J. Tunney, the head of the squad, assigned the new recruit to the "anarchist line" and instructed him to join the Bresci Group and report back regularly. "The situation was disturbing," recalled Tunney. "We had to put a stop to bombing [*sic*] before the anarchists grew bolder and began to kill someone beside themselves."[26]

The twenty-five-year-old Polignani began his mission on the evening of November 27, attending a meeting of the Bresci Group and using the alias "Frank Baldo." He had no difficulty gaining access to the meeting in the group's basement headquarters at 301 East 106th Street in Harlem, "a shabby house in a shabby district east of the New York Central tracks." He spoke with people at the club and then left after about half an hour. Having succeeded in making this first contact with no problems, he continued to attend meetings and became friendly with members of the group, who regarded him as a trusted comrade. He also performed various chores at the headquarters, including cleaning the room, making coal fires, and even one time opening and closing the doors to the meeting place.[27]

His real work, however, began in January 1915 when, according to Polignani, Carmine Carbone, one of the members of the Bresci Group and only eighteen years old, told him about a plot involving himself and another member, Frank Abarno, who was twenty-four years old. Both young Italian immigrants were going to blow up St. Patrick's Cathedral, the target of the earlier bombing in October that caused little damage. This time they wanted to destroy the church, "since it was a *rich* church, and that when the millionaires would walk up and down Fifth Avenue, they would say, 'Oh, [that was] the work of the anarchists.' [Emphasis in the original.]"[28]

Polignani proceeded to help Carbone and Abarno build two bombs. Abarno gave Polignani the *La Salute è in Voi!* (Health is in you!) pamphlet, Luigi Galleani's bomb manual with the deceptive title. Polignani showed it to Tunney, his boss at the Bomb Squad, who made a copy. Polignani then bought some of the ingredients necessary to build the bombs: sulfur, brown sugar, black antimony, and chlorate of potash. This formula was not listed in Galleani's manual but instead was a mixture commonly used in fireworks. The explosive was then packed into soap tins with iron rods bound to the outside to act as shrapnel.[29]

With the bombs concealed under their coats, Polignani and Abarno set off for St. Patrick's Cathedral early in the morning on March 2, 1915. Carbone was going to meet them in the building where they had stored the bombs, but he never showed up, later confessing that he had overslept. The anarchists' plan was to set the bombs off with lit cigars during a mass with hundreds of people in attendance. Polignani had specific instructions from Tunney not to light a fuse at any point. He probably figured that it wouldn't look good from a public relations standpoint for a member of the NYPD to activate a bomb in a church. Tunney also realized that Polignani would be the prosecution's star witness against the two anarchists once they were arrested and brought to trial. If Polignani lit a fuse, that would certainly be exploited by the defense lawyers, who could possibly discredit Polignani's testimony. Having the anarchists light the fuses could only strengthen the prosecution's case and likely lead to longer prison sentences.[30]

It was certainly a dangerous game the police were playing, since hundreds of people could be killed if something went wrong. But Tunney felt confident the bombs wouldn't go off because Polignani had earlier brought to him the fuses they were going to use. Through experiments, it was determined that, based on the length of the cords, it would take ten to fifteen minutes for the bombs to explode, plenty of time for Tunney's officers (who would be strategically situated and disguised inside the church) to extinguish the fuses.[31]

When Polignani and Abarno entered the cathedral at 7:10 a.m., Abarno's cigar was lit. Polignani had put his out on the way to the church without Abarno seeing him do so. They sat down in different places, Abarno several pews in front of Polignani. Abarno soon stood up, walked toward Polignani, and murmured something that Polignani couldn't hear. He then sat down in another pew, placed the bomb underneath a seat, and lit the fuse. Abarno then got up, and as he started to walk up the aisle to exit the church, he was grabbed by a detective disguised, with false hair and a false beard, as an old man. Two other detectives were disguised as scrubwomen, while several others were pretending to be worshippers. The "old man" detective threw Abarno to the two "scrubwomen" detectives behind him, and then he went to where Abarno had just sat. He quickly found the bomb and put out the fuse.[32]

After taking Abarno into custody, the police arrested Carbone at his home and found there a copy of *La Salute è in Voi!* During questioning before he had a lawyer, Abarno, who'd wanted to be a priest at one time in his boyhood, made several statements that the police released in the form of a confession:

> I quit going to church four years ago and since then I have hated the church because it is the enemy of the poor. It pays no taxes and caters to the rich. We anarchists hate the Catholic Church because it fights anarchy all the time. . . . This has been a terrible winter for the poor. Our group decided to do something. We decided to open a campaign against the Catholic and Protestant Episcopal Churches, then to terrorize and perhaps destroy the homes of the Rockefellers, Carnegie [*sic*] and some of the Vanderbilts, and finally, when we had the city terrorized,

> to invade the banks at the head of an army of the poor and help ourselves to the hoards of the rich. We fixed on St. Patrick's Cathedral as the place to start because it is the biggest Catholic church and our demonstration there would attract so much attention.[33]

Abarno would later distance himself from this confession. "We would not have ventured into the scheme if it were not for the urging of Baldo [Polignani]," he said. He also asserted that he and Carbone "were the tools of the police, anxious to make a showing; the victims for a frame-up, and if it had not been for Baldo we would never have gone as far as we did." But during his arraignment, he told the judge, "Just because I've had work . . . didn't make me so blind that I couldn't see those around me who had no work. Rags to wear, and not enough of them. Scraps to eat, and sometimes not even scraps. Those are things you people don't know about. You don't see it as we do. The rich people know and are responsible for all this, but they wouldn't make a change. I guess they will now. We have waked them up." His arrest, along with that of Carbone, was denounced by anarchists everywhere, particularly those in the Bresci Group, who viewed this as a classic case of entrapment and a setup. They, along with the lawyer for Abarno and Carbone, asserted that Polignani had conceived of the plan to bomb the church and had gotten Abarno and Carbone to go along with it. Abarno also claimed that he never lit the fuse to the bomb. Nevertheless, the two anarchists were found guilty in a jury trial just a month after their arrests and were each sentenced to six to twelve years in prison.[34]

One of the anarchists incensed over the Abarno and Carbone case was, not surprisingly, Galleani. He published a series of articles about it in *Cronaca Sovversiva*, labeling Polignani an agent provocateur and printing his photo with each article. While Galleani viewed the bomb plot as a police frame-up, he did not deny that anarchists had planned and implemented the earlier string of bombings and attempted bombings throughout New York. He was encouraged by those acts of violence because they demonstrated to the police "the unexplored world of the 'rebels' without church, without commandments, without priests, extending from the Battery to Harlem, between the two rivers, impalpable, elusive, inexorable, like ether and like destiny." Galleani extolled his readers to "continue the good war, the war that know neither fear nor scruples, neither pity nor truce."[35]

Galleani could finally see that the advice he'd given his followers back in 1905 to start using bombs in their activities was now being put to use. He probably expected it to happen a lot sooner, not for it to take almost a decade since the publication of his bomb manual. Why, then, did it take so long? One possible explanation was that the Galleanists and other anarchists needed some grand event, such as the Ludlow Massacre, with its images of women and children burned to death, to become enraged enough to do something more dramatic and violent than just protests and demonstrations. This was still a minority view, as most anarchists continued to be opposed to the use of violence. But for the Galleanists and other militant anarchists, the cat was now out of the bag in terms of attacking their enemies with bombs. This "good war," as Galleani put it, would only escalate in the coming years.[36]

No God! No Master!

While there would be additional bombings in New York that year, including one at the Bronx Borough Hall in May and one in July at the NYPD headquarters, the latter coming one day after the first anniversary of the Lexington Avenue bombing, by 1916 "the theater of battle shifted from New York to Boston." And that was near to where Galleani was firmly entrenched. He was operating from his new home base in Lynn, Massachusetts, on the outskirts of Boston, having moved there from Barre, Vermont, in 1912. Just as he'd found an enthusiastic group in Barre in 1903, so too did he find a strong circle of supporters in the Boston area.[37]

It wasn't long after he moved there that he became embroiled in a major labor strike. For Galleani, strikes were always viewed as a means to an end, with the end not necessarily being better working conditions, higher wages, and so forth, objectives most labor unions and other labor-friendly organizations wanted. Rather, Galleani's goal was always to transform a strike into an uprising, a social revolution and insurrection that would bring about the anarchist society he was striving for.

So when thousands of textile workers, mostly Italian, Polish, and Lithuanian and many of them women, walked off their jobs in Lawrence, Massachusetts, in January 1912 to protest a wage cut, Galleani saw an opportunity to exploit the situation to further his objectives. By February twenty-three thousand workers out of a total workforce of thirty-two thousand were on strike against the textile mills. When a striker was killed during clashes with the police, the authorities arrested two leaders of the strike, Joseph Ettor and Arturo Giovannitti, for "indirect" responsibility for the striker's death. That led to union leaders from the IWW, including Elizabeth Gurley Flynn and William "Big Bill" Haywood, traveling to Lawrence to continue the strike and demand the release of Ettor and Giovannitti from jail.[38]

Galleani's *Cronaca Sovversiva* published articles supporting the strike and coordinating fundraising efforts and protests. But it was an ingenious idea that his newspaper proposed that not only helped the strikers but also guaranteed nationwide publicity and sympathy for them. More importantly, for Galleani, it was a way to ensure that the strike, and the disruption it was causing in the area, would continue. Parents were understandably worried about the safety and well-being of their children and about putting food on the table while they were out of work. To ensure that the strike would continue, *Cronaca Sovversiva*, along with others, helped organize for the strikers' children to be sent to New York and Barre to live temporarily with supporters there. This became known as the Children's Exodus, a tactic that had been used effectively during strikes in Europe, with children greeted by cheering crowds in the cities they were sent to. Newspapers across the country carried the story of the children's plight, and when the Lawrence authorities violently prevented one group of mothers from sending their children away, the nation was outraged by the scene of mothers and children being clubbed by the police. This led to congressional hearings on industrial conditions in Lawrence and across the country.[39]

In mid-March the strikers won their battle with their employer, the American Woolen Company, and were granted a significant (15 percent) wage increase, double pay for overtime, and amnesty for the strikers. With the strike over, the children were sent back home to their families. But it wasn't a total victory for the workers. The two strike leaders, Ettor and Giovannitti, were still in jail. For Galleani this provided another opportunity to keep the pot boiling by calling "for a mass uprising in order to achieve the liberation of Ettor and Giovannitti."[40]

Galleani and his supporters convinced the workers to go on strike again and take to the streets to protest the scheduled trial of Ettor and Giovannitti. The Italian anarchists among the protesters carried a banner that said, "No God! No Master!" This new walkout by the textile workers led the IWW to call for a twenty-four-hour general strike on September 30, the first day of the trial, but for the strike not to involve street fighting. This did not satisfy Galleani and other militant anarchists who wanted the general strike, and the turmoil in the streets, to continue indefinitely.[41]

The one-day general strike resulted in twelve thousand strikers and operatives demonstrating in Lawrence in support of Ettor and Giovannitti, while sympathy strikes were held elsewhere in Massachusetts, Vermont, Pennsylvania, and Ohio, attracting ten thousand people. In the end the two union leaders were acquitted on November 23, and the Lawrence strike could finally be viewed as a total victory for the workers.[42]

It wasn't a victory, however, for Galleani, who remained angry with fellow Italian anarchist Carlo Tresca. In collaboration with the IWW, Tresca had helped to limit the general strike to just one day, while Galleani and his supporters believed that the workers were ready for more direct action. The Galleanists blamed him for having "eviscerated the enthusiasm of the proletariat" and would attack him intermittently for the rest of his life. Tresca was a prominent anarcho-syndicalist, from a faction of anarchists who "placed their faith in the trade-union movement [that was] shunned by and large by the anarchist communists, [such as Galleani,] who feared the emergence of a boss, a *padrone*, endowed with special privileges and authority."[43]

More than just ideological differences may have been at play in Galleani and Tresca's acrimonious relationship. At one time it had been one of mutual support. According to historian Nunzio Pernicone, jealously may have been a factor because Tresca was seen among Italian anarchists as a rival to Galleani. Tresca's high-profile role in the Lawrence strike and in the defense campaign for Ettor and Giovannitti led to fears among the Galleanists "that he might eclipse Galleani as a radical leader."[44]

Despite the setback in Lawrence, Galleani continued to build his base of support in New England. In 1914 the Gruppo Autonomo (Autonomous Group) of East Boston, a counterpart to the Bresci Group in East Harlem and consisting of Galleani supporters, published a series of articles that Galleani had written for *Cronaca Sovversiva*. The book, *Faccia a Faccia col Nemico* (Face to face with the enemy), defended "propaganda by deed" and praised those who had put it into practice. Each chapter had a picture of an anarchist assassin, and the assassins were portrayed "as martyrs in a holy cause, avenging heroes moved by a spirit of self-sacrifice and a passion for retribution." Among those featured were Gaetano Bresci, who assassinated King Umberto I of Italy in 1900; Sante Caserio, who stabbed to death the French president in 1894; and Michele Angiolillo, who killed the Spanish prime minister in 1897. The U.S. Department of Justice would later describe *Faccia a Faccia col Nemico* as the "glorification of the most anarchistic assassins the world has ever seen." Anybody in possession of the book was likely to be viewed as a dangerous subversive.[45]

The same year that *Faccia a Faccia col Nemico* was published, one of the most famous assassinations in history took place, though it was not perpetrated by an anarchist. On June 28, 1914, Archduke Franz Ferdinand of Austria and his wife, Sophie, were shot and killed by a Bosnian-Serb nationalist, Gavrilo Princip, in Sarajevo, a single act of violence that provided the spark that would lead to World War I shortly afterward. For the antimilitaristic Galleani, the war provided yet another issue he could use, through his impressive oratory and writing skills, to rally people to his cause. He viewed all wars as imperialistic campaigns for power and profit, exploiting workers, who would be the ones to die on the front lines. One of his favorite slogans was "Against the War, Against the Peace, For the Revolution!"[46]

The United States did not enter the war on the side of the Allies (Britain, France, Russia, and Italy) against the Central Powers (Germany, Austria-Hungary, the Ottoman Empire, and Bulgaria) until April 1917. In the lead-up, Galleani (whose writings were published in many Italian-language periodicals throughout Europe, where *Cronaca Sovversiva* also had a wide readership) first focused on portraying the horrors of war by publishing letters from Italian soldiers to their loved ones. He then encouraged desertion for the Italian immigrants who had been called back to Italy to serve in the military. He also wrote a regular column in *Cronaca Sovversiva* aimed at those who had not yet returned to Italy, called "Children, Don't Come Back!" That was also the title of a leaflet signed by the "Mothers of Italy" that was actually written by Galleani and distributed among Italian immigrants. Demonstrating Galleani's flowery writing style and gift for hyperbole, the leaflet reads as follows: "Children, don't come back! They will seize you like thieves, like slaves on the docks, and without allowing you to see again, to embrace, perhaps for the last time, the old folks who gave you life, sincere hearts, and fertile strength, they will sacrifice you up there in the canyons of Ampezzo or on the high plain of the Carso to bring about the triumph of a terrible and bloody deception: the homeland!"[47]

In 1916 America entering the war was becoming a very real possibility. A series of Preparedness Day parades were held across the country to whip up enthusiasm for the likely war effort and to show support for the expansion of the armed forces, the increased manufacturing of armaments, and the planning for a possible military draft. The U.S. military at the time was nowhere near the force it would become in later years. In 1914, when World War I began, "the nation's army remained underwhelming, ranking 19th (or worse, depending on the survey) in both size and competence among the world's forces." The Preparedness Day parades became almost like a national competition in civic pride to see which city could get the most people to march.[48]

An advertisement in a Washington DC newspaper urged everyone to show their patriotism and join the parade scheduled for June. "Washington is going to have a monster preparedness parade," the newspaper claimed on its first page. "Other large cities have held preparedness parades, and certainly there is no date more fitting than Flag day [June 14] for such a demonstration in Washington. We want the citizens of Washington to realize that this is every man's and every woman's responsibility. . . . This is a demonstration for everyone, and none need wait upon an invitation." President Woodrow Wilson led the Washington DC parade that drew sixty thousand marchers.[49]

After New York City held a parade in May that drew a large crowd, a resident of Chicago wrote to the *Chicago Tribune* in anticipation of that city's parade in June. "I have no doubt in the world the parade in Chicago," she wrote, "would outdo that in New York. There were 145,000 in line in New York. There should be 200,000 in line in Chicago. I have always felt in my heart that Chicago [can] do better."[50]

San Francisco joined in on the competition with a parade held on July 22. Organizers, led by the Chamber of Commerce, were undoubtedly hoping for a large turnout in the City by the Bay, a festive and patriotic gathering that would generate banner headlines the next day. Although they got their headlines, the event was not at all what they had hoped for. And it was a faction of the Galleanists that may have been responsible for spoiling the fun.

More than fifty thousand people marched in the streets of San Francisco that afternoon during a procession with fifty-two bands and representatives from more than two thousand organizations, including the military, business groups, local and state government agencies, and other entities. The parade began at 1:30 p.m., with the planners anticipating it would last up to six hours. But just about a half hour later, as a group of Spanish-American War veterans were marching by the Ferry Exchange Saloon, a bomb hidden in a black suitcase that had been placed on the sidewalk near the saloon exploded, killing ten people and injuring forty others. The bomb was a six- to eight-inch pipe containing steel rivets, sections of auto tire, and .22 and .33 caliber bullets. It had been charged with either nitro-toluol, nitroglycerine, or some other high explosive and detonated by a clock. Fragments of the bomb were found as far away as four hundred to five hundred feet from the site of the explosion. It was the worst terrorist attack in San Francisco history.[51]

The search for the perpetrators covered anyone linked to anarchism, radical politics, or labor unions. But it was labor agitators that the authorities, with the backing of the powerful business interests in the city, zeroed in on first as the prime suspects. Prior to the bombing, there had been a series of labor disputes in San Francisco, and there was opposition to the parades within progressive and radical circles, as well as among mainstream labor leaders. The entire preparedness movement was seen by its critics as a means to rush the United States into war and a way to make the rich industrialists even richer through the increased production of munitions and other wartime products. Anything that could discredit the labor movement, like blaming them for the bombing, would be to the advantage of the business and financial sectors of the city, along with business and management interests across the country, where the bombing did indeed generate banner headlines.[52]

What happened next was a miscarriage of justice. Though there was no evidence against them, two leading labor activists, Thomas Mooney and Warren Billings, were nevertheless arrested, tried separately, and convicted of the bombing, with Mooney given a death sentence and Billings life in prison. It was later revealed, however, "that the entire judicial process had been a farce, marked by illegal arrests, perjured and coached witnesses and gross prosecutorial misconduct." In one instance, a witness testified that he had seen Mooney, Billings, and another man place the suitcase with the bomb on the sidewalk near the saloon moments before it exploded. But this witness had not even been in San Francisco at the time of the bombing! Mooney's death sentence was commuted to life in prison in 1918, and he was eventually pardoned and released from prison in January 1939. Ten months later, Billings's sentence was commuted to time served, and he too was released from prison. He was granted a full pardon in 1961.[53]

While it is apparent that Mooney and Billings were framed, there is no agreement among historians and others as to who exactly was responsible for the Preparedness Day bombing. William J. Flynn, head of the U.S. Secret Service at the time of the incident and later director of the Bureau of Investigation, the predecessor to the FBI, was convinced that Luigi Galleani was involved. "Whoever did it was well known to Galleani," Flynn wrote years later, "and Galleani knew it was about to be perpetrated and who was to do the actual work." Flynn further explained how Galleani operated in devious ways: "Galleani . . . will suggest. One of his close companions will pass on the suggestion. The idea will pass hither and yon until eventually a particularly wild man or woman will touch off the bomb or ignite the fire. Trace it back and you become lost in the most complicated labyrinth of indirect statements, evasions and plain lies, and you learn sooner or later you are destined to emerge from the maze at the same spot you entered, having gained nothing."[54]

One of the Galleanist factions that might have gotten the "suggestion," if indeed Galleani made one, was the Gruppo Anarchico Volontà (Anarchist Will Group). This was a new Galleanist group that formed in San Francisco only months before the parade. Modeled after Galleani's anarchist teachings, it met every Saturday evening, with lectures and discussions held in both English and Italian. It also had picnics and maintained a large library, all the time promoting Galleani's ideology. It proudly announced its founding in the pages of *Cronaca Sovversiva*, promising to attract "the sympathy of the mass . . . by forming new youth consciousness that will increase the ranks of the rebels." An April 1916 article in *The Blast*, an anarchist periodical founded by Alexander Berkman, praised Gruppo Anarchico Volontà for "doing things instead of talking about them." The article stated that "nobody even knows how many members this circle has. Each member stands responsible for his own acts, but cooperates with other members, all of whom are equally responsible." The story concludes with this warning: "Fine examples are these youth, fiery, conscious, clear sighted. They know what ails them and they are not going to be overdelicate in putting an end to the nuisance."[55]

At his final deportation hearing in November 1918 (he'd had two others, one in July 1917 and one in May 1918), Galleani, while not admitting that his followers may have been responsible for the bombing, nevertheless told the inspector that the authorities in San Francisco had not apprehended the right people: "It is a very ticklish affair upon which I do not wish to comment; I am positively sure that it was not Mooney who threw the bomb." Galleani also had an "informal conversation" with the immigration inspector and told him that it was an Italian who'd committed the bombing. He further said that the perpetrator had come to him for advice, but Galleani had told him that he "wished not to learn of it." When the inspector asked him to reveal who it was, Galleani replied that it was a secret he could not disclose. It is plausible then that a Galleanist, perhaps from the San Francisco–based Gruppo Anarchico Volontà, traveled to Massachusetts to obtain Galleani's approval of the plot (and perhaps guidance as to how to best carry it out) and that Galleani, always the shrewd operator, simply by saying he did not wish to learn about it, was still interpreted by the mysterious visitor as giving the green light to go ahead with the attack.[56]

Another indication pointing to the possible involvement of Galleanists in the parade bombing was a letter sent to San Francisco's police commissioner, James Woods, after the incident, threatening to kill him for helping to organize the parade. It was the method of killing mentioned that brought to mind a past Galleanist tactic: poisoned soup. Earlier that year, as discussed in the introduction, Nestor Dondoglio, a.k.a. Jean Crones, a Galleani follower, had poisoned the soup of all the guests at a reception in Chicago for Archbishop George Mundelein. A letter had also been sent to the headwaiter at San Francisco's Hotel St. Francis, where Woods additionally worked as the manager, pleading with the waiter to serve Woods the poisoned soup and telling him how easily it could be accomplished given the waiter's job at the hotel. (As hotel manager, Woods had significantly helped San Francisco rebuild following the 1906 earthquake; afterward, he was appointed police commissioner but maintained his position as manager of the hotel.)[57]

The link to the Crones case received national attention. Newspapers around the country reported that police now had a good clue as to who was responsible for the parade bombing. The *Los Angeles Times* ran the story under the title "Think Outrage Work of Jean Crones Gang." The media, police, government officials, and others did not know the true identity of Crones and that he was a Galleanist. But the mention of poisoned soup in the threatening letter to Woods, as well as the request that the waiter at the hotel do the deed, was a red flag, in particular for the Chicago police. They believed, based on the letters, that the plot to bomb the parade had originated in Chicago and that the bomb had been built there. Another clue that pointed them to "the Jean Crones gang" was "the letter-writing proclivity of the supposed murderer after his destructive work." Crones wrote numerous letters taunting the police after the soup poisoning, boasting that they would never capture him. They never did.[58]

But no more letters were sent to Woods or the waiter regarding poisoned soup. The Crones link to the bombing eventually faded as Mooney and Billings became the focus of the authorities. Whoever wrote the letters remained unknown. That it could have been Nestor Dondoglio or some other Galleanist, and that Gruppo Anarchico Volontà could have perpetrated the parade bombing, cannot be dismissed. Historians Paul and Karen Avrich are convinced that the Galleanists were indeed responsible for the blast. "The explosion was the work of the San Francisco members of the Gruppo Anarchico Volonta," they write, "as an act of antimilitarist protest. The perpetrators were disciples of Luigi Galleani, a preacher of terrorism and bombs."[59]

While the country was being swept up in patriotic fever with Preparedness Day parades and other activities held in many cities, those opposed to military preparedness held their own rallies and demonstrations. At one of these in Boston in September 1916, demonstrators clashed with the police, leading to the arrests of three Galleanists on the charge of inciting to riot. Among those arrested was Mario Buda, "an uncompromising militant, who rejected docile submission to the state." He refused to take the oath during his trial and was sentenced to the maximum of five months in prison, a conviction that was reversed on appeal. Protests against the arrests of Buda and the other Galleanists (one was acquitted and the other sentenced to three months in prison) led to another violent struggle on December 6 in which a policeman was stabbed in the hand with a butcher knife, resulting in the arrests of three more militants. In reprisal the Galleanists set off a bomb at the headquarters of the harbor police on December 17, causing substantial physical damage but no injuries.[60]

By the beginning of 1917, the Galleanists were gearing up for what promised to be an even more contentious year, as America moved closer to entering World War I. Galleani and his followers could be expected to voice their opposition through continued protests, demonstrations, and bombings. But was there anything else they could do to hinder the war effort? Galleani would come up with an idea, and when he publicized it, the government began a methodical and relentless campaign to wipe out the group and its leader.

Just Say No

There is usually a fine line that most terrorist groups are careful not to cross—perhaps the number of casualties they inflict, the type of target or people they strike, or even the methods they use. The reason is that many terrorist groups depend upon the support—political, logistical, and financial—of various segments of the population that may not necessarily approve of a group's violent tactics, even though the people support its political, religious, or territorial objectives. That support could erode if the group miscalculates in its attacks and kills too many people. A certain type of attack, such as using a nuclear, biological, or chemical weapon, could also backfire for the group and lead to an unprecedented government crackdown with public approval that puts the group's very existence in jeopardy. Terrorists want to keep the pot boiling, but not to the point where they could be wiped out in retaliation for a specific attack.[61]

The Galleanists had not yet reached that point with their terrorist activity. While they had attacked police stations and churches, poisoned a banquet dinner for an archbishop, and, if they were responsible for the San Francisco parade bombing, also attacked civilians attending a promilitary parade, they had still managed to avoid committing an attack resulting in the full force of the government being brought down upon them. It would, however, be Galleani's insatiable appetite for provocation through his writings that would cross that line in 1917 as far as the government was concerned.

After the United States declared war on the Central Powers on April 6, 1917, and Congress followed up six weeks later by passing a military conscription law, Galleani took to the pages of *Cronaca Sovversiva* to voice his opposition to the compulsory draft and to share an idea with his readers about what they should do. The conscription law required every male between the ages of twenty-one and thirty to register with his local draft board by June 5, regardless of whether he was an American citizen. Although those aliens who had not applied for naturalization were excluded from military service, they still had to register. Failure to register was punishable by a penalty of up to one year in prison.[62]

Galleani saw a trap for immigrants and wrote an article in the May 26 issue of *Cronaca Sovversiva* titled "Matricolati!" (Registrants!). He used the pseudonym "Mentana," the full name of his daughter, Tana. (He had also used that pseudonym for *Faccia a Faccia col Nemico*.) He was shrewd enough not to appear to be advocating for outright draft evasion, something that could get him immediately arrested. "No advice is given on this matter, my children!" he wrote. But he really did give advice, warning his readers about the dangers of registering for the draft. "They register you so they can control your life," he argued, "to take it from you on the first occasion." He explained that while aliens who had not applied for citizenship were not liable to be drafted, there was no guarantee that they wouldn't be in the near future. Once you register, he claimed, the government will know who you are and where to find you.[63]

Galleani's supporters took his advice, many of them assuming new names, quitting their jobs, and moving to different locations, including Mexico and Canada, where they could not be found and arrested for failing to register for the draft. Three days after Galleani's article was published, the office of *Cronaca Sovversiva* in Lynn, Massachusetts, was searched for the first time in its history. Galleani was arrested but released after a few hours of interrogation in Boston. Then, after the Espionage Act was passed on June 15, a law that made aiding the enemy, interfering with the draft, or encouraging disloyalty in the armed forces a crime punishable by up to twenty years imprisonment and fines up to $10,000, the government stepped up the heat on Galleani and his newspaper.[64]

Cronaca Sovversiva was banned from the mails, as the Espionage Act had also given the postmaster general the right to deny the mails to printed matter that urged treason, insurrection, or forcible resistance to federal laws. The newspaper was described by the Department of Justice as "the most rabid, seditious and anarchistic sheet ever published in this country," and Galleani was labeled "the leading anarchist in the United States." The office of *Cronaca Sovversiva* was raided again by federal agents on June 15, and Giovanni Eramo, the newspaper's printer, was arrested. Agents then went to Galleani's home in nearby Wrentham around midnight and arrested him too, in front of his frightened children and partner, Maria. He was taken to Boston, where he and Eramo were indicted for conspiracy to obstruct the draft based on the publication of "Matricolati!" in *Cronaca Sovversiva*. Also indicted on the same charge was the newspaper's publisher, Carlo Valdinoci, who had escaped arrest by first hiding in New Britain, Connecticut, and then fleeing to Mexico.[65]

The trials of Galleani and Eramo were postponed, with both men eventually pleading guilty to the charges and fined $300 and $100, respectively. They also had to appear before the Immigration Commission of Boston in June for deportation hearings for "advocating or teaching the unlawful destruction of property, or advocating or teaching anarchy." Their lawyers protested this action in a letter to the secretary of commerce and labor, implying that others were pulling strings to get the men deported. "We feel that our clients are being persecuted unjustly in the matter," the lawyers wrote, "though this persecution is not due to your department, but that your department is being used for the purposes of accomplishing the riddance of these two men on the recommendation of others, more than any investigation, which has been had by any member of your department."[66]

At Galleani's hearing, the acting immigration inspector, John Ryder, asked him if he had written the "Matricolati!" article in *Cronaca Sovversiva*. Galleani said yes but insisted that he had not advised anyone to not register for the draft. He explained that "it was not my business to advise anybody to commit an act to be sent to jail." When Ryder showed him the article with the words "do not register" in the text, Galleani said he had done nothing wrong: "I said it was up to them to talk it over; see what they want. If they were strong enough to resist registration it was up to them."[67]

Ryder persisted with questions about advocating or teaching anarchy or the unlawful destruction of property, either one a deportable offense:

RYDER: Have you ever taught in writing or speaking anarchistic doctrines?

GALLEANI: In all my speeches, in all my writings I always try to keep away from anarchism because the people are so afraid of it, when they hear the word "anarchy." Not because it is not permissible to write or speak.

RYDER: Did you ever teach or advocate the unlawful destruction of property?

GALLEANI: No, if I shall commit any such crime I would be punished. Our paper has been published for 15 years and we never had any trouble with the authorities.[68]

Ryder wasn't fooled by Galleani's answers. "I find that the alien Luigi Galleani is an anarchist," he wrote in his report. He pointed out that Galleani "is a highly educated man, able to couch cleverly his phrases and by circumlocution and evasion parry the questions asked to obtain his definitions of his belief." Ryder further wrote that "for a man who has such command over words his answers to direct questions on anarchistic doctrines are weak and, in my opinion purposively divergent from the paths which he feared would lead him into incriminating evidence." He concluded that "as charged in the warrant for his arrest . . . [Galleani] has been found advocating or teaching the unlawful destruction of property by his writings in the Cronaca Sovversivva [*sic*]."[69]

Ryder, however, did not recommend deportation. He was influenced by Galleani's past in Italy and his current obligations to his large family: "Owing to the very extenuating circumstances in this case, in that deportation would mean imprisonment in Italy as an escaped exile; the alien's wife [Maria was not legally Galleani's wife] and two children have lived here 16 years, three other children were born here, and his deportation would entail untold sorrow to them besides removing their support I recommend that warrant of deportation be predicated upon his future activities." These activities included Galleani reporting to the immigration office at specified times and submitting a copy "of every article he writes and a copy of every speech he makes." Ryder finished by writing, "In this manner the alien would do no harm here and the alien members of his family would not become public charges."[70]

The commissioner general of immigration, Anthony Caminetti, agreed with Ryder that Galleani should not be deported. He did not believe the government had a strong-enough case. "It appears doubtful if the issuances for a warrant of deportation on the basis of the evidence so far developed is justified," he wrote. Caminetti recommended that the government instead "exercise such surveillance over him as may be possible, with a view to observing his actions." Galleani thus dodged a bullet in his first deportation hearing. He was being given a chance to demonstrate through his words and actions why he should be allowed to remain in the United States. But if anybody really thought that Galleani was going to go quietly into the night now after a lifetime of anarchist agitation, they were mistaken.[71]

Eramo's hearing took place right after Galleani's, but it didn't go as well. The investigator was again Ryder, who was not as impressed with Eramo as he had been with Galleani. The fact that Eramo was single without children worked against him, as there would be no family repercussions if he were deported. He was also not as savvy and evasive as Galleani when answering some of the questions. For example, when Ryder asked him whether he believed the United States to be "a Government by the people," Eramo answered that the government "have had laws against the American constitution." Ryder asked him to explain that comment further. "I have seen strikes where workmen have been ill-treated without any reason," Eramo said. "I have seen married women starving while the husband [*sic*] were serving terms in jail for having asked for a piece of bread; and the Government of the United States has never had any sympathy for the little children who were starving."[72]

Eramo also told Ryder that anarchy could be defined as a "society of free people without government." When asked if he believed in any form of government, Eramo replied, "No. I believe in the welfare of all humanity." He also admitted to Ryder that he attended anarchist meetings. Ryder recommended in his report that Eramo be deported since he found "that the alien . . . is an anarchist; (he says he is one) [and] that he disbelieves in and is opposed to organized government." Ryder further concluded, "I find that . . . he has been founding [*sic*] advocating anarchy, by his bodily presence an [*sic*] anarchistic meetings, approving, or advocating whatsoever might be there taught or espoused."[73]

No date was set for Eramo's deportation, and he would eventually have additional hearings. As for Galleani, even though he had now become a marked man, with every action he took and every word he spoke or wrote bringing with it the risk of arrest again and possible deportation, he didn't slow down. He continued to be involved with *Cronaca Sovversiva*, sending copies by American Express to a network of supporters around the country who then distributed them in their local areas.[74]

Meanwhile, in Mexico, a close bond was formed among some of the approximately sixty Galleanists who had fled there to avoid the draft. They lived in a group of adobe houses near Monterrey and "forged a special relationship . . . binding them together into a tightly knit underground fraternity. Young, energetic, determined, they formed an inner circle of ultra-militants within the larger Galleanist movement." This inner circle included Nicola Sacco and Bartolomeo Vanzetti, who in a few years would become known around the world for a robbery and murders in Massachusetts that they might have committed but for which they were executed after what was universally considered an unfair trial.[75]

Also among the Galleanists in Mexico was Mario Buda, a small, quiet, serious man nicknamed "Nasone" (Big Nose) for his large nose. He, as noted earlier, had been arrested the previous year during the violent demonstration in Boston. Carlo Valdinoci was in Mexico too. He was a tall, jovial, dashing individual with good looks who was always well dressed and well groomed. As different as Buda and Valdinoci were in appearance, they were similar in their uncompromising devotion to Galleani and to the cause. "Both were determined to answer force with force," writes historian Paul Avrich, "not only as a matter of self-defense but of principle and honor. Both were capable, intelligent, and possessed of strong character." And both would play prominent roles in the war between the Galleanists and the U.S. government once they returned to the States.[76]

None of the Galleanists had planned to stay long in Mexico, with many of them believing a social revolution was imminent in Italy and they would soon go there to take part in the uprising. But when that revolution never occurred, they decided to return to America, regardless of the risk of arrest for evading the draft. They were incensed by the harassment of Galleani by the government and its efforts to suppress their beloved newspaper, *Cronaca Sovversiva*. It is not surprising that they would return, as this was a proud, bold, adventurous group of anarchists who could not sit idly by as their leader, mentor, and godfather was under siege by the government.[77]

By October 1917 most of the self-exiled Galleanists were back in the United States, and it didn't take long for some of them to become involved in another skirmish with the "enemy," the battle this time taking place in the heartland. During a prowar, prodraft "loyalty" rally held in Milwaukee in September by Reverend Augusto Giuliani, pastor of the Italian Evangelical Church, members of the Francisco Ferrer Circle, a Galleanist faction, tore down an American flag that was on the stage. Police responded and opened fire on the anarchists, killing two of them. They arrested eleven more and then raided the headquarters of the Ferrer Circle, roughing up its members.[78]

The Galleanists, most likely led by Buda and Valdinoci, planned a revenge attack. On November 24, three days before the trial of those arrested in the September melee was to begin, a bomb was discovered near an exterior wall of Giuliani's church by the eleven-year-old daughter of the church's scrubwoman. The girl's mother informed an aide to Giuliani, who then notified the police. But when the police still had not shown up at the church after several hours, the aide gave the twenty-pound bomb to a young man to deliver to the police station. The device, made of iron pipe and approximately a foot in length and eight inches in diameter, was placed on a table inside the station. As detectives were inspecting it and also joking about it, the bomb exploded, killing nine policemen and a woman who had come to the station on a different matter.[79]

In the aftermath of the bombing, the authorities and the public wanted revenge against the anarchists they suspected of the explosion. When nobody was charged, they took out their anger and frustration on the eleven defendants from the September skirmish. The jury deliberated for only seventeen minutes and found all eleven people guilty of assault with intent to commit murder. They were each sentenced in December to eleven to twenty-five years in prison.[80]

The cycle of violence and retaliation continued, with it now being the Galleanists' turn to seek payback. This time, however, their plot involved using somebody they hoped would not arouse suspicion: a beautiful and dedicated teenaged member of the group. Gabriella Antolini, known as Ella, would soon be portrayed in the media as the "Dynamite Girl." She was very smart with an engaging personality. "She's the cleverest girl I have met in all my experience in investigation," Clinton Clabaugh, Midwest division superintendent of the Bureau of Investigation, would later say. "She is saturated with anarchy; seems to have been raised in its atmosphere."[81]

Clabaugh was correct. Ella's father, brothers, and husband were all anarchists. Born in Italy in 1899, she immigrated to the United States in 1907. She married when she was sixteen and joined the Galleanist faction Gruppo I Liberi (Group I Free) of New Britain, Connecticut, a year later. She participated in many of the group's activities, including dances, picnics, lectures, and theatrical performances. But it was her willingness to do anything for the group, including transporting dynamite between states, that got her in trouble.[82]

The plot involved transporting thirty-six sticks of dynamite from Youngstown, Ohio, to Chicago and then on to Milwaukee, where the probable target was the home of Winfred Zabel, the prosecutor in the case against the eleven anarchists. Carlo Valdinoci was now living in Youngstown after returning to the States from Mexico, and Mario Buda was in Chicago after his summer in self-exile. In January 1918 Valdinoci contacted Ella and asked her to come to Youngstown. Ella was smitten with the debonair Valdinoci, whom she had met at an anarchist dance in New Britain when he was hiding there in June 1917 before going to Mexico. The two exchanged letters that summer, and when he asked her to come to Youngstown at the start of the new year, she immediately went. He then persuaded her to carry the dynamite in a black leather bag to Chicago, where Buda would construct the bomb and bring it to Milwaukee. There, in the code words of the anarchists, he would "plant the poof."[83]

After meeting up with Valdinoci in Youngstown, Ella traveled with him by train to Steubenville, Ohio, apparently in a failed effort to pick up more dynamite. They then spent the night together, and the next day Valdinoci put Ella on the train to Chicago. After placing the black bag with the dynamite in her Pullman car, he kissed her goodbye. A porter, though, became suspicious of the couple, particularly the careful way they'd handled the bag, as well as their gestures and expressions. The porter devised a scheme through which he would be able to inspect the bag without Ella knowing. He shut off the heat in her compartment, telling her that the heating apparatus had broken and that she would have to go into an adjoining Pullman while the system was being fixed. Ella refused at first, but after a while it got so cold that she relented and went into another car without her bag. The porter then opened the bag and discovered the dynamite. He notified the conductor, who contacted the authorities in Chicago. Ella was arrested when the train pulled into the station. She put up a struggle and was very reluctant to surrender one item in her possession: a lock of Valdinoci's hair.[84]

From her jail cell two days after her January 18 arrest, Ella wrote to Valdinoci using his alias, "Carlo Rossini." She used her alias as well, "Linda José." Ella was worried that her parents would become distraught if they learned about her arrest. "Don't let any newspaper get into the house if possible," she wrote. She also asked Valdinoci, who knew her parents, to visit them "and keep them up." She promised in the letter that she would not tell the police who else was involved in the plot because she would never "be a spy and put others in danger." She tried to convince the authorities, whom she knew would read the letter before it was sent, that Valdinoci had nothing to do with the dynamite plot and that all he'd done was "accompany me to the station and kissed me good bye." Clearly in love with Valdinoci, she ended the letter with a prophetic thought: "You know, we kissed for the first time when I left Steubenville and maybe it will be the last too." It was, as the two would never meet again.[85]

Ella pleaded guilty to transporting explosives and was sentenced in October 1918 in federal court in Chicago to eighteen months in prison. She was incarcerated in the Missouri State Penitentiary (female federal prisoners at that time were sent to state prisons), where her prison mates were the famous anarchist Emma Goldman and Kate Richards O'Hare, a prominent Socialist. Both older women took the teenaged Ella under their wings and became very fond of her. O'Hare arranged for her husband to hire a lawyer after Ella had served her term but still faced potential deportation. Immigration officials, however, could not prove that she was an anarchist, and she was set free in April 1920.[86]

What is remarkable about the story of Ella Antolini is that for somebody who played a rather minor role in the Galleanists' campaign of violence, she received nationwide publicity for simply being a courier caught with thirty-six sticks of dynamite. Had she been a man arrested for the same offense, the story might have generated a column in a few newspapers, not the headlines that "Dynamite Girl" received. That the country was fascinated by the image of a beautiful young girl willing to blow up buildings and people revealed the stereotype most Americans had of what an anarchist looked like—a foreign male, usually an Italian, German, or Russian. While the public was aware of eloquent female anarchist propagandists such as Emma Goldman, these women were not usually associated with violent attacks such as bombings in America. The public could therefore only wonder now whether there might be more dynamite girls out there and where they might strike next.

The failure of the dynamite plot, sometimes referred to as the Youngstown conspiracy because that was where the plot was hatched, did not deter the Galleanists from trying again. On April 15, 1918, two bombs, each weighing about twenty pounds and containing enough dynamite and metal slugs to blow up a house and kill everyone inside, were discovered at the home of Winfred Zabel, the Milwaukee prosecutor. One of the bombs was to be detonated by a bottle of sulfuric acid dripping onto the cylinder, while the other had a fuse. The bomb with the sulfuric acid was identical to the one that exploded at the Milwaukee police station in November. This time both bombs were dismantled without them exploding and killing more policemen.[87]

The Galleanists didn't realize it at the time, but the Youngstown conspiracy would mark a turning point in their battle with the government. It would result in an ambitious, midranking federal agent based in the Midwest seizing upon the investigation as a way to advance his career. He would become obsessed with hunting down Galleanists everywhere, and they, in turn, would fight back with some of the most creative and daring terrorist attacks ever committed.

4 You Have Shown No Pity to Us!

There was an obscure advertisement in the January 17, 1961, edition of the *Sun*, a leading Baltimore newspaper. Sandwiched between auction sales notices for furniture, appliances, and other household effects was this listing:

> Administrator's Sale
> Approximately 5,000 Books
> (Estate Rayme Weston Finch)[1]

"Five thousand books!" people reading that item must have muttered to themselves. Who in the world would have so many books for sale? This Rayme Finch, they probably thought, must have been a bookstore owner, a librarian, or maybe just a wealthy man who was able to accumulate thousands of books during his life.

They would have been surprised, though, to learn that this mysterious man was neither wealthy nor a proprietor of books. He was a collector of books, seizing them in raids on anarchist and radical headquarters during his career as a Bureau of Investigation (BI) agent in the 1910s. Perhaps some of them were among the five thousand books in his estate.

Finch did not fit the mold of the typical BI agent. He didn't have the educational pedigree that the bureau looked for in its agents. He had dropped out of Baltimore City College and Johns Hopkins University and had no legal training in his background. He'd worked a number of tedious jobs, including peddling telephone service. His physical appearance was also not very impressive, with an abnormal growth over his left eye and most of his weight in his belly. But he was tenacious, energetic, and smart. He also got lucky and was in the right place at the right time to take advantage of an opportunity to further his career.[2]

After working for several years as an insurance investigator and claims adjustor in Cleveland, basically doing corporate detective work, Finch got a job as a "special employee," or informant, for the BI in Cleveland in 1916. He had on his own been absorbing all the information he could gather about radicals, and this helped him get his foot in the door with the BI. Charles DeWoody, the Cleveland office's special agent in charge, was impressed with Finch's knowledge and initiative and hired him to a permanent position in 1917 as a special agent to investigate activities aimed at disrupting industries that were vital to the war effort.[3]

Between late 1917 and early 1918, Finch visited industrial and coal-mining towns in Ohio, Pennsylvania, and West Virginia looking for anarchists and other radicals and at the same time developing contacts and informants. After Ella Antolini was arrested in Chicago with dynamite in her bag in January 1918, Finch got the big break he'd been hoping for. Ella had inadvertently alerted the authorities that the dynamite plot had a connection to Youngstown, Ohio. As noted in chapter 3, she'd written a letter from her jail cell to "Carlo Rossini" (Carlo Valdinoci's alias), using an address in Youngstown. The Cleveland office of the BI thus took over the case, and DeWoody made Finch the lead investigator.[4]

Finch was elated. Here was a case getting nationwide publicity, an opportunity for him to further impress his bosses at the bureau and hopefully rise up the ranks. He rushed to Youngstown and went to the address that Antolini had used in her letter to Valdinoci. It turned out to be a house where Valdinoci and another Galleanist, Giovanni Scussel, received mail. Further investigation resulted in Finch learning where Valdinoci and Scussel were residing, and a search of that house in Youngstown uncovered material linking the two men to Galleani, including a copy of his book *Faccia a Faccia col Nemico* (Face to face with the enemy), extolling the virtues of using dynamite in anarchist attacks. Finch also found two new .38 caliber Smith & Wesson revolvers among Scussel and Valdinoci's possessions. He arrested Scussel, but Valdinoci once again eluded capture. Finch tried to find Valdinoci, whom he at this point still only knew by his aliases, "Carlo Rossini" and "Carlo Lodi." He searched for him in other towns in Ohio, including the mining camps of eastern Ohio. But Valdinoci was nowhere to be found.[5]

The investigation into the Youngstown conspiracy uncovered other suspects, including Emilio Coda, who had gone to Mexico with Valdinoci, Scussel, and many other Galleanists during the summer of 1917. Coda was arrested, but after several months of questioning, both he and Scussel were released. Thanks to Finch, though, the government now strongly suspected that Galleani and his followers had been involved in the Youngstown dynamite plot. Additional searches of Scussel and Valdinoci's room uncovered correspondence and other material linking them to the Galleani network.[6]

Finch now pressed his superiors to let him take charge of an investigation of Galleani and his newspaper, *Cronaca Sovversiva*, in Massachusetts. They agreed, and he went to Boston to pick the brains of BI agents who had experience with the Galleanists. He learned about the raid on *Cronaca Sovversiva* the previous year and how, even though the newspaper was banned from the mails, it was still being distributed by American Express to people around the country. He further discovered that the person he'd been chasing in the Midwest, whom he knew only by the aliases "Carlo Rossini" and "Carlo Lodi," was in fact the fugitive publisher of *Cronaca Sovversiva* (Carlo Valdinoci), who had escaped arrest after the June 1917 raid on the paper. Finch also met with a former BI agent, Harry Bowen, who had led the June raid. Bowen gave him more information about the Galleanists, including a physical description of Valdinoci, who was in his early twenties and "clean shaven, 195 pounds, black hair worn in a pompadour."[7]

Seeing another opportunity to make a name for himself, Finch proposed to his superiors that he lead a new raid on *Cronaca Sovversiva*'s headquarters in Lynn. Once again they agreed, and on February 22, 1918, after obtaining a search warrant, Finch, along with several BI agents, federal marshals, and local police, descended upon the newspaper's office. They arrested the manager of the paper, Raffaele Schiavina, but Valdinoci was not there. The real find was thousands of documents, letters, books, and other materials. Finch and the other agents searched for the paper's subscription list but were unable to find it. They were, however, able to obtain more than three thousand names and addresses from the labels on copies of the latest issue about to be distributed.[8]

Working with translators, Finch combed through all the documents and other materials seized in the raid. In one of his reports, he made an astute observation about how the Galleanists communicated their ideas to others via *Cronaca Sovversiva*:

> The articles which appear in this paper are written in the almost cryptic style of those who impart knowledge and advice to others unlawfully. It seems to be done in this method purposely in order that the authors of these articles might not be punished. The style is understood by the readers of this paper, however, and it is through this means that Galleani and his associates have been able to import their radical views and ideas to the readers of this paper without openly putting themselves in a position for prosecution. The article "Matricolati[!]," however, was an exception and was written by the author in an open and frank vein.[9]

Finch took issue with acting immigration inspector John Ryder's finding in Galleani's June 1917 deportation hearing that taking him away from his family "would entail untold sorrow to them besides removing their support." He enclosed photographs of Galleani's children and argued that they could take care of themselves without his support: "It is the opinion of this investigator that Galleani's three daughters are old and able enough to provide for the family in the event of the deportation of Galleani for the activities of this man are such that his deportation is not only warranted but quite necessary and, indeed, it would be a bad precedent to be permitted to become established, that much cleverness, cunning and rascality should be protected simply because the perpetrator of them is the father of children."[10]

He also criticized Ryder for giving Galleani the benefit of the doubt and not deporting him as long as he reported to the immigration offices at specified times: "Mr. Ryder's conclusion that the alien could do no harm should he report to the Department or submit copies of his newspaper articles and speeches is misleading. Galleani could easily continue to do as he has always done, that is, travel to anarchistic groups from time to time, teaching his anarchy by correspondence and especially, as he has done in the past, through the individual actions of his lieutenants with whom he appears constantly surrounded."[11]

The deportation of Galleani, Finch concluded, was vital "to the breaking up of the anarchistic element which surrounds him and look up to him for guidance." He was thrilled to see his detailed investigation pay off when the Bureau of Immigration issued approximately one hundred arrest warrants in May 1918 for Galleanists they believed could potentially be deported. Almost half of these anarchists lived in New England, mostly in the Boston area. They were among the most active members of the movement, writing articles and editorials for *Cronaca Sovversiva*, collecting money for political prisoners, taking subscriptions, distributing the paper, and performing other tasks. Many of them would indeed eventually be deported.[12]

Galleani, of course, was on the list of those to be arrested, as was Giovanni Eramo, the newspaper's printer. Both had already had deportation hearings a year earlier. Finch didn't want to miss the big day: "As the arrests of John Eramo and Luigi Galleani, Printer and Editor respectively of the 'Cronaca Sovversiv' [*sic*], Lynn, Mass. were extremely important, I went with inspectors of the Bureau of Immigration to Lynn, Mass. in order to personally cooperate in the apprehension of these two men."[13]

On May 16 Galleani and Eramo were brought before Inspector Ryder for the second time at the immigration office in Boston. The inspector was probably looking forward to another interaction with the always interesting and intelligent Galleani. At the last hearing in June 1917, Ryder got into a discussion with Galleani about topics ranging from the different types of governments that exist around the world to the issue of immigrants assimilating into American society. This time they again discussed democratic virtues, and Ryder asked Galleani about his belief in the United States as a democracy. "The Democratic principle was before this was the United States. We find democracies in Athens, in France, in Italy," Galleani responded. He added that "most people don't know what democracy means."[14]

Galleani may not have been aware that Ryder was sympathetic to his family situation. Otherwise he would not have had the following exchange with Ryder that supported Finch's argument that Galleani's family would be fine financially if he were deported:

> RYDER: Have you other incomes [in addition to income from *Cronaca Sovversiva*]?
>
> GALLEANI: In my house I am the second husband, my wife has got a son who is working and he brings money home. I got another boy who goes to work before and after school and brings money home. I got two older girls; in the summertime one goes to State School in Wrenthem [*sic*], another works on a farm; used to do enough to pay for the money for schooling.[15]

When Ryder asked Galleani if he was still opposed to the principle of authority, as he'd stated in his previous hearing, Galleani replied that one accomplishes more by doing things spontaneously than by being forced to do things. Ryder tried to impress upon Galleani the implications of his views on government and authority: "Mr. Galleani, don't you realize that in these perilous times, men of your mind and your doings must be looked upon as deterrents here?" The ever-sharp Galleani equated his own actions with those of the American revolutionaries: "When the Boston Riot [Boston Tea Party] was here, the tea riot, that time was looked upon them just the same as they look upon me now. At the same time the right used to belong to them."[16]

Galleani's lawyer, who was present at the hearing, asked him if he would obey a government order to suspend further publication of *Cronaca Sovversiva*. "If the Government orders I have nothing to do but obey," Galleani said. But he described his devotion to the newspaper later in the hearing: "When a man works 16 years on a paper he is somewhat attached to the paper; not from a material point of view. I have lost health and a lot on that paper. I would be sorry to see the paper suspended because I am convinced that the paper has never given cause to be suppressed."[17]

As was the case with the last hearing, Ryder again did not recommend deportation. "Galleani has repeatedly expressed his willingness to cease publishing the paper if requested to do by any Government official; but no Government official has evidently such authority," Ryder wrote in his report. He pointed out that if Galleani were deported, *Cronaca Sovversiva* would still be published, but by writers less talented and careful than Galleani and more prone to incite readers. He also argued that since Galleani had written articles critical of the kaiser in Germany, with whom the United States was currently at war, "he has been doing pro–United States war work." Ryder wrote that Galleani "is an independent—belongs to no organization. There is no organization of anarchists in the United States any more than there is of Italian atheists."[18]

Galleani couldn't have hoped for a more sympathetic hearing officer than Ryder. One can only imagine Finch's astonishment when he learned of Ryder's decision and read the transcript of the hearing. He'd thought he had a slam-dunk case against Galleani. That Ryder was impressed with and liked Galleani was evident in the different way he treated Galleani's colleague, Giovanni Eramo. Even though Eramo told him that he had severed all ties with *Cronaca Sovversiva* and that he had not done anything since his last hearing to teach or advocate anarchy in any way, Ryder again recommended deportation. "He is of mild manner," Ryder observed in his report. "From all the evidence it appears his work for the paper is mostly a work of love for socialistic or anarchistic propaganda. Owing to his connection with the paper he becomes accessory to any unlawful matter printed therein for he knows the nature of the paper and admires the brighter minds who write for it." While Galleani was not taken to task by Ryder for writing such passages in his newspaper as "If they send you to the harvest you will destroy the wheat; and that you will destroy the looms and pulleys, bridges, roads, telephones, automobiles, cotton, wool and forage," Eramo, the typesetter for the paper, was. "I find that Giovanni Eramo has been found advocating the unlawful destruction of property and of all forms of law," Ryder concluded. "Again I recommend his deportation."[19]

While Galleani and Eramo were being questioned by Ryder, a new law came into effect aimed at punishing anarchists and other radicals. The Sedition Act of May 16, 1918, extended the penalties of the 1917 Espionage Act (up to twenty years in prison and fines of up to $10,000) to anybody who discouraged recruitment into the armed forces; obstructed the sale of Liberty Bonds; or uttered, printed, wrote, or published any disloyal, profane, scurrilous, or abusive language against the U.S. government, constitution, flag, or military uniforms. In other words, criticizing the country in writing or speeches could now be viewed as illegal. The Sedition Act also included penalties for anyone who advocated curtailing the production of materials needed for World War I.[20]

On July 18, 1918, the government suppressed *Cronaca Sovversiva*. The paper had, up until then, been banned from the mails but had managed to survive by being distributed by railway transport and private means. Now it was to be shut down for good. Yet despite what Galleani had told Ryder at his hearing (that if the paper were suppressed he would obey the order), he secretly shipped the newspaper's printing presses from Lynn to a new location in Providence, Rhode Island, where there was an active group of Galleani supporters. He tried to continue operations but was only able to publish two more issues over the next year.[21]

BI agents like Finch were frustrated seeing anarchists they'd built cases against, such as Galleani, not deported. But they had no jurisdiction over deportations. At that time, deportations were administrative decisions rendered by the Department of Labor, under which the Bureau of Immigration operated. There was input from the Bureau of Investigation, but immigration hearing officers like John Ryder made recommendations to the secretary of labor for the final say. It was not until 1940, when the Bureau of Immigration was transferred to the Department of Justice, that deportation decisions were made by that department.[22]

The criteria the Bureau of Immigration used to determine whether an alien should be deported was whether the person was advocating or teaching anarchy, the unlawful destruction of property, the overthrow of the government by force, or the assassination of public officials. This was included in the Immigration Act of 1917. Yet these charges were often hard to prove. Did the alien actually teach anarchy or specifically call for the overthrow of the government or destruction of property or assassination of government officials? Due to these loopholes, most of the anarchists who appeared at deportation hearings were set free on bail to be called back later.[23]

To make the job of the immigration hearing officers easier and close all loopholes, Congress passed the Anarchist Exclusion Act on October 16, 1918. This new law excluded and expelled from America "aliens who are members of the anarchistic or similar classes." Now all an immigration inspector needed in order to make a recommendation for deportation was to find that an alien simply belonged to or subscribed to the beliefs of an anarchist group or was in possession of anarchist literature for the purposes of propaganda.[24]

There was now little wiggle room left for anarchists such as Galleani and his followers to avoid deportation. To make sure of this, the Department of Labor issued a memorandum to guide the Bureau of Immigration when dealing with Galleanists. It specified that "in the cases of Italian anarchists, evidence of their continued subscription to the *Cronaca Sovversiva*, the leading anarchist newspaper in the United States . . . shall be considered good grounds for deportation on the charge of advocating and teaching anarchy in the United States."[25]

We Will Dynamite You!

As the hammer was lowering on the Galleanists, their nemesis, Rayme Finch, was no longer working exclusively on their cases. During the spring of 1918, he was transferred to the New York office of the Bureau of Investigation, a promotion based on his meticulous investigative work in Boston and Youngstown. Charles DeWoody, who had hired Finch as a BI special agent while running the Cleveland office in 1917, was now in charge of the New York office. He wasn't happy with the agents there. When he wrote to Finch to congratulate him on building cases against the Galleanists, he let him know how he had always "banked on you pretty heavy" but now there was "bad work going on in another bureau." He hoped Finch could "deliver the goods [there] as you did in the Italian cases."[26]

It isn't clear what "bad work" DeWoody was referring to in his letter to Finch. But the New York field office had a much larger and more complex caseload than any other BI division in the country. It wasn't just the Galleanist groups in East Harlem and nearby Paterson, New Jersey, that it had to contend with. Identifying German spies and saboteurs was a top priority for the bureau during World War I. New York BI agents were also watching members of the Union of Russian Workers and the IWW, militant restaurant workers, Irish and Indian nationalists, and Mexican revolutionaries. Even Greenwich Village bohemian anarchists were on the radar of the bureau. New York was also the home base for Emma Goldman and Alexander Berkman.[27]

Finch, who was to monitor all radical activity in the New York area, "felt overworked and underappreciated." He was given just one assistant who also served as a stenographer. He utilized informants when he could find them to gather any evidence that a particular individual or group was violating the Espionage Act or Sedition Act. One of his informants, "B-10," was a single woman in her thirties who spoke Italian and attended meetings, dances, and other activities, oftentimes those of the IWW, hanging out with various radicals until one or two in the morning. Though Finch was not very complimentary about her physical appearance, describing her as "unattractive [and] undersized," he respected her loyalty to the country, writing that "she is prompted by only the most patriotic motives."[28]

Female informants were still a novelty during this period, but Finch recognized their value. "Being a woman," he wrote, "she [B-10] is free from suspicion, and she has made it a point to play up to these men in this movement [IWW] who are active and who know a great deal about what is going on. We have found that these radicals are quite free with their fiancees and believe this is just as good, if not a better way than to have a man in this movement." Finch also noted that B-10 had refused to join any of these movements, even if it would help the Bureau of Investigation, because "it has been repulsive to her to think of carrying a red book." This was no problem, however, since, according to Finch, the radical leaders liked to "have women present at all times as an added attraction to keep the men interested and present at the meetings at all times."[29]

Finch's job with the New York BI office lasted only about a year. He resigned in May 1919 and the next month became the chief investigator for the Lusk Committee, a New York State legislative body that examined seditious activities. That was only a temporary position, though, so when the committee finished its hearings and delivered its final report in April 1920, Finch was out of work. He had already fallen from grace with the Bureau of Investigation, and they rebuffed his efforts to get his old job back. The bureau was suspicious of the close ties he had developed with British intelligence while on the Lusk Committee. The Brits were operating in New York to gather information on Irish nationalists, anti-British Hindu militants, international radical organizations, and other groups or individuals they viewed as threats to Britain. J. Edgar Hoover, then a special assistant to the attorney general and in 1924 the director of the Bureau of Investigation, sent a memo to U.S. military intelligence in February 1921 that included Finch's name on a list of "known British agents and suspects who have come to the attention of this Bureau."[30]

Not long after that memo, a BI report stated that Finch had gone to the office of a counselor of the British Consulate and, while there, ran into another former U.S. government agent. He told this agent "that he was out of a job and in poor financial circumstances; that he had sought to obtain a position with the Department of Justice, and having failed in that he was now trying to connect with the British service." One can only imagine the embarrassment of this former hotshot anarchist hunter as he revealed his misfortunes to his former colleague. He would have been even more embarrassed if he'd seen the title of the BI report on him: "Raymond Finch—Alleged British Agent." "Can't the bureau even get my first name right?" he probably would have muttered to himself.[31]

Finch wound up getting a job with a private detective agency known as the International Library Service. That name was intentionally misleading. The firm was owned by RA&I Company, a nationwide detective agency composed of many ex-BI agents. The agency "specialized in compiling dossiers on radicals." A union publication warned its readers about this "new spy agency plying up old stuff." A company would hire an RA&I detective who would then "make daily reports of everything the other working men do, such as: how much faster it would be possible for them to work, what jobs should be cut, why men lay off [are not working hard], what men are agitators, etc. This is to be done in the six working days in the week, then on Sunday they are supposed to associate with their fellow workers and learn just what they say, do, and think, so as to also report that." It is not known if this was the type of work Finch did for the company, but if so he would have been well suited for it based on his previous investigative experience and his "gift of getting others to talk without revealing anything about himself."[32]

One group of people, though, who knew Finch very well was the Galleanists. After all, he was their main government antagonist, gathering evidence that could lead to their arrests and hearings before the Bureau of Immigration for likely deportation. His investigative work, combined with the repressive October 1918 Anarchist Exclusion Act, marked the beginning of the end for many of Galleani's followers, including the godfather himself. With deportation now based simply on being an alien who belonged to anarchist or similar types of movements or subscribed to *Cronaca Sovversiva*, many Galleanists could see the writing on the wall. But they were not going to go quietly.

When Galleani had another deportation hearing with acting immigration inspector John Ryder just a month after the Anarchist Exclusion Act was passed, there was little that even Ryder, who had previously been sympathetic to Galleani, could do in his favor. The law specified that aliens such as Galleani should be deported, and that is what Ryder recommended. It was at this hearing that Galleani, as noted in chapter 3, told Ryder in an informal conversation that an Italian was responsible for the July 1916 San Francisco Preparedness Day bombing and not Tom Mooney, who, along with Warren Billings, had been convicted of the attack. Knowing it might be his last chance to obtain information from Galleani about that bombing, Ryder pressed on. "When I informed him he would be performing a grand thing for justice to tell all he knew," Ryder wrote, "the said Galleani said the secret was not his to give; that if one Mooney were to suffer capital punishment, the real culprit, if he had any honor would confess."[33]

Meanwhile, Giovanni Eramo, *Cronaca Sovversiva*'s printer, also had another hearing before the Bureau of Immigration in November 1918, and the result was the same as before: a recommendation for deportation. Eramo appeared yet again at a hearing in February 1919, but Inspector Ryder didn't change his decision. However, Anthony Caminetti, the commissioner general of immigration (in Washington DC), overruled Ryder and ordered that a decision in Eramo's case be postponed for one year, during which time Eramo was to report quarterly to the nearest immigration officer to update him regarding his occupation and behavior. Unlike Ryder, Caminetti was impressed that Eramo was no longer associated with *Cronaca Sovversiva* and had cut ties with Galleani. In a memorandum he sent to Acting Secretary of Labor John Abercrombie, Caminetti wrote that "the evidence shows conclusively that Eramo has at all times been the tool and dupe of Galleani; that in the summer of 1918, after both Galleani and Eramo had been taken into custody for the second time by this Bureau, Eramo decided to sever his connections with Galleani and removed his monotype machine from the premises of the Cronaca Sovversiva; that this action made Galleani angry and he wrote an article in his paper against Eramo." Caminetti also pointed out that "the Bureau is inclined to the belief that Eramo's difficulties are due almost entirely to the influence of Galleani and that since he has alienated himself from the latter, it is quite probable that he may be converted into a law abiding citizen."[34]

The government had no such hope that Galleani could ever become a law-abiding citizen. On January 27, 1919, Abercrombie signed the deportation order. It was now only a matter of time before Galleani, out on bail, would be arrested again and sent to Ellis Island to be deported. But before that happened, his followers let the authorities know that they were not going down without a fight.[35]

In February the Galleanists, using the name American Anarchists, distributed a circular throughout New England, titled *Go-Head!* It was a warning to the government of what would happen if they followed through with the deportations of Galleani and other anarchists:

Go-Head!

The senile fossils ruling the United States see red!

Smelling their destruction, they have decided to check the storm by passing the Deportation law affecting all foreign radicals.

We, the American Anarchists, do not protest, for it is futile to waste any energy on feeble minded creatures led by His Majesty Phonograph Wilson.

Do not think that only foreigners are anarchists, we are a great number right here at home.

Deportation will not stop the storm from reaching these shores. The storm is within and very soon will leap and crash and annihilate you in blood and fire.

You have shown no pity to us! We will do likewise.

And deport us! *We will dynamite you!*

Either deport us or free all! [Emphasis in the original.]

The American Anarchists[36]

Mario Buda and Carlo Valdinoci were believed to have been among the authors and distributors of the circular. That same month Galleani, who apparently was accelerating his activities in anticipation of being deported soon, gave a provocative speech to a crowd in Taunton, Massachusetts, a city located near Franklin, where a strike at the American Woolen Company was underway. The following evening, four Galleanists who had attended the speech were blown up when a bomb they were trying to place at the company exploded prematurely. The Bureau of Investigation suspected that Galleani was behind the bombing and that he'd even had one of his daughters, who was an architecture student, draw up a map of Franklin highlighting the location of the factory.[37]

Based on the *Go-Head!* circular and the past activities of the Galleanists, the authorities knew that the "We will dynamite you!" warning was no idle threat. The group had proven itself to be the most dangerous association of anarchists in America. Galleani and his followers had to be planning something big to protest his impending deportation. The Franklin bombing, though, didn't really qualify as the major attack the authorities were expecting. The question was what exactly Galleani and his followers were planning to do and who or what would be the target.

For the Galleanists the challenge was coming up with something new, since the authorities were on the lookout for bombs placed in police stations, courthouses, churches, and other favorite targets of the anarchists. They decided on a plot that would combine their expertise in making bombs with a different way to deliver them: the U.S. postal system. This choice was ironic and perhaps intended as such, since the Galleanist newspaper, *Cronaca Sovversiva*, had been banned from the mails before being shut down completely by the government. Thus it would be the postal service itself that would be the delivery vehicle for one of the most ingenious and ambitious terrorist plots in history.[38]

A Gift for You from Gimbel Brothers

As the Galleanists planned their revenge, America was still in the process of transitioning from the end of World War I to an uncertain peacetime era. After the armistice was signed in November 1918, U.S. soldiers started coming back to a country experiencing price increases and widespread unemployment due to the cancellation of production contracts related to the war effort. There was also labor strife, including a general strike in Seattle in February 1919 that shut down the city and resulted in federal troops being brought in to end it. Meanwhile, the third wave of the deadly 1918 influenza pandemic was about to hit America in the spring of 1919, eventually bringing the death toll to 675,000. And during the summer, racial riots swept through Chicago, Washington, and Detroit, with violent attacks on Black communities in those cities. As historian Beverly Gage observes, "It looked as if American society was tearing itself apart."[39]

Amidst all these negative developments, the fear of a Bolshevik or some other type of radical revolution in America also fueled public anxiety. The "public had been whipped up by patriotic propaganda to a pitch of nativist excitement [during the war years], and such emotion could not be instantly turned off," writes historian Paul Avrich. "Instead, wartime hatred of Germans transformed itself into peacetime horror of radicals, especially alien radicals. If only the menace of un-Americanism could be eliminated, it was widely felt, the nation would be cleansed, its difficulties and tensions mitigated."[40]

This sentiment was obvious on May 1, 1919, a date that annually celebrates working-class solidarity and is known as May Day. Parades in Cleveland and Boston were broken up violently by ex-soldiers and sailors, policemen, and civilians. In New York the offices of the Socialist newspaper the *New York Call* were ransacked, and everyone inside was beaten up with broken chair legs used as clubs. A meeting at Carnegie Hall in support of Tom Mooney was also broken up, while the headquarters of the Union of Russian Workers in Manhattan was attacked by the mob. The Russians there were forced to sing "The Star-Spangled Banner."[41]

Galleani and his followers would do their part to add fuel to the fire during this period that became known as the Red Scare, a public frenzy encouraged by the government, Congress, media, and law enforcement agencies. What the Galleanists had in mind required perfect timing and the element of surprise. They intended to have thirty identical package bombs arrive at destinations around the country on May Day. Doing this, though, involved a lot of luck since there was no guarantee packages sent through the mail toward the end of April would arrive exactly on May 1. If the packages arrived before or after that date, that would be all right as long as all the packages arrived on the same day. If some arrived a day or two before the others, there was a chance the authorities and the public would be alerted and on the lookout for more package bombs sent through the mail.[42]

To ensure that the recipients of the packages would not be suspicious and would open them, the Galleanists cleverly wrapped them in straw-colored paper and used a notable return address: Gimbel Brothers, a famous New York department store. In black, printed letters it read, "Gimbel Brothers, 32nd St. Broadway 33rd Street, New York City." The anarchists also had the words *novelty* and *sample* stamped in red letters on separate areas of each package, and there was an emblem of a mountain climber with a pack on his back and an alpenstock in his hand next to the typed name of the addressee. Each package was about the size and shape of a one-pound candy box.[43]

Underneath the paper wrapping was a green cardboard box that was eight inches long, three inches wide, and two inches deep. Within this box was a dynamite bomb constructed of a small, black, glass vial of sulfuric acid fastened by brass screws to a cork at the top of a wooden cylinder. Opening the lid of the cylinder would force the cork with the screws into the fragile glass vial, breaking it and releasing the acid onto three fulminate-of-mercury percussion caps resting on a stick of dynamite within the cylinder. This would ignite the caps and set off an explosive charge packed with metal slugs at the bottom of the package. It was an ingenious contraption both in design and construction.[44]

The list of people the Galleanists planned to assassinate with their bombs is an impressive one, ranging from cabinet officers and U.S. senators and representatives to governors, mayors, judges, district attorneys, and industrialists. Nobody could accuse the Galleanists of aiming low. The following individuals were the intended recipients of the packages:

A. Mitchell Palmer, attorney general
Albert S. Burleson, postmaster general
William H. Lamar, solicitor of the Post Office Department
Anthony Caminetti, commissioner general of immigration
William B. Wilson, secretary of labor
Frederic C. Howe, commissioner general of immigration, Port of New York (Ellis Island)
Thomas W. Hardwick, former senator from Georgia
John L. Burnett, congressman from Alabama
Albert Johnson, congressman from Washington
Lee S. Overman, senator from North Carolina
William H. King, senator from Utah
Reed Smoot, senator from Utah
Oliver Wendell Holmes Jr., associate justice of the U.S. Supreme Court
Kenesaw Mountain Landis, U.S. district judge, Chicago
Ole Hanson, mayor of Seattle
John F. Hylan, mayor of New York City
Richard E. Enright, police commissioner of New York City
William C. Sproul, governor of Pennsylvania
William I. Schaffer, attorney general of Pennsylvania
T. Larry Eyre, state senator from Pennsylvania
Theodore G. Bilbo, governor of Mississippi
Walter Scott, mayor of Jackson, Mississippi
Frederick Bullmers, editor of the *Jackson Daily News* in Jackson, Mississippi
Frank K. Nebeker, special assistant to the attorney general
Charles M. Fickert, district attorney of San Francisco
Edward A. Cunha, assistant district attorney of San Francisco

William M. Wood, president of the American Woolen Company
John D. Rockefeller, industrialist
J. P. Morgan, financier
R. W. [Rayme] Finch, special agent, Bureau of Investigation[45]

This list was not a random selection of high-profile government, legal, and law enforcement officials. Each person was chosen for a reason—namely, all "in one way or another, had offended the Galleanists." For example, Palmer, as attorney general, was in charge of the Department of Justice and its Bureau of Investigation, the body that had gone after Galleani and other anarchists and radicals for several years. Burleson and Lamar, as top officials of the postal system, had banned radical publications, including *Cronaca Sovversiva*, from the mails. Caminetti and Wilson were key players in the impending deportations of Galleani and some of his supporters, with Caminetti having recommended the warrants for the deportations. Wilson, as secretary of labor, in charge of overseeing the Bureau of Immigration, had signed them. Howe was the top official at Ellis Island, where most of the deportations occurred.[46]

The senators, congressmen, and judges on the list were also viewed by the Galleanists as their enemies, as well as the enemies of all anarchists, Socialists, and IWW militants. Even though the Galleanists had their differences with the IWW and other radicals, they were still viewed as kindred brothers and sisters in the struggle against capitalism and government. Hardwick and Burnett were targeted because they had introduced the law calling for the deportation of alien anarchists and radicals, while Johnson, Overman, King, and Smoot were among the bill's main supporters. Justice Holmes had delivered the Supreme Court decision affirming the conviction of Socialist leader Eugene V. Debs for violating the Espionage Act, while Judge Landis had presided over the trials of IWW militants and Gabriella Antolini, the Galleanist "Dynamite Girl."[47]

Mayor Hanson was included on the list for, among other things, requesting federal troops be sent to Seattle to put down the general strike that had taken place there. Mayor Hylan had ordered raids on meeting places of anarchists and radicals in New York, while Police Commissioner Enright had carried them out. Governor Sproul, Attorney General Schaffer, and State Senator Eyre, all from Pennsylvania, made the list for playing key roles in establishing and enforcing antisedition laws in their state. (Galleani had also been arrested once in Pennsylvania and charged with inciting to riot.) The same was true for the Mississippi contingent on the list. Governor Bilbo, Mayor Scott, and newspaper editor Bullmers were all supporters of antisedition legislation in Mississippi. An example of Bullmers's antianarchist crusade can be seen in the following editorial in his newspaper a little over a month before the package bombs were sent:

> The alien agitators who are to be deported now that the courts of last resort have said that they are subject to deportation are trying to arouse the sympathy of the labor unions in their behalf. But they ought not to be able to do so. They are not being deported because of their "union or strike activities," as claimed but because they are undesirable citizens. That is, they are anarchists and disturbers, and have been declaiming against our form of government.
>
> We have been more lenient in the past with this class of people than we are going to be in the future. We have stood more from them than we ought to have stood. So with the lessons before us in the old world, with a full knowledge of what their kind will do to the government if they get a chance, we are going to send them out of the country, and we are going to make it so hard for their kind to get into the country that we shall save ourselves a lot of trouble.[48]

The remaining names on the list had also done their part to antagonize anarchists and other antigovernment militants. Nebeker had previously been the chief prosecutor at an IWW trial in Chicago, while Fickert and Cunha had prosecuted Tom Mooney and Warren Billings for the Preparedness Day bombing in San Francisco. Wood, as president of the American Woolen Company, had orchestrated a murder charge frame-up of strikers during the Lawrence, Massachusetts, textile strike of 1912 and was on the minds of anarchists due to the recent strike at his factory in Franklin. (Galleani gave the rousing speech there that inspired four of his followers, as noted earlier, to try to bomb the factory, but they were killed when the bomb exploded prematurely.) And of course someone composing a list of hated figures to attack wouldn't leave out John D. Rockefeller and

J. P. Morgan, two of the most prominent capitalists in the country and "symbols of everything the anarchists opposed."[49]

That there are no religious figures on the list is surprising, given the Galleanist hostility toward all religions. What is not surprising, though, is the inclusion of Rayme Finch. Most anarchists and radicals had probably never heard of him. After all, he was not a high-level BI official, and his name didn't appear very often in newspapers. But for the Galleanists, Finch was public enemy number one. His name on the list convinced historian Paul Avrich that it was the Galleanists, not IWW militants, Bolsheviks, or any other possible suspects, who sent the thirty package bombs:

> Should any doubt remain concerning the plotters, the appearance of Finch on the list must dispel it. Why should a lowly Bureau of Investigation operative be selected as a target? The answer seems clear. It was Finch, during the early weeks of 1918, who had arrested Scussel in Youngstown and dogged Valdinoci through the mining camps along the Ohio River. In February 1918, moreover, he had led the raid on *Cronaca Sovversiva* and arrested Raffaele Schiavina. Transferred to New York, he had continued his pursuit of the Galleanists, arresting Andrea Ciofalo in the Bronx. Ciofalo, released on bail, may have been a party to the bomb conspiracy. Like Valdinoci and Schiavina, he bore a special grudge against Agent Finch.[50]

According to Avrich, a small group of Galleanists in New York and Massachusetts was responsible for the package-bomb plot, and Galleani and Schiavina probably participated in the selection of the targets. Experienced bomb makers such as Valdinoci and Buda would have been the most likely candidates for preparing the bombs to explode upon opening. Valdinoci was a carpenter whose skills would have come in handy when constructing a device to hold explosives, while Buda was familiar with explosives, having worked in construction and other industries where dynamite was used. He had also been involved, along with Valdinoci and Antolini, the "Dynamite Girl," in the conspiracy to carry dynamite to Chicago and then to Milwaukee in order to bomb the home of Winfred Zabel, the prosecutor in a case against several anarchists.[51]

After the thirty packages were completed and ready to go, they were dropped into mailboxes on the west side of Manhattan near Gimbel Brothers, between April 22 and April 26. (Putting them in mailboxes far away from Gimbels could have elicited suspicion at the post office about whether the parcels really were from the department store.) The packages destined for farther-away locations such as San Francisco and Seattle were the first ones put in the mailboxes, followed days later by the rest. Now all the Galleanists had to do was wait to hear or read about their bombs exploding all around the country (on the same day, they hoped).[52]

One can only imagine their disappointment when they learned that one of the packages had arrived at the office of Seattle mayor Ole Hanson on the morning of April 28, while no reports emerged about any other bombs being delivered elsewhere that day. If the Seattle incident received a lot of publicity, their whole operation would be at risk, possibly resulting in the rest of their bombs either being intercepted by the postal authorities or not opened by suspicious recipients. To make matters worse for them, Hanson wasn't even at his office when the bomb arrived; he was in Colorado on a speaking tour on behalf of a Victory Loan campaign for the government. With him was his secretary, who usually handled the mail. The chief clerk for the city's building department, M. H. Strouse, was working as acting secretary and opened the package. When he attempted to open the lid of the wooden cylinder, it got stuck. So Strouse turned it upside down and tried again with a firmer tug. This time the lid opened and the glass vial broke, but because he was holding the tube upside down, the acid poured out onto his hand and not the fulminating caps, avoiding setting off the explosives. Police described the bomb as being of sufficient power to blow out the entire side of the County-City Building.[53]

When Louis Gimbel, an executive with Gimbel Brothers, learned of the package bomb that evening, he said that as far as he knew nobody associated with Gimbels had sent any package to Hanson. He also pointed out that it would be easy for a customer to make a purchase in the novelty department of the store and then use the wrappings for the purpose of mailing a package bomb. The next day, another package bomb with a Gimbels return address reached its destination. The intended recipient, former senator Thomas Hardwick, was not at his Atlanta apartment when the bomb was delivered in the afternoon. His wife attempted to open it, but just like Strouse, she had trouble getting the lid off the cylinder holding the explosives. She asked her maid, Ethel Williams, to give it a try. Williams, holding the tube upright, pulled off the lid and the bomb exploded, blowing off both her hands. Hardwick's wife, who was standing nearby, suffered burn injuries to her face and neck. The Galleanists were probably happy that at least one of their bombs had exploded, though severely injuring a maid was likely not their intention. They had to wonder, though, why there hadn't been reports of other bombs going off around the country. "Didn't we send out thirty package bombs? What happened to the rest of them?" they must've thought.[54]

A young postal worker in New York had the answer. He didn't realize it, though, until the wee hours of the morning on April 30. Charles Kaplan was looking forward to going home after his night shift ended at midnight at the main post office located opposite Penn Station on Eighth Avenue and Thirty-Second Street in Manhattan. The twenty-nine-year-old Kaplan lived in the Bronx, so it would be a long subway ride uptown, but at least he knew at this time of night he would be able to get a seat and leisurely read the newspaper. As he was perusing the midnight edition of the *New York Tribune*, he came across a story that startled him. It was about the package bomb that had exploded in former senator Hardwick's apartment in Atlanta. (Kaplan had not read any news items about the earlier Hanson bomb.) The story described in detail the bomb with the Gimbels return address. "Good God!" he exclaimed to himself. "We got sixteen of those damned things down in the Post Office right now waiting for first class postage and addressed to members of the Cabinet, the Mayor, Morgan and a lot of other big men and they may be sent out any minute. You have got to hustle!"[55]

He first thought he should telephone the post office to warn them about the packages. But he decided that wasn't a good idea: "I was afraid they would think I was joking or something so I got off at 110th Street, although I was pretty sleepy, and came back [to the post office]." He got there around 1:30 a.m. and told the night superintendent, Henry Meyer, about the package bombs. Kaplan knew about the packages because two days earlier he had received the items but not passed them on for delivery since they did not have sufficient postage. "We had held the parcels up," Kaplan said, "because they were sealed and that made them first-class mail and they only had parcel post stamps."[56]

Kaplan noticed this problem when he weighed the packages in the basement of the main post office after they arrived on the evening of April 26. Each package weighed six ounces and had a small red seal closing the ends of the wrapping. The seals on the packages made them first-class mail and not the cheaper parcel post mail. At three cents an ounce, each one needed eighteen cents' worth of stamps. However, not one of the sixteen packages Kaplan weighed had more than six cents' worth. So he sent them to the short-payment department located on the main floor of the post office.[57]

And there the sixteen bombs lay for more than two days as thousands of people walked through the building. Gimbels was notified twice about the insufficient postage, but nobody from the store ever responded to the inquiries. That was a lucky break for the intended recipients. Had somebody from Gimbels told the post office to add the required postage and bill the store later, then sixteen more bombs would have been on their way to the unfortunate individuals or the people who opened their mail.[58]

After Kaplan returned to the post office and alerted Meyer about the package bombs, the two men carefully inspected the sixteen packages from the outside and were convinced they were similar to the package that had exploded at former senator Hardwick's home. At this point Kaplan's work was done. The sleepy postal clerk could finally go home. "I don't expect any reward or anything else," he would later say. But he became a national hero, his name and picture plastered all over newspapers throughout the country. And the post office did in fact reward him with a promotion from night clerk to foreman of the parcel post section at the main post office.[59]

It was now 3:00 a.m., and Meyer didn't want to wait until the start of the workday to inform his superiors about the packages. So he called William Cochran, chief inspector for the post office, at his home to tell him about the bombs. Cochran immediately went to the post office and examined the packages. Just like Kaplan and Meyer, he too noticed the similarities of the packages to what was described in the newspaper about the Hardwick bomb. He, of course, wasn't going to open any of the packages.

That was left to one of the foremost bomb experts in the country, Owen Eagan. Attached to the Bureau of Combustibles of the Fire Department, he was the man to call whenever a bomb was discovered in New York. He handled more than seven thousand bombs in his illustrious career. "Bombs," he would later say, "strange as it may seem, have been made by many types of men, in all degrees of education, wealth and state of life." One time he suffered a serious injury when a device exploded, resulting in the loss of his left forefinger and rendering his thumb useless. He nevertheless remained very confident when dismantling bombs, believing that experience was on his side. "There are two opponents," he said, "a bomb and Eagan, but Dame Experience is always with me."[60]

When he arrived at the post office, Eagan examined one of the packages. After tearing off the outer wrappings, he took the wooden cylinder out of the cardboard box. He then attempted to open the cylinder from the bottom end; based on his experience, that was the safest part of a device to tamper with. He figured that the makers of the bomb intended for it to be opened from the top, and that's what would cause the device to explode. He may have also learned about how the bomb sent to Mayor Hanson in Seattle had not exploded when opened from the bottom. Eagan only had a penknife with him, but he fiddled with the cylinder before deciding it would be safer to take the bomb to the firehouse nearby, where he would have more tools to work with. Once there, he and the chief inspector for the Bureau of Combustibles, John Dixon, carefully worked on the bomb until five o'clock that afternoon.[61]

After they'd studied every aspect of the bomb, they couldn't believe what they had seen. Referring to it as an "infernal machine," as bombs were often labeled in those days, Eagan marveled at the workmanship that had gone into creating the devices. "It doesn't resemble any machine I have ever come across," he said. "It is the neatest and, from the standpoint of mechanical arrangement, the cleverest I have ever seen. Whoever perfected this thing must have been an expert mechanic and chemist." When shown the inner workings of the bomb, chief post office inspector Cochran was also impressed: "It is the most devilish contrivance I have ever seen—and I have come across a good many samples of anarchistic deviltry in my time." At that point the U.S. Post Office issued a warning to all post offices, postal inspectors, superintendents of mails, mail clerks on railroad mail cars, and anybody else handling the mail around the country to intercept any packages with a Gimbel Brothers return address and the word *sample* stamped in red letters. It also appealed to the public to not open any unexpected or suspicious packages.[62]

Some of these warnings, however, either were not issued in time or not heeded by everyone. In one case a package bomb addressed to Senator Overman reached the Salisbury, North Carolina, post office on the evening of April 30, just when the nationwide warnings were being disseminated. It was a happy occasion that night for the senator, who was hosting a reception at his home for his two daughters. Both had been married earlier that evening. The entire town had been invited to the public reception, and most showed up. All week long and that day, hundreds of gifts and packages had been delivered to the Overman home from all over the country. The post office planned to make one last delivery that night after the mail arrived, but there were not enough packages addressed to Overman or his daughters to justify a special trip. So the packages, including the one containing a bomb, were held until the next morning. Had the package been delivered, it would likely have been opened at the crowded reception along with all the other gifts and packages. Many people could have been killed or injured. The next morning a postal clerk, who by then like everyone else had heard about the nationwide terrorist plot, saw the package with the Gimbel Brothers return address and notified his superiors, who in turn contacted postal inspectors in Washington DC.[63]

Banner headlines across the country on May 1 ensured that everyone would know about the package bombs. The *San Francisco Chronicle* exclaimed, "Nation-Wide Bomb Plot Aims at U.S. Notables and SF Men." The *Pittsburgh Gazette Times* used the headline "Bomb in Mails Show National Terrorist Plot." The *Miami Herald* wrote across its front page, "Widespread Conspiracy of Terrorists to Assassinate Highly Placed Persons Is Unearthed in New York City." The Galleanists may have failed to have their bombs reach their targets and explode on May Day, but they did at least succeed in scaring the nation. They also angered their targets. "I trust Washington will buck up and clean up and either hang or incarcerate for life all the anarchists in the country," said Mayor Hanson. "If the Government doesn't clean them up I will. I'll give up my mayorship and start through the country. We will hold meetings and have hanging places." Senator King, another person who'd been sent a bomb, introduced a bill that would have made the sending of bombs or other explosives through the mails a capital offense.[64]

The United States had never before experienced a terrorist plot of such proportions. There was shock and indignation throughout the country. Terrorists had demonstrated an ability to launch a coordinated and sophisticated nationwide attack using what had previously been considered a safe and reliable means of communication—the postal system. Whereas package bombs had been shipped before the Galleanists launched their attack, there had never been so many at the same time. And although the targets of the bombs were prominent individuals who had in various ways antagonized anarchists, radicals, Bolsheviks, and other militants, the average citizen could not help but think that innocent people might be the next victims of this new form of terrorism. After all, anarchists and radicals in other countries had killed innocent people in their attacks, so perhaps that would be the next stage in the anarchist or Bolshevik revolution in the United States.[65]

There was also begrudging admiration for the sophistication of the plot, in addition to that expressed by bomb expert Eagan and other officials. The *New York Times*, in an editorial, marveled at the expertise of the bomb makers: "The packages of assassination are ingenious enough, almost too ingenious. Apparently clever mechanics, clever chemists, persons with a certain demoniac carefulness, neatness, almost artistry had a hand in the making. That polished, hard, basswood, carved cylinder in the bright green cardboard box shows skillful and patient labor."[66]

As to be expected, a rash of copycat incidents and practical jokes was perpetrated on various people by sending them ultimately harmless items in packages. In one case where there actually was a bomb, Representative John Burnett of Alabama, before the issuing of the national warning about package bombs, tried to open the device, but the lid got stuck. He then became suspicious and turned it over to the police. His constituents, though, seemed proud that he had been singled out for one of the package bombs. A newspaper in Guntersville, in his district, teased those in the much larger city of Birmingham by writing, "We put one over on Birmingham this time. Our congressman received a bomb in the mail and 'their'n' didn't."[67]

The use of the mails to send the package bombs made the crime an offense against the federal government. Though no one had been killed in the attacks and only Hardwick's maid and wife had been injured, an intensive and large-scale investigation was launched that included the Bureau of Investigation, local and state law enforcement agencies, U.S. postal investigators, the Secret Service, and the U.S. Army and Navy intelligence bureaus. Never before in the history of the country had there been such a large-scale and high-level investigation of a terrorist attack involving multiple federal and local agencies. This was due, in part, to the package bombs being seen by some as the opening salvo in a plot to overthrow the U.S. government. But it also might have been the result of federal and local agencies each wanting a piece of the action in the biggest terrorist story in years and all eager to get the credit for solving the mystery of who was behind it.[68]

One of the first steps taken in the investigation was bringing the wrapping paper used with the packages to Gimbels to see if the department store could provide any information or clues. Executives at Gimbels, however, told investigators that the store had never used and did not currently use wrapping paper that in any way resembled what had been used with the bombs. They also said they could not understand why the perpetrators had chosen the Gimbels name as opposed to other commercial stores in order to trick the recipients of the packages. The wrapping paper and the cardboard paper used for the green boxes were both eventually traced to their suppliers, but that did not result in any meaningful progress in the investigation.[69]

Other clues that initially seemed promising also led nowhere, including an analysis of the typewritten recipient addresses on the packages. An Oliver typewriter had been used, but one with a defective small *k* and an out-of-alignment small *w*. It was also determined that the press used to print the Gimbels name as the return address was an old-style, flatbed variety. The decision by the police to make this information available to newspaper reporters angered federal investigators, who felt doing so only alerted the conspirators to destroy their equipment. "That typewriter is now at the bottom of [the] East River," said one post office inspector, "and the aid it would render in running down the crooks is forever lost."[70]

It was hoped at first that a fingerprint analysis might lead to the identification of the culprits. Since too many people had handled the outer wrappings of the packages, police focused instead on possible fingerprints on the wooden cylinders, the glass vials containing the sulfuric acid, and the sticks of dynamite. However, as had been the case with all the other physical evidence thus far, the authorities found nothing leading them to those responsible for the nationwide terrorist attack.[71]

An analysis of the bomb components also proved fruitless. Naval intelligence officers believed that the bombs had been made in Germany and possibly imported to the United States. They based this belief on the resemblance of the explosive ingredients to those in German naval mines that had been discovered along the Long Island and New Jersey coasts. The German mines, though larger than the package bombs, each had a glass container filled with acid that would break when a ship came in contact with one of the horns of the mine. That would release the acid onto the fulminating caps and cause the dynamite to explode. The cover of the mine was also similar to the outer cylinder of the package bomb. It was also believed that militants in the United States could not have obtained the fulminate of mercury used in the bombs and that this or the completed bombs had been sent from Germany. An analysis by the Bureau of Mines, however, determined that the bombs had been made in America.[72]

As the examination of physical evidence continued, authorities raided the meeting places of anarchists, radicals, Bolsheviks, and the IWW in the New York area, seizing records and membership lists. Those targeted in the raids denied any involvement in the plot, claiming the bombs had been sent by detectives as an excuse to arrest radicals and others who'd planned strikes and demonstrations on May Day. "These bombs are a stupid detective's plant," said Julius Gerba, executive secretary of the New York chapter of the Socialist Party. "If real assassins had sent them they would not have been held up at the postoffice for lack of postage."[73]

Meanwhile, there were arrests of radicals and others in several cities, but these did not uncover anybody connected to the package bombs. Despite the lack of progress in the investigation, authorities kept promising an anxious public that the case would eventually be solved. "This is a tough case," said one high-ranking official a few days after the sixteen packages were discovered at the post office. "But we have every reason to believe that we will be able to run down the persons responsible for the outrage. It may be several days, a week or even a month, but I am confident that we will land every person concerned. No matter how long it takes, this investigation will continue until this case is solved." Then, wanting to offer some positive news, the official added, "We already have several good clues, and we have made very good progress to date."[74]

Finally admitting they were stumped in their efforts to solve the case, the NYPD on May 12 appealed to the public for help by offering "a substantial reward" for information leading to the arrest and conviction of anyone responsible for the package bombs. There were many false leads, as often happens in a major investigation. One of these involved a Spanish anarchist who was a member of the IWW and had been active in Philadelphia and New York. Jose Grau, who used the alias "Arnaldo Sapelano," was editor of the Spanish anarchist newspaper *El Corsario*. He had been arrested along with several other Spanish anarchists for plotting to assassinate President Woodrow Wilson in February 1919 but had been released on account of insufficient evidence. One BI agent believed that Grau was the author of the *Go-Head!* circular that threatened dynamite attacks against the government. There were also witness reports that, on April 14 and April 16, he had purchased from a store in New York the cardboard boxes used to house the wooden cylinders that held the bombs. In addition, witnesses claimed to have seen him in a New York hotel carrying a similar-looking package around the time the package bombs were mailed. However, after spending a lot of time pursuing these leads and trying to locate Grau, the BI learned in July that he had been working on a vessel in Norfolk, Virginia, virtually around the clock between April 11 and May 24. He was therefore ruled out as a suspect.[75]

Surprisingly it does not appear that Galleani or his followers were questioned regarding the package bombs. The group left no doubt, though, about how it felt in an editorial in *Cronaca Sovversiva* on May 1, a piece that has all the bearings of being written by those responsible for the attacks. Titled "Treat Them Rough," the editorial justified the sending of bombs to the various targets, including two top postal officials (Albert Burleson, the postmaster general, and William Lamar, the solicitor of the post office department), for their having, along with others, "strangled" newspapers they did not want people to read. (*Cronaca Sovversiva* was the major anarchist newspaper the government wanted to shut down.) The targeting of John D. Rockefeller was explained as due to the Ludlow Massacre: "It will not be out of place to remember today the flames, the massacre and the imprisonments of Ludlow Co. of April 1914. Nor would it be unlikely to believe that the generous executioners, in preparing to ship the Easter gift to J.D. Rockefeller, wanted [to] reminds [*sic*] him of the gestures of his villains, in the recurrence of those days of cowardice and blood." Yet the editorial also emphasized that the package bombs should not be viewed as a retaliatory attack on any particular person but rather an "open war against a whole system . . . [and] its institutions." The essay concluded by exclaiming that "'Treat them rough' will be the shouted, the motto, . . . today, tomorrow and forever."[76]

In extolling the virtues of the package-bomb plot, the Galleanists made no mention of the suffering of an innocent victim, Ethel Williams, former senator Hardwick's maid who lost both her hands when opening one of the packages. Perhaps they justified her fate as her being part of the "system" by working, even as a maid, for the former senator who had supported legislation calling for the deportation of alien anarchists and radicals. Or they might have believed in the old anarchist creed coined by a French anarchist, Émile Henry: "There are no innocent." In 1894 Henry hurled a bomb into a crowded café in Paris to avenge the recent execution of a fellow anarchist. The bombing resulted in several injuries and one death. When the judges at his trial expressed bewilderment at the crime, pointing out that most of the victims were small shopkeepers, clerks, and workers—people innocent of any wrongdoing—Henry simply replied, "There are no innocent." Most likely, though, the Galleanists probably figured that innocent people dying or being injured by their bombs was one of the unfortunate costs of the war they firmly believed they were engaged in with the government.[77]

The package-bomb plot was ingenious on several levels. First it caught the authorities completely off guard by introducing a new terrorist tactic on a grand scale. Police, BI agents, and others were used to anarchists and others leaving bombs in various places, but they were not on the lookout for bombs sent through the mail disguised as gifts from a well-known department store. The design of the small bombs was creative as well, with attention given to every detail by the Galleanists, including how the explosives would detonate after removing the lids of the cylinders. The wooden cylinders were polished so they would look like gifts. Targeting so many different people with bombs was also a shrewd move by the Galleanists. One package bomb to a prominent individual would probably have gained some attention and reaction from the public and government. Newspaper editorials might still have marveled at the ingenuity and cleverness of the homemade device. But by selecting a diverse array of high-profile figures in government, law enforcement, and business, the Galleanists were able to shock the nation with a new type of terrorism.[78]

The diverse list of targets also ensured that investigators would be puzzled when trying to determine who was responsible for the attacks. Since those who'd received the bombs had not only alienated the Galleanists but also IWW members, Bolsheviks, and other radicals, the investigation indeed went in circles as the authorities kept chasing down different leads involving those other groups. Some of the names included on the package-bomb list might have been there for that specific purpose. The Galleanists always thought they were smarter than those trying to suppress their movement and "took satisfaction in outwitting the authorities." They'd also wanted to send a message with the package bombs—namely, that they could reach and attack anybody in authority, no matter how high level an individual was. This is similar to a message delivered by the Italian leftist terrorist group Red Brigades many decades later when it issued a "strategic resolution" prior to their kidnapping and execution of former prime minister Aldo Moro in 1978. "No target should be defensible," the group wrote. "It should not be possible for any bunker where the agents of the counter-revolution hide to be called 'safe.'"[79]

The terrorist tactic that the Galleanists introduced to America on a grand scale in the spring of 1919, something government officials described as "the most widespread assassination conspiracy in the history of the country," was used in later years by a variety of extremist groups around the world, including Jewish extremists during the late 1940s, Palestinian and Irish extremists during the early 1970s, and lone-wolf operators like Theodore Kaczynski, the infamous "Unabomber," who single-handedly terrorized America for a seventeen-year period beginning in 1978. In more recent years, the sending of biological warfare agents such as anthrax and ricin through the mail by suspected lone-wolf terrorists has become the latest evolution of the letter and package-bomb tactic.[80]

By the end of May, the investigation of the package-bomb plot remained stymied. No arrests had been made in connection with the attacks, and none were on the horizon. The confidence authorities had expressed earlier in the month was no longer heard. They probably figured they'd be working on this case for the rest of the year, if not longer. The only bright spot was that there had not been any additional package bombs sent after the initial wave. That took some of the urgency off the need to solve the case quickly. But politicians and officials kept up the rhetoric aimed at anarchists and other radicals. "I say that the man who wont [*sic*] discharge his duties to his country and who wont [*sic*] fight for his country's rights does not deserve citizenship," future president and then senator from Ohio Warren Harding told a crowd on Memorial Day in Dayton. "I would bar from our shores forever the alien who comes here to enjoy the benefits of our freedom, and then plots against the safety and form of our government. We want a nation of one people, of one government dedicated to that people, and of one language."[81]

Harding didn't know it, but as he spoke, another plot "against the safety and form of our government" was well underway. The Galleanists' next move would again catch the authorities by surprise, and their reaction would lead to one of the country's most shameful periods.

1. Luigi Galleani, circa 1912. Galleani was the charismatic leader of a group of militant Italian anarchists active in the United States during the beginning of the twentieth century. William J. Flynn, chief of the U.S. Secret Service and later director of the Bureau of Investigation (the predecessor to the FBI), described Galleani as "one of the most difficult individuals the United States Secret Service has ever had to deal with because he was the brainiest." International Institute of Social History, Amsterdam.

2. View of Paterson, New Jersey, from Reservoir Park, circa 1890–1901. Galleani arrived here in 1901 and soon became involved in a violent labor strike at the textile mills that forced him to flee to Canada to avoid arrest. Library of Congress, Detroit Publishing Company Collection, LC-D4-11559.

3. Laying pavement in Barre, Vermont, 1904. Galleani settled in Barre in 1902 and built a following both there and around the country with his mesmerizing speeches and prolific writings in his newspaper, *Cronaca Sovversiva*. Photographer: Eaton Studio. Vermont Historical Society.

4. One of the mastheads used for *Cronaca Sovversiva*. The newspaper, published from 1902 until 1918, when it was suppressed by the government, was labeled by the U.S. Department of Justice as "the most rabid, seditious and anarchistic sheet ever published in this country." Courtesy of Silver Special Collections Library, University of Vermont.

5. Carlo Abate, 1943. Abate was a beloved artist, sculptor, and anarchist in Barre who illustrated and wrote articles for *Cronaca Sovversiva*. He also established a drawing school to provide technical training for the young people of Barre so they could obtain jobs that weren't as hazardous as working in the granite quarries. Photographer: Al Comi. Vermont Historical Society.

6. Galleani at police headquarters in Paterson, New Jersey, 1907. He was arrested in Barre, Vermont, and brought to Paterson to face charges for the 1902 riots at the silk mills. A local newspaper described him as "tall, well built, of commanding and intellectual appearance." It also depicted him as looking "like the Italian count of melodrama." © *Morning Call*—USA TODAY NETWORK.

7. Lynn, Massachusetts, 1910. Galleani moved to this industrial city, located near Boston, in 1912. Just as he had found an enthusiastic group of supporters in Barre in 1903, so too did he find a strong circle of followers in the Boston area. Photograph courtesy of the Lynn Museum & Historical Society.

8. Ruins in the aftermath of an attack by the Colorado National Guard on a tent camp of striking miners near Ludlow, Colorado, in April 1914. The camp was set on fire, and the burned remains of eleven children and two women were found in a pit where they'd been hiding. The attack became known as the Ludlow Massacre and was a galvanizing event for anarchists and other militants bent on revenge against John D. Rockefeller Jr., who owned the mining company. Library of Congress, Bain Collection, LC-B2-3035-3.

9. An apartment building in New York City that was wrecked by a bomb on July 4, 1914. The bomb was being prepared for use at the Rockefeller estate in Tarrytown, New York. Three anarchists were killed in the explosion. Library of Congress, Bain Collection, LC-B2-3135-3.

10. A gathering of anarchists in Union Square in New York City on July 11, 1914, to honor those killed in the apartment building explosion. Five thousand anarchists and other radicals filled the square. At the end of the ceremony, the crowd gave three cheers for the men killed and threw their hats wildly into the air. Library of Congress, Bain Collection, LC-B2-3147-11.

11. It was in this kitchen at the University Club in Chicago in February 1916 that Nestor Dondoglio, a Galleanist using the alias "Jean Crones," put arsenic in the soup that was served to guests at an event honoring the newly appointed archbishop of the city, George Mundelein. Dondoglio miscalculated and put in too much arsenic, causing about one hundred diners to vomit, thereby preventing the poison from taking its full effect. Mundelein did not eat the soup and was thus not affected. DN-0065861, Chicago Sun-Times/Chicago Daily News Collection, Chicago History Museum.

12. A Chicago police detective captain and the city's health commissioner examine vials of poison found in Dondoglio's room. Dondoglio disappeared after the banquet and was never found. DN-0065870, Chicago Sun-Times/Chicago Daily News Collection, Chicago History Museum.

13. Owen Eagan was the leading bomb expert in New York during the early part of the twentieth century. In this photo he is holding two bombs recovered from an attempt to blow up St. Patrick's Cathedral on March 2, 1915. Library of Congress, Bain Collection, LC-B2-3399-14.

14. Frank Abarno (*left*) and Carmine Carbone (*right*) were arrested and convicted of plotting to bomb St. Patrick's Cathedral. Both men were members of the Bresci Group, a faction of the Galleanists. An undercover New York City police officer had infiltrated the group and was with Abarno when the bomb was placed in the church. Carbone wasn't present. Library of Congress, Bain Collection, LC-B2-3426-10.

15. Prior to the United States entering World War I in April 1917, several Preparedness Day parades were held across the country to show support for the future war effort. At one of these parades in San Francisco on July 22, 1916, a bomb exploded, killing ten people and injuring forty others. Two labor activists, Thomas Mooney and Warren Billings, were convicted of the bombing even though there was no reliable evidence against them. In this photo Mooney and his wife are shown watching the parade from a rooftop. William Flynn, chief of the Secret Service and later director of the Bureau of Investigation, was convinced that Luigi Galleani was involved in the bombing. "Whoever did it was well known to Galleani," Flynn wrote years later, "and Galleani knew it was about to be perpetrated and who was to do the actual work." Library of Congress, New York World-Telegram and the Sun Newspaper Photograph Collection, LC-DIG-ds-09942.

16. Gabriella (Ella) Antolini (*left*), undated. Antolini was portrayed in the media as the "Dynamite Girl" after she was arrested in Chicago for transporting thirty-six sticks of dynamite from Youngstown, Ohio, to Chicago and then to Milwaukee in a planned Galleanist operation. The likely target was the home of the prosecutor in a case against eleven anarchists. DN-0070468, Chicago Sun-Times/Chicago Daily News Collection, Chicago History Museum.

17. Rayme W. Finch, undated. Finch was a Bureau of Investigation special agent who spent many years pursuing Galleani and his followers. The Galleanists paid him back for that by including him on the list of people they sent package bombs to in 1919. FBI Freedom of Information Act.

18. In late April 1919 the Galleanists sent thirty package bombs to prominent individuals around the country, including cabinet officers, U.S. senators and representatives, governors, mayors, judges, district attorneys, and industrialists. They used fake Gimbel Brothers department store wrappers to make the packages appear to be gifts. Bomb expert Owen Eagan marveled at the workmanship that had gone into creating the devices. "It doesn't resemble any machine [bomb] I have ever come across," he said. "It is the neatest and, from the standpoint of mechanical arrangement, the cleverest I have ever seen." Library of Congress, Bain Collection, LC-B2-5123-5A.

19. The Galleanists followed up the package bombs with one of the most well-coordinated bombing attacks in American history. On the night of June 2, 1919, nine bombs exploded in seven cities. One of the targets was the home (shown here after the bombing) of Attorney General A. Mitchell Palmer, who had also been targeted with a package bomb. Carlo Valdinoci, a Galleanist, was blown up as he attempted to place a bomb at the front of Palmer's home. Library of Congress, New York World-Telegram and the Sun Newspaper Photograph Collection, LC-USZ62-136235.

20. A. Mitchell Palmer, 1920. The June 2 bombings led Palmer to launch a series of raids across the country in November 1919 and January 1920 in which alien radicals were rounded up for deportation. As one historian notes, the Palmer Raids were characterized by "a ruthless invasion of civil rights." Library of Congress, National Photo Company Collection, LC-F8-7487.

21. The *Buford*, a U.S. Army transport ship, was used to deport alien radicals to Russia on December 21, 1919. Among the deportees on the ship that U.S. officials and the media labeled the "Soviet Arc" were the famous anarchists Emma Goldman and Alexander Berkman. Luigi Galleani had already been deported to Italy in June 1919. Library of Congress, Bain Collection, LC-USZ62-40635.

22. Louis F. Post, 1928 or 1929. Post opposed what he called the "deportations delirium." When he became acting secretary of labor in March 1920, he dismissed most of the deportation cases that had been prepared as a result of those swept up in the Palmer Raids. Library of Congress, National Photo Company Collection, LC-F8-43294.

23. William J. Flynn, 1914. Flynn was chief of the U.S. Secret Service from 1912 until 1917 and then director of the Bureau of Investigation from 1919 to 1921. Nicknamed "Bulldog" he was convinced the Galleanists were behind all the major terrorist attacks during this period. Library of Congress, Harris & Ewing Collection, LC-H261-3463.

24. J. Edgar Hoover, 1924. Hoover had a meteoric rise in the Department of Justice, becoming the director of the Bureau of Investigation in 1924 when he was only twenty-nine years old. Prior to that, he was in charge of the Radical Division (also known as the General Intelligence Division) of the bureau, during which time he helped to plan and supervise the Palmer Raids. Library of Congress, National Photo Company Collection, LC-USZ62-92411.

25. Nicola Sacco (*right*) and Bartolomeo Vanzetti (*center*) in handcuffs, being taken from jail to court on April 9, 1927. Sacco and Vanzetti were Galleanists who were tried and convicted for the 1920 robbery-murders of an assistant paymaster and his security guard in South Braintree, Massachusetts. Their trial was widely condemned as unfair, and their case received worldwide attention. Courtesy of the Boston Public Library, Leslie Jones Collection.

26. Funeral procession for Sacco and Vanzetti in Boston. Both men were executed on August 23, 1927. Library of Congress, New York World-Telegram and the Sun Newspaper Photograph Collection, LC-USZ62-136883.

27. On September 16, 1920, a bomb hidden in a horse-drawn wagon exploded in the heart of Wall Street, killing thirty-eight people and injuring hundreds of others. It was the first vehicle bombing in the United States and, at the time, the worst act of domestic terrorism in American history. Nobody was ever brought to trial for the attack, but Mario Buda, a Galleanist, is considered the likely suspect. The bombing occurred just a few days after Sacco and Vanzetti were indicted for the South Braintree murders. Library of Congress, New York World-Telegram and the Sun Newspaper Photograph Collection, LC-USZ62-132521.

5 Roundup

It wasn't a great day for Babe Ruth. The future Hall of Fame baseball legend, who was emerging as the most popular player in the game because of his record-setting home runs and extroverted personality, got only one hit, a single, in an afternoon game played at Griffith Stadium in Washington DC on June 2, 1919. He also got picked off third base. His team, the Boston Red Sox, was shut out 4–0 by the Washington Senators. But another game was scheduled against the Senators the next day, so perhaps Ruth and his teammates were thinking about getting even as they went back to their hotel.[1]

More likely, though, Ruth, "who didn't pay much attention to the team's rules on curfew," was probably thinking about where he would party that night in the nation's capital. Had he been near the Georgetown district around 11:15 p.m., he would have heard a loud explosion that rocked the area. A man had attempted to bomb a house there but either tripped going up the stairs to the front entrance, setting off the explosive, or the bomb he was carrying went off prematurely. He was blown to bits, part of his scalp winding up on a rooftop and his body parts flying all over the neighborhood, including onto the porch of one house and through the window of another. "I never imagined a human body could be so widely scattered by an explosion," said Major Raymond Pullman, superintendent of the Washington DC police. Leaflets that the perpetrator had been carrying were found throughout the area.[2]

It turned out that the house that was attacked wasn't just any house. It belonged to Attorney General A. Mitchell Palmer, who had also been the target of one of the package bombs sent through the mail in late April. Palmer had just finished reading in the library on the first floor and had gone upstairs with his wife to retire to bed when he heard the blast. It demolished the front of his home. "The door against which it was thrown leads into the library in which we had been sitting," Palmer told reporters shortly after the explosion, "and the part of the house blown in was in front of the library." Had Palmer and his wife stayed in the library a little longer, they very well could have been killed or seriously injured by the bombing.[3]

One of the first neighbors to check on Palmer after the blast was Franklin D. Roosevelt, who at the time was assistant secretary of the navy and lived across the street. One of the body parts had landed on his porch. He and his wife, Eleanor, had just gotten home when the blast occurred. "I went over to the attorney general's home immediately after the explosion," Roosevelt said, "and was very much gratified to find that no one had been injured, despite the terrific wreckage of the front of the house." When he went back home, he told Eleanor that he hadn't realized until then that Palmer was a Quaker. How did the future president learn this while checking on his neighbor? Palmer, understandably shaken by the bombing, had reverted to the Quaker language of his childhood when speaking to Roosevelt. "He was 'theeing' and 'thouing' me all over the place, 'Thank thee, Franklin!' and all that," said Roosevelt.[4]

Palmer's house and the surrounding area were soon swarmed by approximately one hundred law enforcement officials and other personnel. Investigators spent the night and next two days combing the area for clues as to who might have been responsible for the attack. Among the evidence they uncovered, in addition to the scalp, were two handguns, one a .32 caliber Smith & Wesson revolver, the other a .32 caliber Colt automatic; fragments of a black imitation leather grip bag; a tan, sandal-type shoe with a rubber heel; pieces of a black pinstripe suit and a white pinstripe shirt; a piece of a shirt collar, size 15½, with the laundry mark *K.B.*; a blue polka-dot necktie; and pieces of two hats, one a black derby and the other a gray fedora. They also found an Italian-American dictionary and two train ticket receipts. One was for a 7:10 p.m. train from Philadelphia to Washington DC, and the other was for an earlier train from New York to Philadelphia. A Washington streetcar transfer was also discovered with a 10:30 p.m. time stamp.[5]

The reason for the attack was explained in the leaflets, printed on pink paper, that the bomber had been carrying. Titled *Plain Words* and signed by "The Anarchist Fighters," it is similar in content and style to the *Go-Head!* leaflets that had been distributed in New England earlier in the year and signed by "The American Anarchists." It was once again a message to the authorities that the anarchists would not be defeated:

> The powers that be make no secret of their will to stop, here in America, the world-wide spread of revolution. The powers that must be reckon that they will have to accept the fight they have provoked. A time has come when the social question's solution can be delayed no longer: class war is on and cannot cease but with a complete victory for the international proletariat. The challenge is an old one, oh "democratic" lords of the autocratic republic. We have been dreaming of freedom, we have talked of liberty, we have aspired to a better world, and you jailed us, you clubbed us, you deported us, you murdered us whenever you could.[6]

The leaflet also refers to the suppression of anarchist and other radical newspapers: "Do not expect us to sit down and pray and cry. . . . We know that the proletariat has the same right to protect itself, since their press has been suffocated, their mouths muzzled, we mean to speak for them the voice of dynamite, through the mouth of guns." "The Anarchist Fighters" informed the authorities that they were not a large group but would battle to the end: "We are not many . . . but are determined to fight to the last . . . and will never rest till your fall is complete, and the laboring masses have taken possession of all that rightly belongs to them." The group made it clear that it would be a violent struggle: "There will have to be bloodshed; we will not dodge; there will have to be murder; we will kill because it is necessary; there will have to be destruction; we will destroy to rid the world of your tyrannical institutions."[7]

The leaflet ends with a warning and a boast: "Never hope that your cops, and your hounds will ever succeed in ridding the country of the anarchistic germ that pulses in our veins. We know how we stand with you and know how to take care of ourselves. Besides, you will never get all of us, and we multiply nowadays. Just wait and resign to your fate, since privilege and riches have turned your heads. Long live the social revolution! Down with tyranny. THE ANARCHIST FIGHTERS."[8]

While investigators were busy gathering evidence in the vicinity of Palmer's home in Washington DC, their colleagues in Philadelphia were doing the same thing but for a different bombing. This one also occurred around 11:15 p.m. that evening. The target in the Philadelphia attack was not a government official but rather the rectory of a church. There were no injuries, but *Plain Words* leaflets were found on the church's lawn. Then, just fifteen minutes later, another bombing took place, this time at the home of Mayor Harry L. Davis in Cleveland. Davis had suppressed a recent May Day celebration and also collaborated in an earlier prosecution of two Galleanists, Giovanni Scussel and Emilio Coda. Davis, his wife, and several friends were seated on the front lawn when the blast occurred in the rear of the house. Inside the house were the Davis family's three-year-old son and their maid, who were not injured. Once again *Plain Words* leaflets were found close by.[9]

In Pittsburgh two more bombings occurred, one at 11:35 p.m. and another ten minutes later. In both cases the anarchists apparently hit the wrong targets. The first bomb exploded at the house of Burton J. Cassady, the general manager of the paint department at a Pittsburgh glass company. There was no obvious reason for targeting him. He did, though, live just two doors away from U.S. District Judge W. H. S. Thompson, who had presided in cases against alien radicals. Both houses were identical in construction and appearance, leading to the belief by the authorities that the terrorists had mistaken Cassady's house for Thompson's. Cassady was out of town on a business trip, but the blast threw his wife and four young children from their beds, although they were not injured.[10]

Then, at 11:45 p.m., a bomb exploded at the home of Herbert E. Joseph, a train dispatcher for a railroad. Joseph's home was directly across the street from the residence of W. W. Sibray, chief inspector of the Bureau of Immigration, who had been active in the deportation of aliens. Officials believed he was the real target of the bombing and that the terrorists had struck the wrong home. The section of the street containing the two houses and others was broken up by a steep hill, and the residences were irregularly numbered, making it hard to find a specific address. Joseph was at work when the blast occurred. His wife and several small children were inside the home but not injured. In both this bombing and the earlier one at the Cassady home, *Plain Words* leaflets were found nearby.[11]

Meanwhile, Boston did not escape the evening of violence. Shortly before midnight, a bomb went off at the residence of Judge Albert F. Hayden, who had dealt harshly with recent May Day demonstrators, sentencing them to prison terms of up to eighteen months for disturbing the peace and stating, "If I could have my way I would send them and their families back to the country from which they came." There were no injuries, as Hayden and his family, except for his twenty-year-old son who was out for the evening, were away at their summer home. The bomb had been placed on the porch, and it destroyed the front and sides of the house and damaged five nearby homes. Another bombing took place a couple of minutes after midnight at the home of State Representative Leland W. Powers, slightly injuring his four-year-old daughter with flying glass. Copies of *Plain Words* were found at the sites of both the Hayden and Powers bombings. Powers was likely targeted due to having introduced an antisedition bill in the Massachusetts legislature.[12]

By this time Palmer and his department, along with the Secret Service and law enforcement personnel, had received word about the bombings in the other cities and the discovery of the same anarchist leaflet at each site. Major Pullman, the police superintendent, sent special guards to the homes of cabinet members and other high-ranking officials. The authorities now realized that they were facing a nationwide bombing campaign that was worse than the package bomb plot of a little more than a month ago. Instead of small bombs sent through the mail that might kill or injure only those opening the packages, now there seemed to be more indiscriminate killings intended by the perpetrators. While there were still specific targets, setting a bomb off at a house meant that whole families and neighbors could be killed. The explosion occurring late at night was designed to ensure that both the target and his family would be in the house. To make matters worse, the terrorists were now using more powerful bombs. Each of the pipe bombs that night contained about twenty pounds of dynamite with a powder fuse and heavy metal slugs for shrapnel.[13]

The tally thus far was seven bombings in five cities, all occurring within forty-five minutes of each other. The evening of violence, however, was not yet over. At 12:20 a.m. a bomb exploded in Paterson, New Jersey, at the downstairs apartment of Harry Klotz, who as president of a silk company and a member of the executive board of a Paterson manufacturers' association had opposed a forty-four-hour workweek for silk workers. Klotz and his family were away at the time of the explosion, and the occupants of the upper floor of the residence were not injured by the blast. It's possible that the target of the bombing was John J. Fitzgerald, secretary of the Paterson Chamber of Commerce and an adversary of radicals. Fitzgerald had been living at the address until a short time before the attack. *Plain Words* leaflets were found at the scene.[14]

The final bombing in the series of attacks took place in New York at 12:55 a.m. An explosion ripped through the basement entrance of the home of Judge Charles C. Nott Jr., who in 1915 had sentenced Frank Abarno and Carmine Carbone, two members of the pro-Galleani Bresci Group, to prison sentences for attempting to blow up St. Patrick's Cathedral. Nott and his three daughters were at their summer home in Connecticut at the time of the bombing, but his wife, a caretaker, and the caretaker's family were all in the dwelling. Although stunned by the explosion that blew in sections of the first and second floors of the brownstone, they were not injured. A security guard, however, for several of the homes on the street was killed. Again, copies of *Plain Words* were found nearby.[15]

Americans woke up on June 3 to the startling news that during the night nine bombs had exploded in seven cities within a two-hour span. No city seemed safe. Years of threats and violence by anarchists, radicals, and others were now at their highest point. The media, politicians, and the public were incensed. The *Atlanta Constitution* ran a headline that read, "Bombing Brigade Very Busy: Effort to Kill Att'y-General Palmer: Terror Reign in Many Cities." Another newspaper headline exclaimed, "Reign of Terror Starts." Typical of the antianarchist sentiment sweeping the country was the following column in the *Washington Post*, published a few days after the bombing and titled "Terrorism Must End":

> Without parallel in the nation's history and brazenly advertised as class war against organized government, the series of bomb outrages occurring simultaneously in eight [*sic*] American cities may now serve as a warning as to what wavering indecision and weakness inevitably lead to in dealing with the new brand of bolshevik-anarchy which is fastening itself like a foul growth on the life of the country. Although still stunned by this latest evidence of organized crime, red-blooded Americans here in and out of public life were aroused yesterday, as they have never been aroused before, to full realization of what this open challenge from "the fighting anarchists" means.[16]

Wounded soldiers being treated at Walter Reed Hospital in Washington DC also expressed their anger in an article published in their newsletter, *The Came-Back*: "We have come back home some of us with empty sleeves and shattered nerves, to enjoy the peace of freedom, for which we have suffered through two red years. We are a peace-loving lot, but we instinctively reach for the musket when we hear slander of the good things for which that old flag stands." After writing that they knew how to "subdue spies and snipers and submarines," the soldiers assured their readers that they could certainly "squelch the sneaking terrorists." Then, in a play on the title of the anarchist leaflet found at all the bomb sites, the soldiers wrote, "That is all of our 'Plain Words.' In the drive on the terrorists you can count on those of us in the uniform of the United States for the front line positions."[17]

One of the targets of the bombings, Mayor Harry Davis of Cleveland, was naturally incensed by the attempt on his life. He ordered the Cleveland police department to take any measures necessary to rid his city of anarchists and radicals. "There is no need to disclose the methods by which this is to be accomplished," he said, "but we will rid Cleveland of this red terror." Another target, Judge Albert Hayden, declared that the bombing "has not intimidated or frightened me in the slightest." He added, "We have got to defeat Bolshevists; we have got to deport them. They should not be allowed in this country. They should all be deported at once."[18]

The angriest man of all was Attorney General Palmer. The two attempts to assassinate him, first with the package bomb plot and now a bomb exploding in front of his house, were a personal insult. He was the highest-ranking Justice Department official, and the anarchists were simply thumbing their noses at him. That they had been able to walk right up to his front door with a bomb was both embarrassing and frightening. With the package-bomb plot still not solved, Palmer was determined not to have the same lack of progress occur with this new investigation. As he recalled later, he was ready "to exercise all the power that was possible to the Department of Justice to run to earth the criminals who were behind that kind of outrage." To accomplish this, he turned to one of the most famous sleuths in the country, a man he said was "the greatest anarchist expert in the United States," one who "knows all the men of that class" and was able to "pretty nearly call them by name." He was counting on this rock-star detective to get results and hopefully get them fast.[19]

Tracking Down the Leads

In a story in the spring of 1918, the *Los Angeles Times* wrote, "William J. Flynn, United States secret service. A name pregnant with romances of international intrigue, haloed by thrilling adventures with desperate counterfeiters and the matching of wits with the keenest brains of the underworld. What boy has read that name and not had a thrill race up his spine as his fertile imagination weaved fancied adventures in the United States secret service. Thousands of boys hold William J. Flynn as the hero of their air-castle adventures." Indeed, Flynn had built his reputation prior to the June 2, 1919, bombings not as an anarchist expert (as Palmer asserted) but rather as a relentless pursuer of German spies and saboteurs prior to U.S. entry into World War I, and before that by apprehending counterfeiters and mob figures.[20]

A native New Yorker with the nickname "Bulldog," Flynn was a large, rotund man with a close-cut mustache and reddish hair often covered under a derby hat. He also carried a large cigar with him. While "not a polished individual" or "glib of speech," he nevertheless commanded a presence whenever he spoke because "his every word and sentence carries a punch and gets to the pith of the subject without verbosity or redundancy." He was born in 1867 and attended New York City public schools. He worked as a tinsmith and a plumber and played semipro baseball before launching his career in law enforcement. His first job in that field was as a jailkeeper at the Ludlow Street Jail in New York, where all federal prisoners in the city were held at the time. While there he learned all that he could about the characteristics and tactics of counterfeiters and other prisoners he watched over.[21]

He used that knowledge to obtain a job with the Secret Service in 1897 and rose rapidly through the ranks to become head of the Eastern Division, where he led investigations resulting in the successful prosecution of Mafia boss Giuseppe Morello and his associates for counterfeiting. He took a brief leave in October 1910 to serve as second deputy commissioner of the New York Police Department. He reorganized and retrained the detective force but resigned about six months later due to interference from his superiors. After returning to his old job, he continued to do well and was appointed chief of the Secret Service in December 1912.[22]

He maintained that position until 1917, when he resigned due to opposition in some quarters regarding the Secret Service's role in general and Flynn's aggressive actions in particular in pursuing German spies in America. He didn't stay unemployed long, as he obtained a position in 1918 with the newly created U.S. Railroad Administration (USRA), where his job was to uncover and investigate threats of sabotage and other criminal activity against the railroads during World War I and also track down stolen freight. He was put in charge of the Secret Service and Police Section of the Division of Operation of the USRA and had at his disposal "the largest police organization in the world," with twenty thousand men working for him.[23]

Wherever and whenever he could, Flynn sounded the alarm about potential German infiltration into the United States. He urged all Americans to be vigilant, "to keep their eyes open for suspicious actions or people." He estimated in 1918 that a quarter million German spies were in the country, "and one of them may be working next to you, waiting on you. A seeming good friend, yet he or she is the most dangerous viper we have in the United States. . . . I again repeat as my best advice, based on my observance of the German espionage system, 'Beware of Spies.' What you know keep to yourself." Among Flynn's celebrated exploits when he was head of the U.S. Secret Service was the uncovering of a German plot to blow up munition ships leaving New York by attaching bombs to the rudders. The Secret Service under his command also discovered a briefcase in New York belonging to the principal financial agent of German activities in the United States. Inside were detailed plans to undermine the Allied cause during World War I, including "bombing munitions areas and factories manufacturing supplies for the allies, monopolizing the supply of liquid chlorine used for poison gas, and a plan to invade New York City."[24]

By the spring of 1919, Flynn was still working with the USRA when Palmer approached him about becoming director of the Bureau of Investigation. The two men had been discussing the job before the June 2 bombings occurred. The attacks presented Palmer with the perfect opportunity to make a grand announcement the next day about the appointment of Flynn to head the BI and solve the case. He gave Flynn "a mandate to crack down on anarchists and Bolsheviks." Flynn did his part to please Palmer, declaring about a month into the investigation that those responsible were "connected with Russian Bolshevism, aided by Hun money." This announcement was made despite the fact that BI agents, and Flynn himself, believed from the beginning that the bombings had been acts of retaliation by a small group of anarchists, most likely the Galleanists, for government actions against them. Palmer, who intended to run for the Democratic presidential nomination in 1920, wanted to portray the June 2 bombings not as the work of a small group with specific grievances but rather as "the first step in a nationwide radical uprising." That would give him a better platform to run on, portraying himself as the one candidate who could protect America from these large, organized revolutionary groups.[25]

There certainly were enough early signs, however, that pointed to either the Galleanists or another small Italian anarchist group as the perpetrators.

First, as noted, the *Plain Words* leaflets left at the bombing sites state that "we are not many" and that their "press has been suffocated," hints that it was a group like the Galleanists, who'd had their newspaper, *Cronaca Sovversiva*, suppressed by the government. An analysis of *Plain Words* by the Military Intelligence Division of the U.S. War Department a few days after the bombings concluded that it was Italians who'd authored the leaflet based on various words and phrases in the text. For example, in one part of the document the author or authors spelled the word *pedestal* as *piedistal*, similar to the Italian word *piedistallo*. Also, the translator pointed out that the word *usurped* in the circular was "far more commonly used in Italian than in English."[26]

The discovery of an Italian-American dictionary at the scene of the bombing at Palmer's home further pointed to the likelihood that it was Italian anarchists, not Bolsheviks, who were responsible for the attacks. But beyond first determining the type of movement behind the attacks, the authorities had to identify who exactly the person blown up at Palmer's home was, the specific group he belonged to, and who else was involved in not just the Washington DC attacks but also those in the six other cities. Investigators had never before faced such a difficult and complex task. And they had to do their work under the constant pressure of producing results for an anxious public and an even more anxious boss, Attorney General Palmer, who didn't want an unsolved terrorist investigation on his résumé.

One of the first things Flynn did after being appointed BI director was convene a meeting of all the federal government agencies, chiefs of police, and detective chiefs in the cities where the bombings had taken place in order to establish cooperative arrangements for the investigations. What it really meant, though, was that Flynn had free reign and would be able "to 'borrow' any man anywhere in the country if he needs him." In an attempt to lower public expectations for a quick resolution to the case, Flynn said a few days after the bombings, "No arrests are in sight at this time. We are looking up the movements of every known anarchist and radical in the country to determine just where they were on Monday night [the night of the bombings]. This task may occupy a month, but I believe it will lead to something."[27]

Based on his experience with the Secret Service and the USRA, it is doubtful that Flynn really believed he could solve the nine bombings in a month. But he had to give the public and the media an optimistic message. He decided upon a two-prong approach to the case. First, the BI and other authorities would investigate known anarchist organizations to determine whether they might have been involved in the plot. Second, they would examine thoroughly all the physical clues available with the hope of identifying any of the perpetrators and, through that identification, uncovering the conspiracy. They were primarily concerned with determining the identity of the individual who tried to kill Palmer. They hoped that by looking at various groups and finding out who was missing and whose whereabouts could not be explained they might be able to discover who the dead bomber was.[28]

The BI looked at four groups of anarchists in the early days of the investigation: the Galleanists, whose headquarters the bureau believed were in Lynn and Boston, Massachusetts, and Barre, Vermont, even though Galleani had left Barre in 1912; the Spanish Pro Prenza group in Philadelphia; the Italian L'Era Nuova group in Paterson, New Jersey; and the individual followers of Emma Goldman and Alexander Berkman. But the Galleanists soon became the prime suspects. BI Special Agent William J. West of Boston wrote in one of his reports on June 21 that Galleani was "the moving spirit of Italian anarchists in this section of the country" and that "if it is believed the present bombing outrages were the work of Italian anarchists, that Galleani would surely be acquainted with perpetrators of these outrages."[29]

West's report was written just a few days before Galleani and eight of his followers, including Raffaele Schiavina, who for a time had been the manager of *Cronaca Sovversiva*, were scheduled to be deported on June 24. On June 23 BI agents went to the East Boston immigration station to question Galleani and the others about the bomb plot. The Galleanists provided the agents with no information beyond stating that they were anarchists. Under the Anarchist Exclusion Act of October 16, 1918, simply admitting to being an anarchist was enough to justify deportation. As such, despite the belief in the bureau that the Galleanists were probably behind the bombings, the deportations were allowed to proceed as scheduled.[30]

It was a major blunder on the part of the government. Almost a year later, there was no question as to who was responsible for the attacks. A BI report in May 1920 concluded, "It is established beyond a reasonable doubt that the bomb plot of June 2nd were [*sic*] conceived and directed by Luigi Galleani and were [*sic*] exploded on the day that he was deported from this country. Naturally persons or his followers who remained in this country were selected to do the deeds and it would appear that he appealed to the more ignorant of his followers, who desired to become martyrs to the cause." Keeping Galleani in the country might have provided valuable intelligence to investigators as they tried to determine the nature and scope of the bombing conspiracy. Galleani's followers might have tried to contact him, inadvertently providing clues to the authorities regarding who else was involved in not only the June 2 bombings but also the package-bomb plot of late April 1919. There was even the possibility, although remote, that Galleani might weaken as time went on and, in exchange for various concessions, including rescinding the deportation order, cooperate with the government's investigation. But deporting him when the government did would be like deporting Osama bin Laden to Afghanistan in the aftermath of the 9/11 attacks, had he been living in America at the time. Opportunities to learn more about the case would be lost.[31]

Galleani, who had been free on bail awaiting his deportation, was arrested shortly after the June 2 bombings. He remained at the immigration station in East Boston until he was transferred to Ellis Island, where he was put on the Italian ship *Duca degli Abruzzi* along with eight other Galleanists and deported to Italy on June 24. Galleani was fifty-seven at the time and left behind Maria, whom he had finally married just a month earlier, and their six children. Since the immigration laws did not allow for families to accompany deportees, he did not know when, if ever, he would see them again.[32]

His ten-year-old daughter, Tana, couldn't understand why he wouldn't lie to the immigration officials to avoid deportation. "When my father was to be deported," she said in a brief memoir recorded at the end of her life, "my parents were discussing it and I went up to their bedroom and said to him, 'why don't you say you don't believe any more [in anarchism]?'

I'll never ever forget the look on his face. Now, I'm so glad he lived the way he did and believed in what he did."[33]

As Galleani set sail for Italy, Flynn continued his search for the identity of the anarchist who set off the bomb at Palmer's home. The partial scalp with curly black hair was brought to a hairdresser, who mounted it on a wooden block and studied all its features. He surmised that the bomber was an Italian man between twenty-six and twenty-eight years old. Attempts were made to trace all the other pieces of evidence found at the bombing scene to their origins. Photographs of the shirt collar with the *K.B.* laundry mark were published in laundry trade journals around the country, while investigators visited all laundries, including steam, hand, and Chinese, in New York, Philadelphia, and Boston. The only clue uncovered was from a Brooklyn laundry—that the customer had lived on a street in the area at one time. A house-to-house canvass of that street as well as neighboring streets did not reveal any further information.[34]

The blue polka-dot necktie of the bomber was traced to a store in New York, where only one of those types of ties had been sold at the end of May. A clerk at the store thought the purchaser was Italian; that customer told him "he was tired of America and was going away." Both the clerk and the owner of the store could not identify the man from photos of various suspects. The clerk also said he believed the man was connected to Italian theatrical companies in New York. This sent investigators to places supplying costumes for performances, members of choruses, musicians, and so forth. The search yielded no results.[35]

What looked like a promising lead was uncovered when the sandal shoe with the rubber heel was shown to cobblers in New York and Boston. This was done with the hope that one of them would remember putting the rubber heel on the shoe. One cobbler in New York said that he had indeed attached a similar rubber heel to a similar sandal sometime before June 2 and that the customer was a foreigner. He gave investigators a description of the foreigner, who turned out to be very much alive and "a loyal citizen of Polish descent."[36]

Following up on the other evidence, including the two hats, two handguns, pieces of clothing, train tickets, and the Italian-American dictionary, did not produce the identity of the dead bomber. But besides BI agents having suspected the Galleanists of orchestrating the attacks (as previously noted), they also believed as early as July 1919, according to one account, that the person blown up at Palmer's house was an unidentified member of that group. At one point the bureau believed that the Galleanists had worked with Spanish anarchists in Philadelphia to plan the attacks. A BI report in October 1919 surmised that "an inner circle exists that lies between the Spanish radicals of Philadelphia and the New York radicals and the Galleana [*sic*] Italian Groups in Massachusetts and that in all probability the Galleani Group are responsible for the June 2nd bomb outrages which seem to be borne out by our reports gathered in Boston."[37]

Using undercover informants, the bureau discovered two suspects for the Palmer bombing who stood out from all the others. Both men were associated with Luigi Galleani, and both wore sandals and had black hair. One of them, Umberto Colarossi, was a bookkeeper and an ultramilitant Galleanist, "young, dark, [and] intense" and committed to revolutionary violence. However, Colarossi had been arrested in Chicago a few days before the Palmer bombing and was in custody awaiting deportation. The other suspect was Carlo Valdinoci, the dapper and handsome twenty-four-year-old Galleanist who had at one time been the publisher of *Cronaca Sovversiva*. He had become legendary in anarchist circles, continually frustrating law enforcement agents who tried to capture him for a variety of offenses, including the 1918 dynamite conspiracy involving Ella Antolini, the "Dynamite Girl" and Valdinoci's lover. His skill in avoiding arrest "had endowed him with a mantle of invincibility and was a source of inspiration and pride."[38]

In addition to fitting the description of the bomber, Valdinoci had disappeared approximately one week before the June 2 bombing, telling a friend that he was going to Washington. A BI informant reported in January 1920 that an anarchist in New York had told him that Valdinoci was the man killed in the Palmer bombing. The informant replied that he didn't think so, but the anarchist said, "It is so, he has never shown up again since that date." In June Attorney General Palmer appeared before Congress and placed into the *Congressional Record* a report from the General Intelligence Division (better known as the Radical Division) of the Bureau of Investigation, which stated that the investigation into the bombings had resulted in "the probable discovery of the man who was killed at the house of the Attorney General." That man, the report indicated, was "Carlo Valdinucci [*sic*] who during 1917–18 was a trusted lieutenant of Galliani [*sic*] while the latter was printing Cronaca Sovversiva." It would not be until 1922 that BI Special Agent West would drop the word "probable" and report with confidence that "the person killed in Washington, D.C. on June 2, 1919, was CARLO VALDINOCI."[39]

Discovering the identity of the dead bomber was only one piece, though an important one, in the puzzle of the June 2 bombings. Palmer and Flynn also needed to know who else among the Galleanists and their supporters had been involved in the conspiracy and where they could be found. They used informers throughout the country who tried to gain the confidence of anarchists and then reported back anything of importance. One such informer turned out to be quite valuable. Eugenio Ravarini, an Italian immigrant given the code name "D-5" by the bureau, fed them information over a seven-month period beginning in September 1919. He was trusted by Italian militants in Boston, New York, and New Jersey. He posed as a "violent itinerant anarchist" and claimed that the revolution was imminent and that "the time for action was now." He managed to infiltrate key Galleanist groups, including the Gruppo Autonomo of East Boston and the Bresci Group of East Harlem. It was Ravarini who learned from a New York anarchist that Valdinoci was the Washington bomber. He also learned from his spying activities that the package-bomb plot of late April and the June 2 bombings were "only one affair, done by the same people."[40]

Ravarini also penetrated the Gruppo L'Era Nuova of Paterson, New Jersey, an Italian anarchist group not affiliated with the Galleanists. Based on information from Ravarini, BI agents in February 1920 raided the group's headquarters and arrested twenty-nine of its members. They also went to a printing shop where the group's newspaper had previously been published until it was suppressed by the government in 1917. There they discovered a batch of pink papers similar to those used for the *Plain Words* leaflets. The shop's owner, Beniamino Mazzotta, denied any connection to those leaflets. He told BI agents that the same type of paper was used by Roberto Elia, who worked at a printing shop in Brooklyn, New York, and published an underground Italian journal.[41]

Among those arrested in the L'Era Nuova raid was Ludovico Caminita, a leading anarchist and editor who was familiar with many Galleanists and their roles in the June 2 bombings. In exchange for not being deported, he cooperated with the government. He confirmed Mazzotta's belief that Elia might be the person who'd printed *Plain Words*, and he also gave them several other names of Galleanists he thought might have been involved in the bombings. J. Edgar Hoover, who had been put in charge of the Radical Division, wrote in a memo that Caminita "is a very high-class Italian and can not be handled in any third degree manner," adding that he had provided "some very valuable information" about the bombings. Caminita even told the agents where he believed the bombs had been made and who'd made them: at Galleani's home in Wrentham, Massachusetts, by a Galleanist named Nicola Recchi, who was missing four fingers on his left hand, compliments of previous bombmaking activities. Caminita also promised to review a list of subscribers to *Cronaca Sovversiva* and identify the names of "dangerous individuals."[42]

The bureau was never able to find Recchi, but they did locate and arrest Elia and soon after that Andrea Salsedo, who, like Elia, was a close associate of Galleani and had worked in the past on *Cronaca Sovversiva*. Then, much like the U.S. government would do during the height of the "war on terrorism" in the years after the 9/11 attacks, when it secretly held and interrogated suspected foreign terrorists in detention centers in friendly foreign countries, in 1920 Flynn "hid" his two prize prisoners, secretly placing them in the bureau field office on the fourteenth floor of a building on Park Row in lower Manhattan. He kept them there for two months, from March until May, as BI agents tried to gain as much information as possible regarding the bombing conspiracy. After initially refusing to answer any questions, both men eventually cooperated, identifying photos of various members of the Galleanists and of other anarchists. They admitted that they had printed *Plain Words* and that they knew Galleani and Recchi. They also told the agents that "they were certain that these men, along with a handful of others, had planned and carried out the June 2 plot."[43]

Flynn hoped that, by keeping secret that he had Elia and Salsedo in custody, the rest of the Galleanists and other anarchists would not get suspicious that the two men might be talking and thereby placing all of them at risk of being arrested. But word did get out, and during the two months that Elia and Salsedo were kept in the bureau's New York office, many of the Galleanists began to scatter, depriving Flynn of his opportunity to make a series of grand arrests. Among those who fled the country during this period were Recchi, Giuseppe Sberna, and Filippo Caci, "all key figures in the bomb plot." Two other Galleanists, Nicola Sacco and Bartolomeo Vanzetti, were also planning to leave. They did not, however, and would soon become the key figures in a different case that became one of the most infamous trials in American history.[44]

Elia and Salsedo were held for those two months without warrants or any other legal justification. They had been threatened by the BI agents with deportation, but they were not transferred over to the Bureau of Immigration for the customary deportation hearings. They were also not "given a hearing, indicted on any criminal charge, or put in jail. They were in effect private prisoners, practically incommunicado, held secretly in the offices of the Bureau of Investigation." Salsedo's friends and family claimed he was beaten during his interrogation. He became depressed as time went on, feeling guilty for betraying his comrades and also fearful that they might seek revenge. The long confinement also took its toll. Unable to take it anymore, at 4:20 a.m. on the morning of May 3, he committed suicide by jumping out of the window from his sleeping quarters on the fourteenth floor of the bureau's New York office. He thereby, in the words of the Radical Division's report, "put an end to his part of the arrangement" in terms of cooperating. There were accusations by some that he was pushed out the window by agents, but this has been refuted by most historians.[45]

The publicity surrounding Salsedo's death—it was front-page news in many papers—led the bureau to quickly move Elia to Ellis Island for a deportation hearing. His lawyer advised him that if he would simply deny being an anarchist, he might be able to stay in the United States, much like Galleani's ten-year-old daughter had urged her father to do on the eve of his deportation. Elia's reaction was similar to Galleani's. He told his attorney that being an anarchist was his "only title of honor." He was deported to Italy in August, where he resumed his anarchist activities.[46]

Ludovico Caminita remained under the threat of deportation for four more years. He was held on Ellis Island, then released on bond, and then rearrested again at least two times. His deportation warrant was finally canceled in 1924. He would later write about the emotional experience of first being put on the ferry that would take him and the other arrested anarchists to Ellis Island. "The boat set off and during the crossing [to Ellis Island] I watched, heartsick, as New York receded; New York, the great, immense, beautiful metropolis, where I had enjoyed so much and suffered so much; New York, that I loved the way one loves the city of one's birth!"[47]

Meanwhile, Eugenio Ravarini, the "D-5" spy for the bureau, became "very much scared" in March 1920 that Italian anarchists in Massachusetts suspected he was working for the government and might try to kill him. Carlo Tresca, a leading anarchist in New York, had earlier denounced him and accused him of being a spy, something Ravarini denied. He was also proving difficult to work with, as he wanted to be put in charge and expressed disappointment that Director Flynn had not taken him into his confidence. All of this led one of the BI agents to characterize Ravarini "as in a very poor frame of mind" and "of no immediate help to us" anymore. He recommended that he be sent back to New York. Ravarini eventually "vanished from sight."[48]

By the time Palmer appeared before Congress on the first anniversary of the June 2 bombings, the investigation into the attacks had pretty much run its course. This was evident in the Radical Division's report that Palmer placed into the *Congressional Record*: "The net results of the investigations of the bomb plot of June 2, therefore, are that every physical clue has been run out to the last possible extreme. . . . The perpetrators of the crime have succeeded in leaving the country, with the possible exception of one or two, and that the principal source of information is now closed by virtue of the suicide of Salsedo. Nevertheless there are several avenues of information yet to be explored and which hold out fairly substantial hopes that ultimately the plot will be solved."[49]

The plot, however, has never been completely unraveled. Not a single suspect was ever brought to trial. Historian Paul Avrich's theory is the best explanation for how the Galleanists probably pulled it off. According to Avrich, the idea for the simultaneous bombings originated with Carlo Valdinoci and Mario Buda, two of the most militant Galleanists. Plans were discussed within the Gruppo Autonomo of East Boston, whose members came from the surrounding area. Nearly all of them took part in some way in the conspiracy, including Sacco and Vanzetti. The principal bomb maker was Nicola Recchi, and as previously noted and according to Ludovico Caminita, the bombs were likely made at Galleani's home in Wrentham, Massachusetts.[50]

Armed with the bombs and the *Plain Words* leaflets that had been printed by Elia and Salsedo, Valdinoci and Buda set out to distribute them in different cities. Valdinoci traveled to New York, Paterson, and Philadelphia, dropping off the bombs and leaflets with Galleanists who operated there, with instructions to set off the bombs at about the same time, around midnight on June 2. The New York conspirators were most likely members of the Bresci Group, including Giuseppe Sberna, Andrea Ciofalo, and Alfredo Conti, all of whom had gone to Mexico along with Valdinoci in the summer of 1917 to avoid the draft. The Paterson contingent were members of the group Gli Insorti (The Insurgents), with Filippo Caci, Gemma Mello, and Ruggero Baccini the key conspirators in that city.[51]

While Valdinoci was meeting with his comrades in New York, Paterson, and Philadelphia before going to Washington DC, another Galleanist from Boston, most likely Buda, traveled to Pittsburgh and Cleveland to deliver the bombs and leaflets in those cities, possibly to fellow Galleanists Emilio Coda and Giovanni Scussel. He may also have been carrying a bomb to drop off in Chicago in order to target the home of Judge Kenesaw Mountain Landis. However, there had been a raid of an Italian anarchist meeting in Chicago just a few days before the planned attacks. Umberto Colarossi, a militant Galleanist who, as noted earlier, had been a suspect in the bombing at Palmer's home, was among those arrested. Buda had apparently been present at that meeting but avoided being caught. If there had been plans to set off a bomb in Chicago, this canceled them.[52]

All told, about fifty to sixty Galleanists were involved in the plot. Their roles varied from making the bombs and planting them to choosing the targets and providing shelter and financial support. Galleani himself was certainly aware of the plot, whether or not the bombs were made at his house. He may even have been the one to "suggest" something along the lines of multicity bombings to Valdinoci and Buda. As noted in chapter 3, BI chief William Flynn observed, "I doubt very much whether Galleani or any other prominent anarchist in this country . . . worked up a bomb outrage from a definite plan. . . . They work deviously. Galleani, for instance, will suggest. One of his close companions will pass on the suggestion."[53]

The most astonishing aspect of the June 2 bombings is how it was kept secret from the authorities. After all, they had a number of informers, undercover agents, and others constantly feeding them information about Italian anarchists around the country. Yet the Galleanists, who "all lived in constant fear of detection, of being discovered by federal agents or local police," were able to accomplish one of the most sophisticated and coordinated terrorist attacks in history. Carrying out near-simultaneous bombings in a few cities is impressive for any terrorist organization, whether in 1919 or today. But doing it in seven cities without the plan ever leaking (with the possible exception of the Chicago raid, if that was indeed related to the plot) is simply startling. It's also impressive that they were able to strike on the heels of the nationwide package-bomb attacks when one would think that the authorities would be on the lookout for another major, multicity attack by anarchists. There were so many points where the operation could have been discovered, from the meetings in Boston, where the conspiracy was first discussed, to traveling to different cities to drop off the bombs and leaflets to other Galleanists and then those militants hiding the bombs until they brought them to the specific targets to set them off.[54]

That the Galleanists succeeded in their audacious plan for a multicity attack was a testament to their craftiness and well-honed skills in thinking up creative ideas for operations that would catch everyone off guard. They had demonstrated this with the poisoned soup incident in 1916 and then with the nationwide package-bomb plot in the late spring of 1919. But they also succeeded in part because the authorities were more concerned with the threat posed by Bolsheviks, Communists, and others that they claimed were plotting to destroy capitalism and overthrow the U.S. government. That was what most of the intelligence and law enforcement personnel and resources were focused on. This in turn provided the opportunity for a small, dedicated, militant organization like the Galleanists to plan and carry out major terrorist attacks without being detected.[55]

A Most Shameful Period

The bombings on the evening of June 2, 1919, were initially a boon to the careers of three men: A. Mitchell Palmer, William J. Flynn, and J. Edgar Hoover. Palmer instantly became a sympathetic figure across the country, having twice been the target of assassins. He had only recently become attorney general, President Woodrow Wilson appointing him in March 1919. A liberal Pennsylvania Democrat who served three terms in the House of Representatives, Palmer was a favorite of Wilson's. The president had once offered him the position of secretary of war, a role he declined due to his pacifist Quaker beliefs. Based on his record as a congressman, including sponsoring bills limiting child labor and supporting women's suffrage, it would have been reasonable to assume that as attorney general, he would favor progressive causes. But after the two attempts on his life and the widespread sentiment in the country about cracking down on agitators of all types, including Bolsheviks, Communists, Socialists, anarchists, labor activists, and others, Palmer likely realized that launching a war on radicalism could be the springboard he was looking for to win the 1920 Democratic nomination for president. He began to write articles and give speeches warning of the danger posed by radicals. He also obtained additional congressional funds for the Department of Justice. And his name and picture appeared frequently in newspapers, something any public figure with presidential aspirations would covet.[56]

Flynn also benefited from the bombings. Already famous when appointed by Palmer to head the Bureau of Investigation, he could anticipate his legacy only growing further as he tracked down those responsible for the attacks. During World War I, when he led the U.S. Secret Service, he relished keeping America safe from German saboteurs and spies. Now he could use those skills to keep America safe from radicals. His job with the U.S. Railroad Administration was just not as prestigious as what Palmer was offering him. Becoming chief of the BI put him back in the game at a top level and resurrected his career.[57]

The biggest winner of all, however, in the aftermath of the June 2 bombings was the young Hoover. Ambitious, energetic, and smart, even he could not have imagined when he was working as a clerk in the Library of Congress in 1916 that in just a few short years he would become one of the more powerful figures in Washington. He had attended law school at night and joined the Department of Justice in 1917 with a master's degree in law from George Washington University. He gained a reputation for thoroughness and hard work in the Alien Enemy Registration Section that dealt primarily with German aliens during World War I. He rose quickly through the ranks and became the head of that section only five months after starting at the Justice Department. But it was in August 1919 when he experienced a meteoric rise, when Palmer promoted Hoover, then only twenty-four years old, to become director of the newly created Radical Division within the BI. Palmer had recently also given him the title of special assistant to the attorney general.[58]

The Radical Division was a domestic intelligence network "created to keep tabs on political dissent." Hoover's job was "to gather and organize all information about radicals in America." Coming on the heels of the June 2 bombings, this put him front and center in the investigation. But Hoover had visions of much more than just finding out who the culprits of that night of terror were. He wanted to uncover what he believed, or at least wanted to portray to the public, was an ongoing, nationwide plot by radicals to overthrow the government. He had already "acquired what became his lifelong conviction that Russian Communism controlled an organized conspiracy to destroy American values." While he was technically under the supervision of his boss, William Flynn, who remained nominally in command of the bombing investigation and other matters, Hoover actually directed the war on radicalism campaign that unfolded. All reports and correspondence from BI agents regarding the bombings or radical activities were seen by Hoover; even those addressed to Flynn were marked as "Attention Mr. Hoover." The young Hoover was "in complete charge of planning the attack on radicalism during the summer and fall of 1919."[59]

Hoover drew on his experience as a cataloguer at the Library of Congress. He later wrote that this "gave me an excellent foundation for my work in the FBI where it has been necessary to collate information and evidence." He created the "Editorial Card Index" that contained over 200,000 entries of individual radicals, radical groups, and radical publications. The file grew to 450,000 index cards by December 1921. Name cards included each individual's address, nationality, citizenship, BI file number where the original field report on the individual could be found, and a brief summary of the individual's political activities. One didn't even have to be radical to make the list. There was no attempt to verify the information supplied to the bureau, meaning "that any person who had been mentioned in Bureau reports, whether on the basis of rumors, by informers, as a participant in a public meeting, or as a subscriber to a radical paper, was carefully indexed." Index cards for all organizations, societies, and clubs believed to be radical included information on their membership, meetings, and activities. Radical publications were indexed with information on their publishers, editors, circulations, and general content. Each state, city, and foreign country had an index card with a summary of the radical situation there as well as the individuals and organizations active in the locale. The card index system that Hoover created allowed him and his staff to quickly retrieve key information on individuals, organizations, activities, and publications and transmit it to investigators in the field.[60]

Hoover was definitely ahead of his time in realizing that those who control information can wield a great amount of power. Armed with the who, what, and where of radical movements throughout the United States, he drew up plans for raids and deportations. What became known as the "Palmer Raids," though actually planned and supervised by Hoover, began on the evening of November 7, 1919, when BI agents raided offices of the Union of Russian Workers, a group the bureau viewed as a radical organization, in several cities across America. In New York about two hundred men and women were taken outside of the Russian People's House after several had been beaten badly. They could be seen with their heads wrapped in bloodstained bandages. The inside of the building was ransacked—doors smashed, books and other publications strewn about, desks broken open. All the raids "were carried out with utter indifference to legality," and most of the time "arrests were made without warrants."

More than a thousand people were arrested and interrogated as a result of the nationwide raids.[61]

Then, on December 21, Hoover saw his efforts to rid the country of alien radicals pay off when the *Buford*, a U.S. Army transport ship that had been used in the Spanish-American War and World War I, set sail from New York to Finland, where the 249 deportees aboard would be taken by train to Russia. Also on the ship were two hundred soldiers, each armed with a rifle and two pistols, guarding the deportees and preventing a potential mutiny. The passengers were not allowed to leave their cabins except for meals. Among the deportees on the ship Hoover and the media labeled the "Soviet Arc" were Emma Goldman and Alexander Berkman. William Flynn described all the deportees as "the brains of the ultra-radical movement." Hoover, who'd arranged for the loan of the ship from the army, basked in the glory of the moment. He was on the dock when the *Buford* began its long voyage. He also gave interviews and was mentioned in major newspapers, thereby taking "the first step toward his own fame."[62]

The deportees had just a few hours' notice that they were about to be put on the *Buford*, giving them no opportunity to contact their loved ones. This resulted in "many pathetic instances of family separation." The deportations also left many wives and children in dire straits. The women were dependent on their husbands for financial support, and now that was gone. As Louis Post, the assistant secretary of labor, would later write, "To their consequent suffering, and quite irrespective of such mental anguish as the bewildered husbands and fathers may have endured, only a hard-boiled alien-hater could be indifferent."[63]

Hoover, Palmer, and Flynn were not necessarily "alien haters," but they felt no sympathy for those they were banishing from America. They viewed their actions as just the first step in a series of additional raids and deportations planned for the new year. Accordingly, on January 2, 1921, between six thousand and ten thousand people—the exact number has never been known—were arrested, many without warrants, in raids in more than thirty cities across the country. The targets were members of the Communist Party of America and the Communist Labor Party. Club houses, restaurants, bowling alleys, poolhalls, and even bedrooms were raided by BI agents and local police, and those arrested were transported to detention centers in the different cities. Many were beaten and held in overcrowded jails and detention facilities, separated from their families for weeks and in some cases even months. In New England approximately eight hundred people were arrested, half of them forced to march through the streets of Boston in chains as they were taken to Deer Island in Boston Harbor. An immigration official who disapproved of this display by the BI agents and police commented sarcastically that the only thing missing was "a brass band." A mother and her little child were arrested in one of the raids in New England, and the child was released but left alone to find her way home at midnight. The mother was held captive for a month. In East St. Louis, Illinois, located across the Mississippi River from St. Louis, Missouri, BI agents drove around the foreign section of the city at night, arbitrarily arresting alien residents in their homes and places of work. Large numbers of those arrested around the country turned out not to be connected in any way with anarchism, Communism, or Bolshevism.[64]

Nevertheless, BI director Flynn claimed that the radicals had suffered a major defeat due to the raids. "We have succeeded, I think, in breaking the backbone of the radical revolutionary movement in America," he said. "These raids mark the beginning of the decline of organized, rabid revolutionarism [*sic*] throughout the country. We planned this move very carefully and the results have exceeded our expectations." He, Hoover, and Palmer anticipated clear sailing when the cases of the thousands of aliens arrested were sent up the chain of command for approval for deportation. The final authority was the secretary of labor or his representative, since the Labor Department was in charge of the Bureau of Immigration, the entity that held deportation hearings. In the past there hadn't been many cancellations of deportation warrants reviewed by the Labor Department. But in one of those twists of fate that makes history so intriguing, a bespectacled, seventy-one-year-old man with a Van Dyke beard suddenly appeared on the scene and threw the deportation plans into turmoil. It was something Hoover, Palmer, and Flynn never saw coming.[65]

Louis F. Post was a distinguished-looking, progressive liberal who, after a long career in law and journalism, joined the newly created Department of Labor in 1913. He served as assistant secretary of labor until March 1920. He then for a two-month period became the acting secretary when Secretary of Labor William Wilson took a leave of absence to care for his sick wife. At the same time, the solicitor for the department, John Abercrombie, resigned. That was significant because he had been in charge of immigration matters, including approving or canceling deportation warrants, work Abercrombie found "extremely disturbing." His resignation meant that all immigration responsibilities were turned over to Post, thrusting him, in his own words, into "a hurricane of Congressional politics and newspaper vituperation."[66]

Post dismissed most of the deportation cases that Hoover's Radical Division had prepared as a result of the Palmer Raids. He found that many of those arrested had not been given proper counsel and that the evidence against them had often been illegally obtained and was insufficient to justify deportation. He also found that many people were not even aware that they were listed by the Communist Party or the Communist Labor Party as members. Many belonged to the Socialist Party. Years earlier, when factions broke away and formed the two communist parties, these new parties wanted to portray themselves as having large membership bases, so they simply listed a lot of the Socialists as members without their knowledge. Some of those detained had simply wandered into a Communist Party meeting that night out of curiosity and were not members, but they got swept up in the raids.[67]

Post later wrote about "the lawlessness and the cruelty" of the Palmer Raids in his book *The Deportations Delirium of Nineteen-Twenty*:

> From Detroit westward and southward to the Mississippi and the Ohio, and eastward through Pennsylvania and New York into Philadelphia, New Jersey, New York City and New England, that "red" crusade was conducted with so little respect for law and order as to discredit the patriotic boast that ours is "a government of law and not of men." The popular approval it received at the time lies beyond the range of any reasonable explanation other than that the public mind was under the influence of what must always be regarded as a monstrous social delirium. Such deliriums cannot continue even in milder forms, nor often recur, without disastrous social consequences.[68]

He was particularly upset about the popular image that had emerged that those arrested and set for deportations were all revolutionaries:

> As a rule the [deportation] hearings showed the aliens arrested to be workingmen of good character, who had never been arrested before, who were not anarchists nor revolutionists nor obnoxious to the spirit of our laws in any other sense. Many of them were faithful fathers of American-born children. Nearly all had been subjected to arbitrary arrest, to long detention in default of bail beyond the means of hard-working wage-earners to furnish, and for nothing more reprehensible, so far as intent counted, than affiliating with friends of their own race, country and language. Cases in which there was substantial proof of any unlawful act with sinister intent or guilty knowledge were exceptions—very rare exceptions.[69]

Hoover, Palmer, and Flynn were naturally alarmed by Post's actions regarding the deportation cases. BI field offices received a telegram from headquarters in March 1920 instructing them that upon learning of the cancellations of deportation warrants for individuals in their cities, they were to "forward Special Delivery Attention Hoover detailed statement facts in each case where cancellation has been made [and that it was] important that this be given prompt and immediate attention daily." A relentless campaign against Post was launched by the Justice Department, with Palmer denouncing Post as having a "perverted sympathy for the criminal anarchists" and Hoover creating a 350-page file on Post aimed at discrediting him. They tried to get him impeached by Congress, but after hearing Post's testimony, the House Rules Committee found no grounds for impeachment. One conservative newspaper, the *Spokesman-Review* from Spokane, Washington, a news outlet not expected to be favorable to Post, was impressed with his performance and reported the following to its readers in a series of headlines: "Post Hurls Broadside at Foes, in Self-Defense—Wins Round One—Lands 'Terrific Wallops' on Critics of His Policy in 'Deporting Reds'—Is 71, Full of Fight—Flays Attorney General's Work of Persecuting Men Found Innocent of Wrong."[70]

Meanwhile, public sentiment began turning against the Red Scare tactics and warnings of a Bolshevik revolution in America emanating from the Department of Justice. One congressman denounced the Palmer Raids by saying that those arrested and targeted for deportation "probably didn't know the difference between bolshevism and rheumatism." But a key turning point for the public and others was when nothing happened following warnings from the Justice Department that there would be a violent nationwide uprising by Communists on May Day in 1920. That "deflated the national hysteria about arresting and deporting 'Reds.'" There was also a scathing report issued in May by the National Popular Government League (NPGL) that outlined the illegalities of the Palmer Raids. Titled *To the American People: Report upon the Illegal Practices of the United States Department of Justice*, the group, composed of twelve prominent lawyers and professors, including Felix Frankfurter, a future Supreme Court justice, wrote, "We are concerned solely with bringing to the attention of the American people the utterly illegal acts which have been committed by those charged with the highest duty of enforcing the laws—acts which have caused widespread suffering and unrest, have struck at the foundation of American free institutions, and have brought the name of our country into disrepute."[71]

The NPGL accused the Department of Justice of violating the Constitution and having "under the guise of a campaign for the suppression of radical activities . . . committed continual illegal acts." Their report included sworn statements from witnesses and photographs of prisoners who had been beaten during the raids. They also took Palmer and his department to task for trying to manipulate public opinion: "In support of these illegal acts, and to create sentiment in its favor, the Department of Justice has also constituted itself a propaganda bureau, and has sent to newspapers and magazines of this country quantities of material designed to excite public opinion against radicals, all at the expense of the government and outside the scope of the Attorney General's duties."[72]

By the summer of 1920, the Red Scare was, for all practical purposes, over. Warren Harding, who would become the Republican nominee for president and win the 1920 election, campaigned for a "return to normalcy," declaring that "too much has been said about bolshevism in America." Palmer's presidential aspirations were also over, as his warnings of impending doom at the hands of Bolsheviks and Communists never materialized and the publicity regarding the Justice Department's tactics in hunting down radicals tarnished his reputation. He withdrew his name from nomination at the Democratic National Convention in San Francisco in late June after failing to win the nomination following forty-four ballots. With him at the convention was Hoover, who somehow survived the Palmer Raids without damaging his career, even though the raids could just as easily have been labeled the "Palmer and Hoover Raids." For years he denied any role in the illegalities of those raids, demonstrating his understanding "that secrecy and deception were essential to political warfare." Flynn also mostly escaped recriminations, but his public image nevertheless took a hit. It had been more than a year since the June 2, 1919, bombings, and the famous detective had failed to bring any of the bombers to justice.[73]

Flynn faced a handicap in his pursuit of anarchists, including the Galleanists. He had to deal with Palmer and Hoover's belief that even if the Galleanists were responsible for the attacks on June 2, they were only fronting for a larger and more politically significant revolutionary group, such as the Third International, also known as the Communist International or Comintern, an association of national communist parties under the control of the Soviet Union with the goal of promoting world revolution. That meant that a majority of the Justice Department's manpower and resources were devoted to the Bolshevik and Communist threat and not to the actual threat posed by the group that perpetrated the attacks. "It was that assumption," writes historian Charles McCormick, "that provided the excuse for the Red Scare dragnets aimed at groups that investigators well knew had no direct connection with the actual bombings. Weighted down with such baggage, the bomb investigations were compromised and perhaps doomed to fail by the Justice Department's political imperative to go beyond the evidence that pointed to a revenge motive animating a small group of Italian-American anarchists against a government that was prosecuting and deporting them."[74]

Though the Galleanists benefited from the government's focus on Bolsheviks and Communists during the Red Scare, they were in disarray by the spring of 1920. As noted earlier, many had scattered or left the country, fearful of what Roberto Elia and Andrea Salsedo might have told the government while they were being held in the BI office in New York. Yet in terrorism it does not take many to conceive of a plot and then follow through with a devastating attack. One of the remaining Galleanists made sure of that in what became one of the worst terrorist incidents in U.S. history.

6 Final Blow

"Sacco and Vanzetti were the best friends I had in America," Mario Buda said in an interview in Italy in February 1928, almost six months after the two men were executed at the Charlestown State Prison in Boston. More commonly known just by their last names, Nicola Sacco and Bartolomeo Vanzetti were fervent, dedicated Galleanists, just like Buda. But the crime for which they paid with their lives, and for which their trial was universally condemned as unfair, had nothing to do with the bombings that the Galleanists had committed in the past. Rather it was a robbery-murder case that reverberated around the world.[1]

Sacco, Vanzetti, and Buda had all immigrated to the United States from Italy around the same time—Buda in 1907 and Sacco and Vanzetti one year later. Buda was twenty-four years old, Sacco was sixteen, and Vanzetti was twenty when they arrived. None of them had grown up in poverty, but they were not wealthy. Still, they were better off than most of the Italian immigrants who came to America. And unlike the man they would follow with complete devotion, Luigi Galleani, they had not been anarchists in their home country. Their experiences in the United States transformed them.[2]

For Sacco, who worked in a shoe factory in Milford, Massachusetts, it was "the conditions he saw in America [that] turned him towards anarchism. Comparatively well off though he was, he was not blind to the sufferings of others [and] the poverty and squalor in the midst of plenty. . . . He could not ignore those less fortunate than himself." One of those unfortunates was Vanzetti, whom he would not meet until 1917, when they and several other Galleanists went to Mexico to avoid registering for the military draft. Vanzetti's turn to anarchism was based on his difficult life in America, "one of hard, unrelenting toil, with periods of unemployment and near starvation." Vanzetti, who first settled in New York and then moved to Connecticut and Massachusetts, loved to read social and political books and articles. Based on his readings and personal experiences, he decided that "only the anarchists, in contrast to other radicals, favored the abolition of government, the chief sources of tyranny and subjugation." In November 1912 he sent a contribution of twenty-five cents to *Cronaca Sovversiva*, and from then on, "the overthrow of the existing social and political order became an avowed object of his life."[3]

Buda, who first lived in Boston after arriving in the United States, also led a vagabond life like Vanzetti. He worked various jobs in construction, gardening, and freight-car building and then moved to Colorado in search of higher wages. He could not find work there, so he traveled to Illinois, where he found a job but still slept in a box car to save money. "About this time I became an anarchist," Buda said. "The kind of life I was leading gave me something to think about." He moved back to Italy in 1911 and worked for a while with his father but returned to America in 1913, settling in the Roxbury district of Boston, where many Galleanists lived. He first met Sacco during a strike in 1913 and then Vanzetti during another strike in 1916. But as described in chapter 3, it was in Mexico between the spring and fall of 1917 where Buda, Sacco, and Vanzetti formed a close bond, as they did with the approximately sixty other followers of Galleani who'd gone there in order to avoid the draft. Most of them eventually decided to secretly reenter the United States and take their chances avoiding arrest. Buda first went to Chicago and then Iron River, Michigan; Sacco to Cambridge, Massachusetts; and Vanzetti to St. Louis and then Youngstown, Ohio.[4]

The three men stayed in touch and took part in the Galleanists' campaign of terror around the United States, including the June 2, 1919, near-simultaneous bombings in seven cities. That's why it's ironic that on the night of May 5, 1920, Sacco and Vanzetti were arrested in Brockton, Massachusetts, not for their prior terrorist activity but in a trap the police had set for Buda following a robbery and murders that had taken place a few weeks earlier in South Braintree. Prior to the night they were arrested, the police had not even heard of Sacco and Vanzetti.[5]

The event that would link Saco and Vanzetti together in history occurred on the afternoon of April 15, 1920, in South Braintree, an industrial town about fourteen miles south of Boston. It was payday for the workers at the Slater & Morrill Shoe Company factory. At around three o'clock, Frederick Parmenter, the assistant paymaster, and Alessandro Berardelli, a security guard, began the short walk down the street from the company's office building to the factory, where the workers were anxiously awaiting their weekly wages. Men and women watched from the factory windows as "the roll" (how they referred to their paychecks) was on its way to their eager hands. Parmenter and Berardelli were each carrying a heavy steel box containing a combined total of $15,776.51 in bills and coins separated into five hundred pay envelopes.[6]

As Parmenter and Berardelli crossed in front of the factory, they were attacked by two men who had been standing by a fence. One of the men shot Berardelli and, after he fell to the ground, fired three more bullets into him. Berardelli died at the scene. Parmenter was also shot, two times, and he died the next morning. The gunmen fired at a bystander, missing him, and, after taking the payroll boxes, jumped into a getaway car with three other men. The entire crime unfolded in less than one minute.[7]

These were the days when not all police departments had automobiles. The Braintree Police Department would not obtain its first vehicle until 1931, so the robbers had no trouble fleeing in their stolen Buick. Just to be safe, though, they dropped tacks onto the road from the windows of their car, figuring that would cause flat tires for any pursuing police vehicles. Only one person, the chief of the Braintree Fire Department, followed them, but he was not able to overtake them and soon gave up his pursuit.[8]

There had been a similar robbery attempt at a factory in nearby Bridgewater on December 24, 1919, so Bridgewater's chief of police, Michael Stewart, suspected the same gang of being involved in both incidents. In the Bridgewater attack, gunmen fired at a truck delivering over $30,000 in cash to the L. Q. White Shoe Company, but the guard fired back, and the driver of the truck was able to elude the would-be robbers, who then fled in their getaway car. There were no injuries in that attack.[9]

On April 17 the getaway Buick was found abandoned in the woods in West Bridgewater, about thirteen miles from South Braintree. A day earlier Stewart had been to the home of Ferruccio Coacci, a Galleanist, whom he had arrested in May 1918 following a raid on *Cronaca Sovversiva*. Coacci missed a deportation hearing on April 15, the day of the South Braintree ambush, and federal officials asked Stewart to check on Coacci, who lived in West Bridgewater. When Stewart found him at home, Coacci requested immediate deportation, and the government complied by deporting him a couple of days later. It's surprising that he was deported so quickly since, at that time, Stewart suspected him of involvement in both the Bridgewater and South Braintree attacks. He also suspected Mario Buda, who was using the alias "Mike Boda" and living in the same house as Coacci. When small tire tracks were found next to the abandoned Buick (which had large tires), Stewart figured a smaller car must have been the second getaway car used to transport the South Braintree perpetrators away from where they'd ditched the stolen Buick in the woods. Since Buda had such a car, an Overland, that was in a garage in West Bridgewater awaiting repairs, Stewart believed the second getaway car was probably Buda's. Stewart told the garage owner, Simon Johnson, to notify the police as soon as anybody came to retrieve the vehicle.[10]

That happened on the evening of May 5, when Buda, Sacco, Vanzetti, and Riccardo Orciani, a fellow Galleanist, went to the garage to pick up Buda's car. There was an urgency to their task. Just two days earlier, Andrea Salsedo, another Galleanist, had jumped to his death from the fourteenth floor of the Bureau of Investigation building in Manhattan, where he and Roberto Elia had been held and interrogated by federal agents. (See chapter 5 for a discussion of the Salsedo case.) The *New York Times* and *Boston Globe*, among other newspapers, reported the next day about the suicide, stating that Salsedo had cooperated with the authorities and implicated the Galleanists in the June 2 bombing attacks. The story in the *Boston Globe*, a paper Sacco read every day, was titled "Suicide Betrayed Lynn Anarchists." Fearing that federal agents might track them down and arrest them at any moment, they knew they needed to dispose of all the anarchist literature, and likely dynamite, that they and other Galleanists in the area had. And they needed a car to do the job.[11]

Sacco and Vanzetti took a streetcar to Johnson's garage, while Buda went with Orciani, riding in the sidecar of Orciani's motorcycle. The garage was closed, so they went to Johnson's nearby home to speak with him. While Buda and Johnson were talking, Johnson's wife went to a neighbor's house to call the police. Johnson, stalling for time, told Buda that although the repairs on the car were done, the vehicle did not have 1920 license plates and he shouldn't drive it without them. Buda at first said he didn't care but then changed his mind and told Johnson he would have somebody come by the next day to pick it up. By the time Chief of Police Stewart arrived, all four men were gone. Buda had left with Orciani on the motorcycle, and Sacco and Vanzetti had walked away and boarded a streetcar destined for Brockton. Stewart telephoned the Brockton police and told them to be on the lookout for two foreigners on the streetcar from Bridgewater whom he claimed had just tried to steal an automobile.[12]

The policemen found Sacco and Vanzetti on the streetcar when it made a stop, and they arrested them. When the two men asked why they were being taken into custody, they were told it was because they were "suspicious characters." Because of this, they believed the reason for their arrest was due to their anarchist activity. Stewart made no mention of either the South Braintree or Bridgewater attacks when he interrogated them at the police station. Worried about deportation or criminal prosecution for being anarchists, not to mention trying to dispose of anarchist literature and possibly dynamite on the night they were arrested, as well as not wanting to implicate other Galleanists in anarchist activities, they lied in their answers to Stewart. They gave false or evasive responses to questions about whether they knew Buda or Coacci, whether they were Communists or anarchists, whether they subscribed to anarchist literature, whether they had been to Simon Johnson's house, and so forth. Their behavior in the interrogation, coupled with the fact that both men had been armed with weapons at the time of their arrest, was used by the prosecution at their trial, as well as by the judge in his instructions to the jury, to argue that Sacco and Vanzetti displayed a "consciousness of guilt," indicating their responsibility for the South Braintree crime. However, as historian Paul Avrich points out, "It seems reasonable . . . to conclude that the guilt of which they were conscious was that of anarchism, not of robbery and murder."[13]

Vanzetti was brought to trial during the summer of 1920 for the Bridgewater holdup in which nobody had been injured nor any money stolen. Sacco was not, as he had an alibi for that day. He'd been at work at a factory and had a time stamp to prove it. In a prelude to what would occur in Sacco and Vanzetti's later trial for the South Braintree attack, the trial for the Bridgewater crime was characterized by "contempt for Italian immigrants and Italian culture" and questionable eyewitness testimony for the prosecution. Vanzetti was convicted and sentenced by Judge Webster Thayer to the maximum term of twelve to fifteen years in prison for attempted robbery.[14]

Sacco and Vanzetti's trial began on May 31, 1921, and ended with a guilty verdict of murder in the first degree for both defendants on July 14. Many observers believed that they had been convicted not on the basis of evidence proving criminal guilt but rather because they were immigrants espousing anarchist beliefs. It was an unfair trial, characterized by "an atmosphere of intense hostility toward the defendants." District Attorney Frederick G. Katzmann "conducted a highly unscrupulous prosecution, coaching and badgering witnesses, withholding exculpatory evidence from the defense, and perhaps even tampering with physical evidence." The judge in the trial and the subsequent appeals was again Webster Thayer, who never tried to hide his bias against the defendants. He once stated outside the courtroom, "Did you see what I did with those anarchistic bastards the other day? I guess that will hold them for a while."[15]

After several years of unsuccessful appeals, Sacco and Vanzetti were sentenced to death by Thayer on April 9, 1927. They were executed a few months later, just after midnight on August 23, at the Charlestown State

Prison. Their case garnered worldwide attention, becoming "a rallying point for labor and the Left nationally and internationally" and resulting in protests and demonstrations both before and after their execution. Sacco and Vanzetti also drew support from liberals, intellectuals, and workers who were appalled at the unfairness of the trial and the sentence of death. Nearly two hundred thousand people watched the funeral procession as it wound its way through the streets of Boston, with seven thousand mourners marching behind two hearses. "Massachusetts and America murdered them," exclaimed Mary Donovan, secretary of the Sacco-Vanzetti Defense Committee, who delivered the eulogy at the crematory. While there is a consensus that the trial of Sacco and Vanzetti was unfair, there is no consensus among historians and others as to whether or not these two Galleanists were actually guilty of the crime for which they were convicted. "Nearly seven decades after their trial," Avrich wrote in 1991, "the case against them remains unproved. Nor, on the other hand, can their innocence be established beyond any shadow of doubt.... The issue of guilt or innocence awaits definitive treatment, but, alas, it may never receive it."[16]

Mario Buda, for whom police had set the trap at the garage in West Bridgewater in May 1920 (resulting in Sacco and Vanzetti getting arrested instead), eluded the authorities and eventually went back to Italy later in 1920. Edward Houlton James interviewed Buda in 1928 on the island of Lipari, where he was a political prisoner, having been arrested the previous year as a "dangerous anarchist" and given a five-year sentence for antifascist activities. James had a pointed question for Buda: "Since you came back to Savignano, during all the years that the Sacco-Vanzetti case was going on, did you do anything to help them?" Buda seemed surprised. "Well, what could I have to say?" he replied. "If they would not believe all the Italians who spoke for them, would they believe me? You have to reform the government in America."[17]

James, a fervent supporter of Sacco and Vanzetti and also the nephew of the philosopher William James and the novelist Henry James, came away from the interview disappointed. He wanted to hear something from Buda that would clear the names of the two men, even in death. He wrote that Buda "does not yet realize the moral importance to the whole world of the complete, decisive and final rehabilitation of Sacco and Vanzetti, which to a great extent lies in his own hands." To James, if Buda could prove he had not been involved in the South Braintree attack, then Sacco and Vanzetti's names would be cleared:

> It will be remembered that Sacco and Vanzetti were arrested in a net which the police of Bridgewater had spread for the purpose of catching "Boda." It will be remembered that the Lowell Commission [the body that investigated the case at the request of Massachusetts Governor Alvan Fuller after Sacco and Vanzetti were sentenced to death] based their condemnation of Sacco and Vanzetti on the foregone conclusion that Boda was the ringleader of the bandit gang, that his house was the bandit headquarters, that the Buick car in which Sacco and Vanzetti were accused of committing the crimes had been stolen by Boda and concealed in the shed adjoining Boda's house. The clue for the arrest of Sacco and Vanzetti therefore centered around Boda. If Boda was guilty, the State of Massachusetts had a prima facie case against Sacco and Vanzetti. If Boda was not guilty, the State of Massachusetts had no case at all against Sacco and Vanzetti, and the friends of Sacco and Vanzetti become justified in the hypothesis that the case against Sacco and Vanzetti was, from its inception to its conclusion, a mistake or a "frame-up."[18]

James interviewed Buda again in April 1932, a few months before Buda's prison sentence was scheduled to end, bringing with him this time Sacco's teenaged son, Dante, whom Buda embraced warmly. The interview took place on the island of Ponza, where Buda had been transferred. The results of this interview were much more satisfying for James, who told reporters afterward that Buda was planning to return to the United States to prove the innocence of Sacco and Vanzetti. James said he was going to ask Italian Premier Benito Mussolini, who had given him permission to interview Buda both times, to help facilitate Buda's return to America.[19]

The possibility of Buda returning was greeted with anticipation by the media. "News from Naples that Mario Buda has been released from an Italian penal colony and that he plans to come to the United States will revive the hope held by many persons throughout the world that the names of Sacco and Vanzetti will finally be cleared," wrote the *St. Louis Post-Dispatch*. The newspaper, however, cautioned its readers that it was not known what effect his return would ultimately have on the case: "It may be for him to add a footnote to the tragic story of the shoemaker [Sacco] and the fish peddler [Vanzetti], and then again, he may open up a new and important chapter. It is a development that will be watched with interest around the globe."[20]

U.S. government officials were skeptical about the reports of Buda planning to return. "Boda [*sic*] will have a hard time to get back to the United States," said Mary Tillinghast, New England's commissioner of immigration. "It is entirely in the hands of the American consulate in Italy—and from experience, I would say that the consulate will not look very favorably upon any such application. He must expressly tell why he wants to come to this country and I cannot imagine any great approval there of his story to establish the innocence of Sacco and Vanzetti. It sounds too much like a chestnut."[21]

Buda never returned to the United States. It is unlikely that he was ever serious about doing so. Bridgewater police chief Michael Stewart and others believed that he was with the group that committed the South Braintree robbery and murders, was perhaps even the ringleader, and had taken the stolen money, which was never recovered, to Italy. Despite this, there were no outstanding charges against him. Buda, however, could not be sure that the authorities would not charge him if he returned since there was no statute of limitations for murder.[22]

But Buda would have to be concerned about another crime, should he ever return. It was one that he had thus far gotten away with. When James asked him in the 1928 interview if he had done anything to help Sacco and Vanzetti, Buda probably thought to himself, "If only I could tell him what I actually did." It wasn't something aimed at helping his "best friends" in America; it was, however, intended to avenge their likely fate after their indictment for the South Braintree murders. It would be his last act of violence in America before fleeing the country.

Terror on Wall Street

They were young veterans of the Great War, as World War I was known at the time. One of them, Bernard Kennedy, had been gassed and wounded by shrapnel in the knee while serving with the American Expeditionary

Forces (AEF) in France. The other, T. Montgomery Osprey, also with the AEF, had been wounded in the right arm and eye by shrapnel at Beaucourt and, after returning home in December 1918, spent a long time recuperating in a hospital. When he was finally released, his right arm was still paralyzed.[23]

Both men were working for the same brokerage firm as clerks when, on September 16, 1920, around noon, they walked together by the J. P. Morgan and Company headquarters building on the corner of Broad and Wall Streets in New York City. They were carrying securities valued at $170,000 to be delivered to other stock-exchange firms. They never made it to their destinations. After surviving the horrors of war, they now met death on the streets of New York at the hands of a terrorist bomb. So too did other World War I veterans, young women, and teenage boys, most of whom were walking to lunch and other places on that fateful, late-summer day. Thirty-eight people were killed and hundreds wounded in the bombing.[24]

The explosion was preceded by a blinding flash of bluish-white light that illuminated the sky above Wall Street. Then a deafening sound reverberated throughout the area as the bomb, composed of one hundred pounds of explosives and five hundred pounds of heavy, cast-iron slugs, exploded from a horse and wagon parked in front of the U.S. Assay Office, right next to the Sub-Treasury Building and just across the street from the Morgan headquarters. It was 12:01 p.m., and the bells from nearby Trinity Church were still ringing out the hour when the blast occurred. The vehicle bomb, equipped with a timer, smashed windows to bits, causing glass to shower down over the fronts of several buildings and also blow back into offices. The cast-iron slugs were hurled in all directions. A cloud of smoke engulfed the site of the explosion, while another cloud of dust covered the entire street. People ran in terror, and when they looked back moments after the smoke and dust had cleared, they were horrified to see people lying on the street and sidewalk. Thousands of people ran back to the scene of the carnage to try to help those who were injured. Hospitals close by soon resembled field hospitals in a war zone, overcrowded with victims either dead or dying, as well as the lucky ones who with treatment would survive. Army cots were set up in all areas of the hospitals. Several of the injured were carried there on the shoulders of pedestrians. A seventeen-year-old office boy who had been knocked over and cut by the blast got up and commandeered an abandoned automobile. He loaded as many of the injured into the vehicle as he could. He made four trips, carrying more than thirty people to one of the hospitals.[25]

Meanwhile, the interior of the Morgan building was wrecked, the property damage exceeding $2 million. The horse and wagon were blown apart. Since most of the victims were couriers, stenographers, and clerks, the *New York Times* observed that "the conspirators in large measure failed of whatever direct objects they had beyond sheer terrorization. They evidently timed their infernal machine for an hour when the streets of the financial district were crowded, but they chose as well the hour when not the captains of industry but their clerks and messengers were on the street. J. P. Morgan himself . . . was in Europe."[26]

For a public that had grown accustomed to anarchist violence targeting mainly high-profile government, law enforcement, and business personnel, the number of innocent victims in this attack was shocking. Yet to militant anarchists and other radicals, anybody working on Wall Street was viewed as a legitimate target. In the words of the French anarchist Émile Henry (as noted in chapter 4), "There are no innocent." Leaflets found in a public mailbox a short distance away by a mail carrier around the time of the blast warned of more attacks: "Remember we will not tolerate any longer. Free the political prisoners or it will be sure death for all of you." The leaflet was signed "American Anarchist Fighters" and was similar to the *Go-Head!* flyers the Galleanists had circulated in New England in February 1919 and the *Plain Words* pamphlets they had left at the sites of the June 2, 1919, explosions. Even the name American Anarchist Fighters pointed to the Galleanists since it was a combination of the names signed to *Go-Head!* (The American Anarchists) and *Plain Words* (The Anarchist Fighters).[27]

The New York Chamber of Commerce called the bombings an "act of war." Newspaper headlines left no doubt for the public who the culprits were. The *Chicago Daily Tribune* led with the headline "Red Bomb in NY." The *Washington Herald* declared, "30 Die in Wall St Blast; Traced to Red Bomb." And the *Los Angeles Times* used the headline "Blame Reds in

Wall St. Horror." The *New York Times*, however, in an editorial titled "To Put Down Terrorists," cautioned against playing into the hands of the perpetrators by overreacting:

> First of all, there must be no yielding to panic fear. That would be to make the assassins believe that they had half succeeded. They aim to intimidate. The community must show that it is not to be intimidated. Of course, there are great and constant risks to be run. More bombs may be exploded. Other lives may be taken. But these are only hazards of a war which the enemies of society have chosen to declare, and must be faced calmly by those who are ready to defend law and the right of the individual to the fruits of his toil, and if necessary to die in that defense. There must be no blenching, no showing of the white feather in the presence of the terrorists. By keeping cool and firm we begin their defeat.[28]

In the same editorial, however, the *Times* expressed the anger many Americans were feeling:

> Next comes the duty to oppose anarchistic force with the greater force of organized society. These callous and cowardly murderers must be made to feel that every resource of civilization will be employed against them. They will be hunted down in their lairs like wild animals. Every device and stratagem of detection will be put in operation against them. Their confederates and accomplices will be swept into the net of the public prosecutor. They will live in daily fear of betrayal and punishment. They will be made to know that the hand of every honest man is against them. So that, in the end the greatest terror will be their own. They will experience the dread of the law and darker dread of condemnation by the universal judgment and conscience of mankind.[29]

The Wall Street bombing thrust back into the limelight some of the notable names from the recent Red Scare period. Attorney General A. Mitchell Palmer, who'd seen his political ambitions and reputation take a big hit with the public and congressional backlash to the mass arrests and deportations, now had a new calling—a major bombing to solve. He viewed the attack as part of a "gigantic plot" to overthrow the capitalist system. He didn't waste any time before blaming congressional cuts to his budget as the reason the bombing occurred in the first place. Having had to trim his operational staff by one-third because of the reduction in funds, he claimed that "we are not able to keep in as close touch with ultra-radicals as we were some six months ago or keep as well informed on what is taking place or about to take place." He hoped this incident would result in support for new deportations. "If it is found that this was a criminal act," he said, "beyond question we may, with the support of public opinion, be enabled to take more drastic action with relation to deportations of alien criminal anarchists, which is the only class we have been deporting." Palmer also viewed the bombing as vindication and justification for the Red Scare campaign that he and his department had pursued.[30]

William Flynn, the director of the Bureau of Investigation, likewise seized upon the bombing to continue his pursuit of anarchists and other militants. He had thus far failed to bring anyone to justice for the April 1919 package bombs sent through the mail or the June 2, 1919, bombings in seven cities. Now was his chance to prove to everyone that he was up to the task and would have better results this time. A media darling, reporters were probably happy that Flynn was back in the news. Expectations were once again raised that the great detective would be able to solve the case. "Chief William Flynn, the famous 'Big Bill,' hurried to New York to assume personally the task of the unraveling of the mystery," the *Los Angeles Times* reported. Flynn laid the blame for the bombing on the Galleanists, telling the media shortly after the incident that the plot had been hatched by the same group responsible for the June 2, 1919, bombings. The motive for the Wall Street attack, according to Flynn, was revenge for the prosecution of Sacco and Vanzetti, who just a few days earlier, on September 11, had been indicted for the South Braintree murders. "It was the Galleani Reds who conceived and carried out the Wall street outrage," Flynn would write a couple of years later. He even suggested that Galleani, now living in Italy, had orchestrated the plot: "I learned from sources too impressive and reliable to be disbelieved that it was Galleani who not only sowed the seed that grew into the attack upon Wall street but he plotted the thing and forwarded his suggestions to America."[31]

The Wall Street bombing also propelled back into the public eye another high-profile detective, William J. Burns. Even more famous than Flynn, Burns "was quick-witted, glib, and in love with the spotlight." He also resembled Flynn physically with his "broad belly, thick moustache, [and] large jowls." Burns had gained fame around the country after tracking down and bringing to justice the McNamara brothers, John and James, two labor activists responsible for bombing the *Los Angeles Times* building in 1910, causing the deaths of twenty-one nonunion workers. The Burns International Detective Agency grew over the years, but by 1920 Burns's luster wasn't the same as it had been a decade earlier. He wasn't generating the high praise and acclaim that he had grown accustomed to. A major terrorist attack that he and his detective agency could investigate was just what he needed.[32]

The headquarters for his company was in the Woolworth Building, located not far from the Financial District, where the bomb went off. Burns wasted no time getting to Wall Street. One newspaper wrote he "was personally on the scene conducting an investigation within a few minutes after the explosion occurred." When reporters asked him why he was there, he replied that he was working for the Morgan bank, something the bank did not confirm. It really didn't matter, though, because he was so well known that he could operate independently at any crime scene with little interference or opposition from official agencies. Not one to miss an opportunity for publicity, he boldly predicted that the case would probably be solved in just ten days. He also implied that the Morgan bank was not the sole target of the attack. "It was an attempt to startle the world by exploding these bombs in the very heart of the financial district," he said, "where they would damage the assay office, the subtreasury, the Morgan office and the Stock Exchange at the same time."[33]

With high-profile figures such as Palmer, Flynn, and Burns on the case, as well as others ranging from the New York Police Department to the Treasury Department's Secret Service agents, it was going to be a competitive battle to see who would be first to capture the terrorists and bring them to justice. Investigators were at a disadvantage from the start, however, in their search for the bomber or bombers. Pressure from the business community to open Wall Street the very next day as though nothing had happened resulted in cleaning crews, repairmen, and others working through the night to get rid of all the debris to make everything look as normal as possible, thereby losing potentially valuable physical evidence. When workers returned to the Financial District on September 17, "they encountered an eloquently sanitized scene." Corporate America was determined to get back to "business as usual," and hand-lettered signs with those exact words were hung in the doorways of buildings in the district, encouraging everybody to put the tragedy behind them. The Stock Exchange had closed after the explosion but was back in business the next day.[34]

One of the first tasks for investigators was interviewing eyewitnesses. As is usually the case with multiple witnesses of a crime, there were varying accounts. But BI agents were nevertheless able to reach a consensus on a few points from a sample of twenty-one eyewitnesses. Most of them agreed that the wagon was parked in front of or near the U.S. Assay Office and that it was old and dilapidated, with sides of about one foot in height. The body of the wagon was dark or dirty gray with paint worn off, while the wheels were dark red. The horse, a dark bay, was aged, thin, and in poor condition, its front knees badly sprung. The witnesses, however, were not able to provide sufficient information regarding a description of the driver.[35]

Many different people were interviewed about what they saw on the morning of the explosion. According to one witness who had a view of the street from his office window, the wagon was parked outside the Assay Office unattended for at least an hour. He had looked out the window at various times between 11:00 a.m. and noon, and each time he saw the unattended wagon. If true this meant that a dilapidated, beat-up wagon with an old horse sat in the heart of the Financial District of New York for an hour and did not raise suspicions regarding what it was doing there in the first place. Security awareness was apparently nonexistent among both the public and law enforcement on that fateful day. The *Wall Street Journal* took the New York City government to task, criticizing its officials for not policing the Financial District as it should have been, thereby allowing something like the bombing to occur. At the same time, the *Journal* also praised the resilience of Wall Street and noted the futility of whoever was responsible for the bombing. "The relations between capital and labor will not be changed," the paper wrote, "not even for the worse as regards labor; for no one but a fool has ever doubted Wall Street's courage."[36]

Investigators were interested in learning whether any of the people killed or injured had been involved in the bombing. It'd only been a little more than a year since the perpetrator of the bombing at Attorney General Palmer's home, Carlo Valdinoci, was blown up as he tried to place a bomb at Palmer's front door. Perhaps something similar had happened this time and would lead investigators to the individual or group responsible for the attack. But after looking into whether any of the dead or injured had owned or operated a horse-drawn wagon, they found nothing and abandoned that line of investigation. The BI also used confidential informants to determine whether radical groups in New York, including the Union of Russian Workers and the IWW, were involved in the bombing and concluded that they were not. Special Agent Charles J. Scully, in charge of the BI's New York Radical Division, wrote to Flynn in October that "it would appear that . . . the explosion was the work of either Italian Anarchists or Italian Terrorists."[37]

This came as no surprise to Flynn, who, as mentioned, believed from the start that the Galleanists were the ones behind the bombing. Flynn reorganized the New York BI office in late September to help the search for the Galleanists. A special unit was established with the sole purpose of investigating the attack. Scully examined the subscription lists for *Cronaca Sovversiva*, the Galleanist newspaper; divided them up by city; and sent the names off to several BI offices on the East Coast, including ones in Boston, Providence, Buffalo, and New York City. He instructed the agents to determine the locations and recent activities of their particular city's subscribers. More than two thousand suspected Italian anarchists were checked out, but none had any connection to the bombing.[38]

To Flynn, Palmer, and others, this was beginning look like the late spring and early summer of 1919 all over again—high-profile terrorist attacks, high-profile investigations, and high-profile failures to bring anybody to justice for the crimes. A number of people had been detained shortly after the Wall Street bombing, but they were all soon after released. One of these was a mentally ill former tennis star, Edwin Fischer, who had written to friends who worked in the Financial District to warn them to stay away from Wall Street on September 15. He had also told Thomas Delahunty, a caretaker at a tennis court, "Tom, I want to tell you a secret. We are going to blow up Wall Street on the 15th. We got them where we want them." Even though he had the wrong date by one day, his letters and statement got the attention of the authorities. But after questioning him extensively, they released him and sent him to the psychiatric ward at Bellevue Hospital in New York City after deducing that he had no prior knowledge of the explosion and that he truly believed he had received telepathic messages from God regarding the attack.[39]

Not everybody, however, thought Fischer was crazy. Dr. Walter F. Prince, the acting director of the American Institute for Scientific Research, said it was feasible for somebody to have psychic knowledge of an impending disaster. "It is reasonable to suppose," Prince said, "that Fischer's mind being 'tuned' in harmony with the workings of the minds of those who planned the disaster, received the important fact that such an occurrence was to happen but misread the signals as to the exact time, which accounted for the fact that his written warnings fixed the time of the disaster about twenty-four hours ahead of its actual happening." Needless to say, dealing with the issue of psychic powers was not something investigators were interested in pursuing.[40]

Another person arrested at the beginning of the investigation was Florean Zelenko. He had recently moved from Brooklyn to Whitman, West Virginia, for a job but quit after a few days. He then traveled to Cincinnati in search of work but could not land a job there. Next, Zelenko left Cincinnati for Pittsburgh by train, and that is where his trouble began. A traveling companion told authorities in Pittsburgh that Zelenko had talked to him knowingly about the Wall Street bombing and that he was carrying dynamite with him. When police searched Zelenko's hotel room in Pittsburgh, they indeed found seven sticks of dynamite. Zelenko's arrest and possible link to the bombing became national news.[41]

It turned out that Zelenko, a Polish immigrant, was an itinerant miner who, like other miners, was often required to buy the dynamite, fuse, and percussion caps needed for his work from the mine operators. Zelenko was simply carrying the unused sticks of dynamite with him on the train from a previous job. When BI agents searched his recent residence in Brooklyn, they found some radical literature, but nothing of a significant nature. Director Flynn eliminated Zelenko as a suspect, stating that his agents had investigated Zelenko's activities in New York prior to the bombing and were convinced that he had no connections with any radical movements. He was, though, still convicted in a federal court in Pittsburgh for interstate transportation of explosives. But given the notoriety Zelenko had to endure, with the nationwide publicity linking him to the Wall Street bombing, the judge showed compassion and sentenced him to only one day in prison.[42]

Just as the search for suspects had been futile, so too was the attempt to trace the owner of the horse and wagon that exploded on Wall Street. BI agents visited various businesses that handled explosives in the area and found that all the wagons operated by these companies had been accounted for and that they had not delivered any explosives to or near Wall Street on the day of the bombing. Stables were also checked to determine whether any were missing a horse and wagon, but none were. In addition, more than two thousand nearby retail stores were visited, but none had sold the rubber letter stamps used to print the leaflets found in the mailbox around the time of the bombing.[43]

Meanwhile, a request was put out to all news crews that had taken either still or moving pictures of the bomb scene on Wall Street to send the images to J. Edgar Hoover at the Bureau of Investigation. It is not known if this phase of the investigation resulted in any meaningful leads. Interestingly, though, one of the most famous photographs of the bombing shows an overturned car, an ambulance with "Volunteer Hospital" stamped on the back, and a large crowd of people gathered at the site of the explosion. Also, a large white sign is in the background advertising a demolition firm that was working on the new Stock Exchange Annex located near the Morgan headquarters building. "House Wreckers," the sign exclaims in big letters. Having such a sign where buildings were damaged, large crowds would gather, and news organizations would take photographs was ironic—and fortuitous for the company, in terms of publicity and possible future business (see photo 27).[44]

In November an investigation by a New York newspaper, the *Evening World*, published under the banner headline "Wall Street Explosion Solved," claimed that it was the house-wrecking firm's workers themselves and others at the demolition site who were the actual targets of the Wall Street bombing. The newspaper said that members or sympathizers of a union whose workers had been kicked off the site by another union and not allowed to work at other sites in the area were the perpetrators of the attack. BI agents, however, investigated the story and, while confirming that there was trouble between the two unions, concluded that there was no foundation to the *Evening World*'s allegations.[45]

One promising lead ultimately led to disappointment for investigators. They found two charred horse hooves, with the shoes still on, near Trinity Church. Detectives brought the horseshoes to thousands of blacksmiths up and down the East Coast in the hope that someone would recognize them. A blacksmith in New York's Little Italy section did indeed recognize them and told the investigators that a man he described as a Sicilian had come to his shop with his horse and wagon the day before the bombing and requested a new pair of shoes for his horse. BI agents then showed him more than three thousand photographs of known radicals. The blacksmith studied the photos for two weeks and identified five people that he said looked like the man who had come to his stable. A composite photo was drawn up and sent to police chiefs around the United States. Hundreds of people were questioned and some of them arrested. Most were eventually released due to lack of evidence, although one of those arrested, Tito Ligi, pleaded guilty to draft evasion and was sentenced to a year in prison. Flynn had pinned his hopes on implicating Ligi, a follower of Galleani, in the bombing, but the case against him fell apart because of an unreliable witness.[46]

By March 1921 Flynn realized that his days as BI chief were numbered. The new president, Warren Harding, had replaced one of Flynn's biggest supporters, Attorney General A. Mitchell Palmer, with Harry M. Daugherty. There were rumors that Daugherty, in turn, planned to put his old friend William Burns in charge of the BI. That happened in August when, while Flynn was on vacation, a telegram arrived at his New York office from Daugherty, informing him that his services in the government were no longer needed. Burns was going to take over, and Flynn, who had spent almost a year investigating the Wall Street bombing and had little to show for his efforts, now had to watch as his rival tried to succeed where he had failed.[47]

Flynn, however, needn't have worried about being upstaged by Burns. It didn't take long for the other great sleuth to also be embarrassed in his attempt to find those responsible for the bombing. Unlike Flynn, who was convinced it was the Galleanists behind the attack, Burns focused instead on Russian-based Communists as the culprits. When newspapers reported in December 1921 that a Polish-born radical, William Linde, also known as "Wolf Lindenfield," had been arrested in Warsaw and had stated that the Third International (an association of communist parties in other countries controlled by the Soviet Union) had supplied members of the Communist Party of the United States with $30,000 to finance the bombing, it appeared that Burns would be vindicated in his beliefs. He took the glory for this revelation, telling reporters that that "we [now] have the proper solution of this mystery." Linde, though, a prior informant for the Burns Detective Agency who was still being used by Burns to gather information regarding the Wall Street bombing, had made up the whole story. He was known to friends and others as "a fantasist and probably a swindler to boot," yet Burns had placed great stock and confidence in him. Burns never fully recovered from this fiasco, becoming transformed in the public's eye from "hero to laughingstock." He was forced to resign as head of the BI in May 1924.[48]

The new BI director, J. Edgar Hoover, did not pursue the Wall Street bombing case with the same fervor that Flynn and Burns had shown. He focused more on Prohibition and antitrust campaigns after he was appointed BI chief in 1924. Hoover was a survivor. In contrast to Flynn and Burns before him, as well as Palmer, he was not going to let himself get swallowed up following one false lead after another and in the process possibly lose his job for a case that was already fading from public discussion. While he never totally abandoned the investigation, nothing of significance was ever uncovered in the ensuing years. The last time the FBI (the BI's name was changed to FBI in 1935) looked into the bombing was 1944, and once again no results were obtained. The worst terrorist attack in America until the 1995 Oklahoma City bombing was destined to remain one of the most famous cold cases in history.[49]

Buda's Revenge

But it wasn't entirely cold. The FBI's New York office in a 1944 summarizing memo repeated the contention made just a month after the attack by Charles Scully, the BI special agent in charge of the New York office, that "Italian Anarchists or Italian Terrorists" were responsible for the bombing. And Flynn himself, as mentioned, believed that Luigi Galleani, who had been deported in June 1919 and was living in Italy at the time of the Wall Street bombing, had conceived of the operation and sent his suggestions to the remaining Galleanists still in the United States.[50]

One of those still in America in 1920 was among the most militant of them all. Mario Buda would not need any suggestions from Galleani about what to do in this case. An expert bomb maker, Buda was the one the others turned to when they needed somebody to "plant the poof" (how the anarchists referred to constructing and setting off bombs). Buda was "quiet and thoughtful and not given to any excitement or agitation." But this outward temperament hid the fire that burned inside him, a commitment "to answer force with force, not only as a matter of self-defense but of principle and honor." He was involved in most, if not all, of the Galleanist terrorist attacks. Buda "manufactured explosive devices, drafted leaflets, prepared hiding places for comrades wanted by the police, [and] selected the targets of the attacks." With most of the Galleanists either being deported or eluding the authorities and escaping to Italy by the summer of 1920, Buda was left to carry on the struggle alone. He saw "himself as a romantic hero, incessantly fighting against injustices, capable of risking his own physical safety as well as immolate anyone in the name of those ideals which for him constituted an urgent reason for living."[51]

Buda had a special motivation for wanting to strike back after Sacco and Vanzetti were indicted on September 11, 1920, for the Braintree murders. It wasn't just because they were fellow Galleanists, or even because they were his best friends in the United States. It was also likely due to a sense of personal guilt and responsibility for the trouble they were in. The only reason they were arrested on the evening of May 5 was because they had accompanied him when he went to pick up his car that was being repaired, not realizing that police had set a trap for Buda since they suspected him of not only the Braintree attack but also involvement in an armed robbery in Bridgewater in December 1919. Sacco and Vanzetti had not even been known to the police before their arrest that night.[52]

Buda may also have felt guilty if he was, along with Sacco and Vanzetti, responsible for the South Braintree murders. He had gotten away with it, but they might face the death penalty. Added to that was his seething anger over the deportation of his leader, Galleani, the year before, as well as anger about the systematic hunting down of his fellow anarchists and radicals by the government for many years. The indictment of Sacco and Vanzetti for the Braintree murders can thus be seen as the last straw for Buda, the last push he needed to do something big to avenge the fates of his friends and all his other comrades.

After eluding the police the night Sacco and Vanzetti were arrested, Buda went back to East Boston, where he was living. "The next morning I saw the arrest of Sacco and Vanzetti in the paper," Buda told Edward Houlton James in their 1928 interview. But he did not see his name mentioned, so "I stayed in east Boston three or four months." He then went to Portsmouth, New Hampshire, "where I stayed about two months. After that I went to Providence [Rhode Island], got a passport under the name of Mario Buda [he had been using the alias 'Mike Boda' at the time] from an Italian Vice-Consul close to Providence and sailed from Providence on a French boat and landed in Naples. I know I was back in Savignano some time before Christmas—about the last of November, 1920, it must have been."[53]

What Buda didn't tell James was that he'd made a brief trip from Portsmouth to Boston before leaving for Italy. In Boston he decided exactly how he would retaliate for the indictment of Sacco and Vanzetti. Then, after choosing his target, he proceeded to New York City to make final preparations. After reaching New York, he acquired an old horse and wagon and placed a bomb equipped with a timer and filled with heavy cast-iron slugs into the wagon. He drove it "to the corner of Wall and Broad Streets, the symbolic center of American capitalism." There, after parking it in front of the U.S. Assay Office and across the street from the Morgan headquarters, he walked away. "For the last time, then," historian Paul Avrich writes, "Buda had planted 'the poof.'"[54]

Avrich acknowledges that no irrefutable evidence links Buda to the bombing: "That Buda was the Wall Street bomber cannot be proved; documentary evidence is lacking. But it fits with what we know of him and his movements. I have it, moreover, from a reliable source and believe it to be true." Many historians, journalists, and others agree with Avrich's conclusion that Buda was likely responsible for the carnage on Wall Street that mid-September day. The man "who had appointed himself the avenging angel of the imprisoned and deported anarchists" would soon vanish from the country and watch from abroad as the futile Wall Street bombing investigation ensued but never pointed to him as the culprit. Buda had demonstrated what the Galleanists always believed—namely, that they were smarter than the authorities and enjoyed outwitting them.[55]

With Buda's escape to Italy, the remaining Galleanists in the United States lost one of their main bomb makers and strategists. While there were occasional bombings in future years believed to have been perpetrated by the group or others sympathetic to the Sacco and Vanzetti case (including bombings of the homes of the judge in the trial, Webster Thayer, and the executioner of the two men, Robert G. Elliott), none of these incidents generated the intense attention and reaction across the country that the Galleanists' previous attacks had stirred up. Despite the relatively brief period of time that the Galleanists were a force to reckon with in the United States, they left a legacy that can still be felt today. There are many lessons to be learned from America's experience with the Galleanists.[56]

7 The Legacy of the Galleanists

Every September 11 since 2001, America observes the anniversary of the hijacking-suicide airplane attacks that claimed the lives of almost three thousand people. Speeches, ceremonies, and moments of silence occur around the country each year, all aimed at ensuring that people never forget the tragedy of that day. A museum and a wall displaying the names of all the victims stand at Ground Zero in New York City, the site where the Twin Towers once stood. Remembering tragedies and trying to learn lessons from them have long been American traditions.

Yet the 1920 Wall Street bombing, the worst terrorist attack ever on American soil at the time, was quickly forgotten by the public, media, and government officials. No ceremonies commemorated the first anniversary of the attack, and by the middle of the decade, there was hardly a mention of it in newspapers or from public officials. No plaque listing the names of the victims was ever placed at the corner of Wall and Broad Streets. The only physical reminder of the bombing is the damage on the side of the Morgan headquarters caused by the cast-iron slugs from the explosive device. It has never been repaired. Thousands of New Yorkers pass by the building every day, most of them never glancing at the pockmarks or, if they do, not knowing how they got there.[1]

One of the reasons why the Wall Street bombing faded so quickly from the public consciousness was that no subsequent major terrorist attacks in the United States were attributed to anarchists or other militants, with the exception, as noted in chapter 6, of the occasional bombings in the late 1920s related to the Sacco and Vanzetti case. That allayed any fears people had that the Wall Street bombing was going to usher in another wave of terrorism, as had occurred in 1919. It also kept discussions about terrorism at a minimum because there were no more incidents to talk about. The Red Scare had essentially run its course, the public tired of the continual and unfounded warnings by the government about a potential anarchist or Bolshevik revolution in America. All this contributed to the Wall Street bombing appearing to the public and others to be an outlier, the last attack by the defeated anarchists. Why relive that awful day?[2]

Another reason the bombing quickly became a distant memory was that the business community, particularly the Morgan bank, wanted it that way. They made a concerted effort to move on as quickly as possible, starting with the immediate cleanup of the bomb site (and inadvertent destruction of potential evidence) and continuing with a "business as usual" approach, including little discussion of the attack. It wasn't good for business to talk about a bombing in the heart of Wall Street.[3]

And it certainly wasn't good for business to talk about the reasons why Wall Street had been the target of a bombing. Following the events of 9/11, in addition to calls from the public, government, media, and others for retaliation, there were also discussions about why Islamic extremists such as Osama bin Laden and al Qaeda hate America and would perpetrate such attacks. That did not occur after the Wall Street bombing. People did not want to hear about the possible reasons for such a horrendous attack. "Coming at the end of the Progressive era, when Wall Street's power was the subject of fierce political contest," writes historian Beverly Gage, "the explosion helped to affirm the idea that loyalty to America meant loyalty to capitalism as well. Critics of the country's economic system were denounced for supporting violence and terror." Everybody seemed eager to get on with life and embrace the Roaring Twenties after the turbulent decade they had just lived through, with its labor strife, bombings, and World War I.[4]

Just as the Wall Street bombing has for the most part been forgotten, the same can be said about the Galleanists. They are the most prominent forgotten terrorist group in history. Most books and articles about terrorism, with a few exceptions, never mention them, despite the fact that they introduced terrorist tactics and strategies still in use today. Their rise and fall hold many lessons for understanding the dynamics of global terrorism.[5]

Innovative and Creative Terrorist Attacks Can Catch Governments by Surprise

The Galleanists demonstrated the value for terrorists of coming up with innovative and creative attacks. Security against terrorism has often been a reactive process. The development of new detection devices and other measures is usually based upon what terrorists did in the past, particularly the latest incident. However, when terrorists depart significantly from previous operations, they can usually catch authorities by surprise. This is what occurred on 9/11. By combining the tactic of hijacking with the tactic of suicide attacks, al Qaeda introduced a new terrorist tactic that had never been used before—suicide attacks from the air in hijacked passenger planes. Similarly, the Galleanists' use of the postal system in 1919 to send thirty package bombs across the country in innocent-looking Gimbel Brothers gift boxes was not anticipated by the authorities. Never before had a group sent package bombs through the mail on such a wide scale, targeting judges, senators, law enforcement officials, and other high-profile individuals. No security measures were in place to prevent that type of terrorist strike.[6]

The same was true for the Wall Street bombing. There had never before been a car or vehicle bombing in the United States. When Mario Buda, the likely perpetrator, parked his horse-drawn wagon in the heart of Wall Street, no one thought there might be a bomb inside. While there should have been somebody looking into what an old horse and dilapidated wagon were doing in such a prosperous district of New York, the idea of a terrorist bomb exploding from a wagon did not occur to anybody. Buda had thought up a terrorist tactic never before attempted in America, and that increased his chances for success.[7]

Another example of a terrorist coming up with something nobody had done before is the case of Muharem Kurbegovic, also known as the "Alphabet Bomber." He set off a bomb at Los Angeles International Airport on August 6, 1974, killing three people and injuring thirty-five others. It was the first time an airport was bombed anywhere in the world. Kurbegovic devised a new way to perpetrate a terrorist attack—namely, placing an explosive device in a locker at a crowded airport. Because this hadn't been done before, no security was around the lockers.[8]

This is why it's important to anticipate and prepare for new types of terrorist attacks. There is a tendency to think about terrorism from the perspective of what happened in the past rather than thinking "outside the box" as to what may occur in the future. The history of terrorism teaches us that terrorists continually strive to find new and more devastating ways to perpetrate their violence. Al Qaeda demonstrated this with the 9/11 attacks, the Alphabet Bomber with the airport attack, and the Galleanists with the package-bomb plot and the first vehicle bombing in the United States. Thinking up new ways to commit violence will continue to be a characteristic of terrorists everywhere.[9]

There Isn't Always Closure to a Terrorist Attack

Living with uncertainty can be frustrating and upsetting—a breakup without knowing why it happened, the death of a loved one without getting the chance to talk about unresolved issues, doubts about a decision one made. Everyone feels the need for closure, "the desire for an answer that leaves no room for uncertainty," at some point in life. Closure represents "finality; a letting go of what once was." A lack of closure can prevent people from moving on with their lives.[10]

For survivors of a terrorist attack, there may never be closure. The psychological and physical scars can last for the rest of their lives. Charles Epstein was a geneticist at the University of California, San Francisco when, on June 22, 1993, he opened a package that had been sent to his home. The package exploded, and he lost several fingers and suffered permanent hearing loss. He went to court to watch as Theodore Kaczynski, the "Unabomber" responsible for sending package bombs through the mail for a period of seventeen years, resulting in the deaths of three people and injuries to twenty-three others, including Epstein, pleaded guilty to his crimes in January 1998. He described Kaczynski to reporters as "the personification of evil" and that while he was glad the case was over, he did not expect to heal emotionally anytime soon. "There's never closure," Epstein said. "I mean, every time I look at my hand [the effect of the bombing] is still there; every time I have to ask someone to speak up, it's still there."[11]

Witnessing a terrorist attack can also haunt a person for the rest of his or her life. Jacob Roth was on his way to lunch on September 16, 1920, when the bomb exploded on Wall Street. He had moved to New York from Canton, Ohio, in June to work for National Bank. He was not injured by the blast but was traumatized by what he saw. "The glass rained from the skyscrapers for fully five minutes," he wrote in a letter to his parents later that day. "As soon as I convinced myself that I was not having a nightmare and something dreadful had happened, I rushed for Wall Street [to help the victims]." He saw some people "blown beyond recognition, others struggling to their feet, only to be knocked down by the mobs pouring from the buildings, bleeding and frightened, howling, 'Run for your life! There's another one planted. It goes off at 12:30!'" Roth told his parents that he broke down crying. "I am ashamed to say, that I started to cry and cried like a baby, but I could not help thinking of the narrow escape I had. I escaped with only a damaged hat and a torn pair of trousers." Roth wrote that he would never forget the carnage of that tragic day.[12]

Closure may also be elusive for the families of those killed by terrorists. An important aspect of coming to grips with the loss of a loved one in such a way is at least knowing who carried out the attack and why they did it. Family members and friends of those who lost their lives in the Wall Street bombing, as well as the surviving victims, never obtained that finality. As noted in chapter 6, the bombing was never solved, even though William Flynn, the director of the Bureau of Investigation, was convinced that the Galleanists were behind the attack. Historian Paul Avrich made a compelling case decades later, attributing the bombing to a single Galleanist, Mario Buda. But this has never been officially acknowledged.

Several other unsolved terrorist attacks have claimed many lives since the 1920 Wall Street explosion, including, among others, the 1975 bombing in the baggage-claim section of LaGuardia Airport in New York that killed eleven people and wounded seventy-five others and the 1982 Tylenol poisoning in the Chicago area, where seven people died after taking cyanide-laced Tylenol capsules. Even when the perpetrator of an attack is known, a motive may never be uncovered. Stephen Paddock killed fifty-eight people and injured nearly seven hundred others at an outdoor country music festival in Las Vegas on October 1, 2017. Despite more than a year of investigation by the FBI, it was not determined why Paddock, who killed himself before he could be arrested, committed the worst mass shooting in U.S. history. Living with that uncertainty will remain an extra burden for those who have already suffered because of the tragedy.[13]

Extremist Groups Can Remain Dangerous Even after Their Leaders Are Eliminated

The Galleanists demonstrated that even while their charismatic and inspirational leader was awaiting deportation and being watched closely by the authorities, they could still plan and commit major terrorist attacks. Luigi Galleani had built a decentralized movement that tapped into widespread alienation and frustration among Italian immigrants who were being discriminated against and working long hours for low wages (or, for many, not finding any work at all). The better life they'd hoped for when they came to America never materialized. The vast majority of Galleani's followers were enthusiastic recipients of his revolutionary message about abolishing capitalism and government and creating a society consisting of "the autonomy of the individual within the freedom of association." They flocked to his speaking engagements, read his (and other anarchists') numerous writings in *Cronaca Sovversiva*, and praised him whenever they could. Most of them, though, never conspired to commit a violent act.[14]

The same wasn't true, however, for a small group of Galleanists, numbering between fifty and sixty hard-core militants. They were the ones who plotted the attacks and set off the bombs. And they could operate without guidance from the top. The militant Galleanist cells were scattered throughout the country, although the most influential ones were the Gruppo Autonomo of East Boston and the Bresci Group of New York. The shutting down of *Cronaca Sovversiva* in 1918 and the deportation of Galleani in June 1919 were aimed at dealing a severe blow to the

Galleanists, a "policy of decapitation [that] would leave those who rode the Galleani current without a pilot." But the Galleanists were still able to send package bombs around the country in April 1919, set off bombings in multiple cities in June while Galleani awaited deportation, and then, more than a year later, commit the Wall Street bombing while he was in Italy.[15]

The decentralized model of extremism that Galleani built for his followers can be seen today in many other terrorist movements, including al Qaeda and the Islamic State of Iraq and Syria (ISIS). Both started out with a central command, with al Qaeda in Afghanistan and ISIS in Iraq and Syria. But they morphed into global, decentralized groups—al Qaeda after the U.S. invasion of Afghanistan following the 9/11 attacks and ISIS after it was defeated on the ground in Iraq and Syria by U.S.-led coalition forces from 2017 to 2019. The killings of al Qaeda's leader, Osama bin Laden, in 2011 and ISIS leader Abu Bakr al-Baghdadi in 2019 have not diminished the terrorist threats posed by both groups. They've continued to perpetrate attacks in many countries. Each group also utilizes social media and the internet to call on lone wolves everywhere to attack targets by whatever means they can wherever they can. They do not need a central command or specific leader to convey that message, as any member of the group can do the job.

Far-right extremist movements also operate today without a central command structure. In fact, the term "leaderless resistance" was first coined by a white supremacist, Louis Beam, in the 1990s. Beam argued that a new strategy was needed "to defeat state tyranny." He called for the creation of autonomous groups driven by ideology and shared beliefs rather than the direction of leaders. At that time electronic bulletin boards and websites provided the means by which white supremacists, neo-Nazis, anti-government groups, and others could communicate with each other and recruit new members. Today these movements use a variety of alternative social media and messaging apps to post hate speech and call for violent action, all done without any leaders directing their activities.[16]

Lulls in Terrorist Attacks Can Be Misleading

Throughout the history of terrorism, there have been periods when the public and government in a particular country thought the worst was over because a certain amount of time had passed since the last major incident. This occurred in the United States in the early 1990s, when, after decades of terrorist attacks against U.S. targets overseas, things seemed to be getting better. Those years brought the end of the Cold War and the return of American hostages from Lebanon. Even the Persian Gulf War in Iraq, with threats of Saddam Hussein–inspired retaliatory terrorist attacks against the United States, did not shatter the belief that a corner had been turned in the battle against terrorism. But then a car bombing at the World Trade Center in New York in February 1993 killed six people and injured a thousand others, mostly due to smoke inhalation. When there were no more major terrorist attacks on U.S. soil for a couple of years, people once again breathed a sigh of relief. But in April 1995 a homegrown terrorist, Timothy McVeigh (working with another homegrown terrorist, Terry Nichols), set off a truck bomb at the federal building in Oklahoma City in April 1995, killing 168 people. There was then another lull before the next major terrorist event in the United States—the 9/11 attacks.[17]

The Wall Street bombing in September 1920 also followed a lull in terrorist attacks. More than a year had passed since the Galleanists struck with the June 2, 1919, bombings in several cities. The lack of additional major attacks since that date by any group, combined with the Palmer Raids and the mass deportations that followed, likely created a false sense of security among the public and authorities regarding the possibility of future incidents. Terrorists, however, always have the advantage of having to perpetrate just one major attack to put terrorism back at the forefront of public consciousness and reverse all perceptions of progress in the battle against terrorism. That is why governments should never be fooled into thinking they are winning a "war" against terrorists when terrorism can involve just one person, like Mario Buda, with a bomb and a cause.[18]

The Wall Street bombing also illustrated what the Irish Republican Army would state many decades later. After a failed attempt to assassinate British prime minister Margaret Thatcher in 1984, the IRA stated, "Today we were unlucky, but remember, we only have to be lucky once. You will have to be lucky always." America was not lucky on September 16, 1920, due in part perhaps to overconfidence by government officials and security personnel that the threat of terrorism had ended.[19]

Repressive Measures Can Work, but at a Severe Cost

The Galleanists are among those terrorist groups in history that were defeated after a relatively short period of violent activity. Although some Galleanists were still active in the 1920s and 1930s, the group's major terror campaign existed only from 1914, when (along with other anarchists) it set off bombs in New York City, to 1920, when Mario Buda likely committed the Wall Street bombing. Many other terrorist groups in later years, such as the Palestine Liberation Organization, the Red Army Faction, the Red Brigades, and the Revolutionary Organization 17 November, were able to survive for decades as viable and violent organizations.

The Galleanists' demise coincided with the end of what terrorism scholar David Rapoport labels the first wave of modern terrorism, the Anarchist Wave, from the 1880s until the 1920s. The defeat of the Galleanists was mainly due to a concerted effort by the government to wipe them out, along with other radical movements and individuals, in what is considered by many to have been one of the most "ruthless invasion[s] of civil rights" in U.S. history. The abuses, as noted in the introduction and chapter 5, included taking innocent people into custody, detentions without warrants, denials of proper counsel, forced confessions, beatings, illegally obtained evidence, and, in many cases, unjustified deportations. What took place during the Palmer Raids of November 1919 and January 1920 was appalling, as Assistant Secretary of Labor Lewis Post, who opposed and eventually stopped the deportations, would later describe:

> So detectives of the Department of Justice ruthlessly invaded peaceable homes, in the small hours of the morning, without warrants but upon a pretense of imminent danger to the community, and arresting inmates in their beds, searched their rooms, seized lawful private property, and hurried their prisoners to police stations where, before the sun had risen, they subjected them to "third degree" examinations in efforts to discover evidence of a guilt that apparently did not exist. So, also, those detectives made sweeping arrests of whole audiences at public meetings, rounding up citizens and aliens without discrimination, and standing them against meeting-room walls, searched them threateningly after the manner of highwaymen robbing groups of travelers. After the

search they usually turned citizens loose, but the aliens they marched off to prison, and at least once conspicuously in manacles and chains.[20]

Among the illegal measures taken by the government during this period was the secret detention of two Galleanists, Andrea Salsedo and Roberto Elia, who were held without a warrant and interrogated in the New York field office of the Bureau of Investigation from March until May 1920. They eventually cooperated with the BI agents and identified several Galleanists as being involved in the June 2, 1919, bombings. As explained in chapter 5, when word got out that Salsedo and Elia were telling all they knew to the agents, many Galleanists either went underground or left the country in order to avoid arrest. Salsedo's suicide (by jumping from a window on the fourteenth floor of the BI office) became front-page news and led to even more Galleanists learning about Salsedo and Elia's detention and thus going into hiding.[21]

It wasn't just the Galleanists, of course, who were on the run during the Red Scare. The Palmer Raids and the deportation policies "achieved many of their aims, driving hundreds, if not thousands of revolutionaries either underground or out of the country altogether. . . . After the early 1920s, fractured and bereft of outside support, neither the anarchists or the Wobblies ever successfully regrouped. In that sense, the Red Scare did eliminate those groups most often described as the nation's chief acolytes of 'terrorism.'"[22]

The public initially supported the raids and deportations and didn't seem too concerned about the violations of civil liberties. This is not surprising, as we see similar public attitudes today in the aftermath of a major terrorist incident. For example, in a nationwide Gallup Poll conducted a little more than four months after the 9/11 attacks, respondents were asked the following question: "Which comes closer to your view—(the government should take all steps necessary to prevent additional acts of terrorism in the U.S. even if it means your basic civil liberties would be violated, (or) the government should take steps to prevent additional acts of terrorism but not if those steps would violate your basic civil liberties)?" Forty-seven percent of the respondents answered that the government should take steps even if civil liberties would be violated, while 49 percent answered that the government should take steps but not violate civil liberties. That almost half of the respondents were willing to have their civil liberties violated reflects how terrorist attacks today can generate fear in society and support for government and law enforcement agencies to do anything necessary to prevent further attacks. There were no public opinion polls at the time of the Red Scare, but public support for the launch of the Palmer Raids in the aftermath of the June 2 bombings, including one at Attorney General Palmer's home, indicates that had such a poll existed then, similar answers to questions about violating civil liberties would likely have been obtained.[23]

America's experience with the Galleanists highlights a still relevant issue: how to balance the protection of civil liberties with the need for tough measures against terrorists. The arrests and deportations of alien anarchists, radicals, and others during the time of the Galleanists represented a total disregard by the authorities for fundamental democratic values. Some of that disregard was apparent again in the aftermath of the 9/11 attacks, with, among other things, the government's use of domestic eavesdropping as well as prisoner abuse at Abu Ghraib prison in Iraq during the Iraq War. Guarding against the compromise of civil liberties and safeguarding core democratic values will continue to be challenges in the design and implementation of policies aimed at preventing and responding to terrorism in the years ahead.[24]

The Importance of Revenge in Explaining Terrorist Attacks

"If a single common emotion drives the individual or group to terrorism, it is vengeance," observes terrorism scholar Martha Crenshaw. Indeed, while there are many different motivations for a terrorist attack (including the desire to create fear in a society, disrupt peace processes, gain publicity for a cause and recruit new members, create repressive measures by the target government in response and turn parts of the public against the government, and so forth), it is revenge that appears to be the most prominent.[25]

Revenge helps to explain why terrorism is an endless conflict. There will always be a group or individual that believes, often justifiably, that the group or individual was wronged by another group, individual, or government, or by a situation or incident that occurred, and views terrorism as the best way to respond. When terrorism is part of ethnic-nationalist or religious conflicts, the hatreds that exist between different groups can be handed down from generation to generation, creating endless cycles of attacks and reprisals. Furthermore, "cultures that place a high value on revenge offer more social support to avengers."[26]

For the Galleanists, terrorism was used mainly as a tool for revenge. As noted in chapter 2, Luigi Galleani provided his followers with instructions for how to make a dynamite bomb, cleverly disguising the contents of his 1905 manual with a misleading title, *La Salute è in Voi!* (Health is in you!). As discussed, the Galleanists, however, did not start their terrorism campaign until 1914, and the precipitating cause was revenge for the Ludlow Massacre, in which eleven children and two women burned to death during a strike at a Colorado mining company owned by John D. Rockefeller Jr. *Cronaca Sovversiva* labeled Rockefeller the "tormentor billionaire." A New York faction of the Galleanists, Gruppo Gaetano Bresci, also known as the Bresci Group, worked with other anarchists to bomb the Rockefeller estate in Tarrytown, New York, but their device exploded on July 4, 1914, as it was being prepared in a New York City apartment. Three anarchists were killed. A series of bombings and bomb plots targeting churches and courthouses in New York followed throughout the rest of the year and part of the next. Police suspected the Galleanist faction of involvement.[27]

Revenge was also the motivating factor in three more of the Galleanist terrorist attacks. The April 1919 letter-bomb plot and the June 1919 bombings were perpetrated in retaliation for the impending deportation of Galleani and the shutting down of *Cronaca Sovversiva*. The September 1920 Wall Street bombing was likely committed by Mario Buda as retribution for the murder indictment of Sacco and Vanzetti. Avenging the fate of a group's leader or comrades is a common occurrence in the world of terrorism. Hamza bin Laden, the son of Osama bin Laden, called for revenge for the killing of his father in 2011. "I invite Muslims generally to take revenge on the Americans, the murderers of the Sheikh, specifically from those who participated in this heinous crime," he said in 2017 in an audio recording released by al Qaeda. (Hamza was later killed in a U.S. counterterrorist operation in the Afghanistan/Pakistan region.) ISIS in West Africa, an affiliate of the Islamic State of Iraq and Syria terrorist group, posted a video in December 2019 claiming responsibility for the killing of eleven kidnapped Nigerian Christians. They stated that revenge for the death of ISIS leader Abu Bakr al-Baghdadi, who killed himself during a raid by U.S. commandos in October of that year, was the reason for the murders.[28]

The Galleanists illustrated years ago how powerful a motivating factor revenge can be when launching a terror campaign. Since there is no expiration date on revenge—it can be taken years or even centuries after a precipitating event—it will remain a major reason why terrorists perpetrate violence around the world.

Counterextremism Programs Likely Would Not Have Worked against the Galleanists

A major effort has been underway in recent years in the United States and many other countries to prevent individuals from joining or supporting extremist groups. One such program established by the U.S. government in 2011, the Strategic Implementation Plan for Countering Violent Extremism (CVE), had among its objectives the goal of providing "alternative messages and options to terrorist or violent extremist recruitment and radicalization efforts through civic engagement." A U.S. Government Accountability Office report in 2017, however, cast doubt on the effectiveness of the program, noting that "it was not able to determine if the United States is better off today than it was in 2011."[29]

Had such programs been in existence during the time of the Galleanists, it is doubtful that they would have been effective against them. The Galleanists foreshadowed the problems governments and law enforcement agencies would face in trying to prevent radicalization in communities susceptible to extremist recruitment. Just as there's distrust of the government and police in many cities today, as well as a perception that CVE programs primarily targeted Muslim communities to the exclusion of others, so too would there have been resistance in the Italian communities in New York, Boston, Paterson, and other cities to any attempt by the government to counter the messages of defiance and rebellion flowing from Galleani. With widespread discrimination against Italian immigrants, low wages, and poor working conditions, there would have been little hope that the government could prevent a large number of people from being receptive to Galleani's preaching. Furthermore, Galleani's prodigious writings, mainly through his weekly publication of *Cronaca Sovversiva* that reached thousands of subscribers across the country, and his spellbinding speeches would have been very difficult hurdles for any "countering violent extremism" program to overcome.

The Galleanists, like their leader, were also never willing to compromise. Mario Buda and Carlo Valdinoci, two of the most notable members of the ultramilitant core of the group, were "anarchists of an intransigent stripe." Galleani himself "set an example of righteous intolerance that few of his coadjutors could match." As discussed in chapter 5, when Galleani's ten-year-old daughter, Tana, asked him on the eve of his deportation why he wouldn't tell the government that he didn't believe in anarchism anymore to avoid being sent away, he gave her a look of astonishment that she could ask him such a question. There could be no compromise on his part, even if it meant possibly never seeing his family again.[30]

"There is no doubt that he advocated violent means when he thought them necessary," wrote Sean Sayers about his grandfather, Luigi Galleani. "I do not seek to defend him for this. However, if one is to understand him one must see that he lived through extremely violent times and it was clear to many of the working people and immigrants for whom he spoke that the main perpetrators of this violence were the police and the state." That Galleani energized and gave hope to thousands of his followers with a message that they deserved better cannot be denied. Whether he could have done this without encouraging violence is open to debate. He was a gifted writer, orator, intellect, and communicator. Had he channeled those gifts into nonviolent purposes, he probably could have accomplished anything he set his mind to. But he chose a life of anarchist rebellion and, in so doing, became the leader of one of the most intriguing and pioneering terrorist groups in history.[31]

8 Back Home Again

"To avoid my arrest, I have to keep in hiding," Luigi Galleani wrote from Italy to Giuseppe "Joe" Russo, a friend and loyal supporter in the United States, in November 1920. "I am tired and sick of this life—one of these days I will be put in jail, whence I may not come out as I am sixty years old and in bad health. If I die in prison be sure that my last thought will be of you and other comrades who have fought with me, and who would not betray the cause for anything."[1]

Galleani had been in Italy since his June 1919 deportation. It's not surprising that he soon found himself on the run. There was no way the lifelong anarchist was going to lead a quiet existence back in the old country. With assistance from Raffaele Schiavina, who had been deported at the same time as Galleani, he revived his beloved *Cronaca Sovversiva* in Turin in January 1920. Issues of the newspaper were smuggled into the United States under the title *A Stormo!* (To the flock!). Galleani threw himself into his work, though he was suffering from diabetes. "No one can deliver me from it," he wrote to Russo. "I already see signs in my left calf that will lead to the final struggle, which does not frighten me. I am sixty years old and man cannot aspire to eternity." Russo helped raise funds in America to have Galleani's printing press shipped to Italy. The idea of spending money for that while Sacco and Vanzetti were facing the possibility of the death penalty and needed defense money met with some resistance among the anarchists in America. "Now we have to save these two comrades from the gallows for the life of two comrades is worth more than all the paper printed or to be printed," wrote one potential donor to Russo. He also objected to wasting money in order "to ship a pile of iron" overseas.[2]

Galleani was able to get several issues of the paper printed before he ran into trouble with the Italian government. An arrest warrant was issued for him in the fall of 1920 for "defamation of state institutions and instigation of military rebellion and class hatred" based on articles published in *Cronaca Sovversiva*. The newspaper was subsequently suppressed, bringing an end to its long history. Galleani went into hiding and eluded the authorities for two years until he decided to turn himself in at the prison in Turin in October 1922. Schiavina, who'd also gone into hiding after being accused of belonging to an antifascist militant group, escaped to Paris in 1923 and eventually secretly returned to the United States.[3]

It wasn't just the Italian government looking for Galleani while he was on the run. So too was William Flynn, the director of the Bureau of Investigation and a firm believer that the Galleanists were behind not only the April and June 1919 bombings but also the Wall Street explosion. With that investigation at a standstill by the end of 1920, he tried a Hail Mary and sent one of his informants undercover to Italy to track down Galleani and question him about the Wall Street bombing. The irony, of course, was that had the U.S. government not deported Galleani in the first place, they wouldn't have to look for him overseas.[4]

The task of finding Galleani fell to Salvatore Clemente, code name "Mull," a trusted informant. Several years earlier, Flynn, while in charge of the U.S. Secret Service, had assigned him to infiltrate Galleani's supporters in Vermont and Massachusetts. Clemente left for Italy at the end of December 1920 and eventually located the home of Galleani's sister, Carolina, in Vercelli. When he inquired about her brother, she told him that Galleani "had to leave the country." Galleani, however, most likely had not left the country and was in hiding in different parts of Italy at this time, although exactly where is unknown. Unable to find Galleani, Clemente returned to the United States empty-handed and without any information about the Wall Street bombing. But he had been able to confirm in a conversation with a Galleanist in Italy that Carlo Valdinoci was the anarchist killed in the bombing at Attorney General Palmer's home in June 1919.[5]

After turning himself in to the authorities in Turin in October 1922, Galleani was tried and convicted on charges of sedition and sentenced to fourteen months in prison. By this time Benito Mussolini and the fascists were on the verge of assuming power. Galleani had written earlier of his despair at witnessing the rise of fascism in Italy. "I saw the blackshirts sweep aside everything and everyone," he wrote in a letter in September 1922. "The filthy crowds were supported, sustained, urged by the authorities, defended by the royal guards, by the armored cars that passed under my windows."[6]

Galleani's health continued to deteriorate, his diabetes made worse by the diet he was given while incarcerated. When he was released from prison at the end of 1923, he was exhausted but still full of fight and put his energies into writing. He finished up "The End of Anarchism?" series of articles he had started for *Cronaca Sovversiva* in 1907 in response to Francesco Saverio Merlino's claim that anarchism was dead. (See chapter 2 for a discussion of this.) He added new material, and this was published by his comrades in the United States as a book with the same title in 1925.[7]

The publication of *The End of Anarchism?* did not please the Mussolini government. One can imagine its reaction to passages like: "The soul of the anarchist movement is the ardent desire for a society of free and equal people, which the anarchists know cannot be attained without the inevitably violent destruction of the existing order of things." Galleani, who spent a month during the spring of 1925 in a hospital in Vercelli due to his worsening diabetes, was arrested again in November 1926 and briefly put in prison, this time as a precautionary measure following the October 31 assassination attempt on Mussolini in Bologna by a fifteen-year-old anarchist.[8]

Galleani's life in Italy was a lonely one, even though he lived with his sister at various times in Vercelli and then resided near his daughter Cossyra, who had married and moved to Sori, Ligura, a village not far from Genoa. But he missed his wife and other children, who remained in the United States. He also missed his old comrades. "The thought of those left behind in America, who are continually shadowed, spied by detectives and who are always fighting with tomorrow, it is a thought that gnaws me ceaselessly," he wrote in a letter to Russo. "Here I am completely surrounded by sorrows."[9]

Among the comrades left behind were Sacco and Vanzetti. Galleani had no doubts about their fate and expressed his anger over the matter in a letter to Schiavina in 1925, two years before they were executed. Viewing the case as a "humiliating and terrible defeat," he called upon Sacco and Vanzetti's supporters to take revenge by publishing a circular "briefly emphasizing the evidence of the innocence of the two victims [Sacco and Vanzetti] and underneath that put, in large letters, the first and last names and home addresses of all the magistrates, of all the jurors, simply inviting the workers to go there to pay their respects and thank them . . . as they deserve."[10]

Galleani also expressed frustration in his letter about not being able to do anything to help Sacco and Vanzetti: "In my heart I have so much bitterness, so much desolation that I wonder if it would not have been better to intervene in the debate with my usual unflinching honesty. Instead I always abstained from uttering a single word out of fear that appearing to be their friend would aggravate the legal situation for them both." Galleani, however, was not far from the thoughts of Sacco and Vanzetti. After the Supreme Judicial Court of Massachusetts upheld the guilty verdict and denied their motions for a new trial in May 1926, the Sacco-Vanzetti Defense Committee printed an article in its newsletter in June that was written by Vanzetti and signed by both Sacco and Vanzetti. It called for a type of retaliation that would've pleased Galleani. "Remember, *La Salute è in Voi!*" the article concluded, invoking the title of Galleani's bomb manual to encourage readers to act.[11]

In July 1927 Galleani was sentenced to three years of internal exile on the island of Lipari, off the Sicilian coast, for being "a danger to the order of the state." No sooner had he arrived on the island than he got into further trouble, this time for insulting Mussolini. He was overheard talking to Giuseppe Russo, the friend he'd corresponded with in the United States.

Russo had been deported and was now also serving a sentence of internal exile in Lipari. Galleani supposedly commented on an inscription on the Lipari Castle. The inscription read, "It is necessary to respect the Head of the government His Excellency Benito Mussolini." Galleani allegedly said derisively, "Wooden head." He was sentenced to an additional six months, this time to be served in the island's prison, for that comment.[12]

Upon release from prison in February 1928, Galleani still had to serve his three-year term of internal exile in Lipari. Also there, in addition to Russo, was Mario Buda. After escaping from the United States following the Wall Street bombing, he had resumed his anarchist activities in Italy and eventually found himself in the same predicament as Galleani. The two veterans of anarchist battles in America spent time together in Lipari until Buda was transferred to another island, Ponza, in 1929. When Buda was finally released from internal exile and allowed to return to the mainland in 1932, he reportedly began working as a spy for the Mussolini government, infiltrating antifascist groups in Switzerland and France. For the militant anarchist, this was certainly a change of heart in terms of his beliefs. But, since his activities as a spy lasted only for a few months and he did not give anyone away, some observers argue that Buda did this only to avoid further imprisonment in Italy.[13]

Meanwhile, Galleani, whom one cannot imagine spying for any government, remained in Lipari until February 1930, when he was released under a general amnesty for hundreds of political prisoners who had served two-thirds of their sentences. His health, however, had deteriorated further due to the lack of medical treatment while he was in exile. He was brought to Genoa and allowed to go free, though his freedom was severely restricted. He was watched constantly by the police, who even followed him when he took walks by himself. He first stayed with his daughter Cossyra in Sori for a brief time and then moved in with his sister Carolina in Vercelli. Not wanting to continue exposing her to the round-the-clock police surveillance, he soon left and eventually settled near the mountain village of Caprigliola.[14]

Galleani spent his days reading and taking half-hour walks. It was a lonely existence, but despite weakness from the diabetes, he remained strong in spirit and defiant to the end. Upon his seventieth birthday in

August 1931, Galleani wrote to some of the people who'd sent him birthday greetings. He shared the following message: "The faith and the banner of the first day are still those of the last. . . . I am happy with myself, even if along the way they have devastated everything, my home, my family, my health, and at seventy years I feel in exile here in this wild valley, without even a dog for company."[15]

During one of his walks, on November 4, 1931, Galleani suffered a heart attack and died two hours later. His sister and daughter attended the funeral, as did the police, to make sure there were no anarchist flags or other related signs and symbols exhibited. He was buried in the village of Albiano, and a marble funeral monument was erected in his memory when it was safe for the anarchists in the area to do so. That occurred after the death of Mussolini and the end of World War II.[16]

There is no inscription on the monument except for Galleani's name and dates of birth and death. Few passersby have any idea who he was. Had there been an epitaph, perhaps the best one would have been a few quotes from his devoted followers, who described him as "the soul of the movement," someone who "spoke directly to my heart" and "expressed what I wanted to say but couldn't because I didn't have the words"—characteristics any leader would be proud to have.[17]

NOTES

ABBREVIATIONS

BI, FOIA   Bureau of Investigation, Records of the Federal Bureau of Investigation, obtained through the Freedom of Information Act.

RG 60, DJ Central Files, Straight Numerical Files, NARA   Record Group 60, DJ (Department of Justice) Central Files, Straight Numerical Files, National Archives and Records Administration, College Park MD.

RG 65, BS, M1085, Fold3, NARA   Record Group 65, Bureau Section Files [1909–21], Bureau of Investigation, Records of the Federal Bureau of Investigation, Microfilm Publication Number M1085, Fold3, National Archives and Records Administration, College Park MD.

RG 65, OG, M1085, Fold3, NARA   Record Group 65, Old German Files [1909–21], Investigative Case Files of the Bureau of Investigation 1908–1922, Records of the Federal Bureau of Investigation, Microfilm Publication Number M1085, Fold3, National Archives and Records Administration, College Park MD.

RG 85, INS, NARA   Record Group 85, Records of the Immigration and Naturalization Service, National Archives and Records Administration, Washington DC.

INTRODUCTION

1. "Nation-Wide Search for 'Poison' Chef," *Washington Times*, February 13, 1916.
2. "Poison Plot Laid to Chicago Chef," *New York Times*, February 13, 1916.
3. "Boasts of Poison Plot, Threatens Deaths in Letter," *New York Times*, February 17, 1916.
4. "Crones's Signature in Letter Here Identified," *New York Sun*, February 18, 1916; "Crones Flaunts Police in Second Letter to Times," *New York Times*, February 18, 1916.
5. Stephen J. Taylor, "The Anarchist Soup Plot," Hoosier State Chronicles, September 4, 2015, https://blog.newspapers.library.in.gov/the-anarchist-soup-plot/; "Crones Flaunts Police"; "Crones Now Gives 2 Days to Get Him," *New York Times*, February 19, 1916.
6. Taylor, "Anarchist Soup Plot"; Mark Jacob, "A Century Ago Today, an Anarchist Tried to Kill Chicago's Archbishop with Soup," *Chicago Tribune*, February 10,

2016, https://www.chicagotribune.com/news/ct-poison-soup-anniversary-met-20160209-story.html; "Latest Crones Story, As Usual, Nets Goose Egg," *Chicago Tribune*, June 1, 1919.

7. "Chicago Drops Charges Against Alleged Poisoner," *New York Tribune*, November 14, 1919; "Jean Crones Is Indicted," *New York Times*, March 22, 1916; Taylor, "Anarchist Soup Plot"; Avrich, *Sacco and Vanzetti*, 98. The followers of Galleani have also been referred to by some scholars and others as "Galleanisti."
8. Avrich, *Anarchist Voices*, 316; Avrich, *Sacco and Vanzetti*, 48–50; Simon, "Forgotten Terrorists," 197.
9. Avrich, *Anarchist Voices*, 107, 111, 120, 132, 157–58; William J. Flynn, "On the Trail of the Anarchist Band—Chief Flynn," *New York Herald*, March 5, 1922.
10. Davis, *Buda's Wagon*, 1–2; Avrich, *Sacco and Vanzetti*, 51–52, 55, 97, 99; Simon, "Forgotten Terrorists," 197.
11. Galleani, *End of Anarchism?*, 73–74; Avrich, *Anarchist Voices*, 147; Pernicone, "Luigi Galleani," 472.
12. "Propaganda by deed" is "the theory that individual acts of terrorism, from bomb plots to assassination attempts, offered a vital way for the working class to liberate itself from the tyranny of capital." See Gage, *The Day Wall Street Exploded*, 41.
13. Gage, *The Day Wall Street Exploded*, 2; Galleani, *End of Anarchism?*, 60–61.
14. Avrich, *Sacco and Vanzetti*, 95, 175.
15. Avrich, *Sacco and Vanzetti*, 196–97, 204–7.
16. Simon, "Forgotten Terrorists," 195, 209–11. Among the few scholars who discuss Galleani in their excellent books are Paul Avrich, Beverly Gage, Charles McCormick, Antonio Senta, Susan Tejada, and Bruce Watson. See Avrich, *Sacco and Vanzetti*; Gage, *The Day Wall Street Exploded*; McCormick, *Hopeless Cases*; Senta, *Luigi Galleani*; Tejada, *In Search of Sacco and Vanzetti*; and Watson, *Sacco and Vanzetti*. There is also an excellent unpublished doctoral dissertation by Andrew Douglas Hoyt on Galleani's newspaper, *Cronaca Sovversiva*. See Hoyt, "And They Called Them 'Galleanisti.'" George W. Carey, Michael A. Gordon, Nunzio Pernicone, and Robin Hazard Ray also discuss Galleani in their scholarly articles. See Carey, "Vessel"; Gordon, "'To Make a Clean Sweep'"; Pernicone, "Luigi Galleani"; and Ray, "No License to Serve."
17. Galleani, *End of Anarchism?*, 93.

1. THE SOUL OF THE MOVEMENT

1. Jim Dobson, "The Hidden Italian Island of Pantelleria: The New Sikelia Hotel and Inside Giorgio Armani's Villa," *Forbes*, July 19, 2017, https://www.forbes.com/sites/jimdobson/2017/07/19/the-hidden-italian-island-of-pantelleria-the-new-sikelia

-hotel-and-inside-giorgio-armanis-villa/#21e131fc6395; Simon Usborne, "Pantelleria: Black Pearl of the Mediterranean," *Financial Times*, August 8, 2017, https://www.ft.com/content/10ed7baa-7915-11e7-a3e8-60495fe6ca71; "Resort Acropoli," Resortacropoli.com, no date, https://www.resortacropoli.com/en-gb/photo-gallery.

2. Ray, "No License to Serve," 7–8; Pernicone, "Luigi Galleani," 473; Sayers, foreword, 2.
3. Sayers, foreword, 1; Avrich, *Sacco and Vanzetti*, 48–49; Pernicone, "Luigi Galleani," 472–73.
4. Pernicone, "Luigi Galleani," 473; Avrich, *Sacco and Vanzetti*, 49; Senta, *Luigi Galleani*, 39–40.
5. Avrich, *Sacco and Vanzetti*, 49; Simon, *Terrorist Trap*, 40. Eight people were convicted of the bombing. Four were hung, one committed suicide, and the remaining three prisoners were eventually pardoned.
6. Senta, *Luigi Galleani*, 45–46, 49–50, 58–59.
7. Senta, *Luigi Galleani*, 62–68; "Fascio siciliano," *Encyclopedia Britannica*, July 20, 1998, https://www.britannica.com/topic/fascio-siciliano; Tomchuk, *Transnational Radicals*, 42; Topp, *Those without a Country*, 29.
8. Senta, *Luigi Galleani*, 63.
9. Senta, *Luigi Galleani*, 63, 65, 68; Sartin [pseudonym], introduction, 11; Pernicone, "Luigi Galleani," 473–74. The introduction for the first English translation of Galleani's *The End of Anarchism?*, credited to the pseudonym Max Sartin, was actually authored by Raffaele Schiavina, a member of the Galleanists.
10. Senta, *Luigi Galleani*, 71–78.
11. Senta, *Luigi Galleani*, 74–75, 78.
12. Galleani, *End of Anarchism?*, 11–12; Ray, "No License to Serve," 8–10; Pernicone, "Luigi Galleani," 474.
13. Senta, *Luigi Galleani*, 78–79; Sayers, foreword, 2. The Federal Bureau of Investigation would later describe Maria as "the wife of his jailor." See Ray, "No License to Serve," 9. In May 1919 the couple finally got married, most likely in an attempt to delay the impending deportation of Galleani from the United States to Italy. See Senta, *Luigi Galleani*, 184.
14. Senta, *Luigi Galleani*, 82, 84–86.
15. Senta, *Luigi Galleani*, 87.
16. Senta, *Luigi Galleani*, 87–90.
17. Senta, *Luigi Galleani*, 86, 93–96, 99; Sartin [pseudonym], introduction, 12; Avrich, *Sacco and Vanzetti*, 49; Pernicone, "Luigi Galleani," 474.
18. Avrich, *Anarchist Voices*, 157.
19. Simon, *Lone Wolf Terrorism*, 159.
20. Simon, *Lone Wolf Terrorism*, 162.
21. Simon, *Lone Wolf Terrorism*, 163.

22. "Immigration and Relocation in U.S. History," Library of Congress, no date, https://www.loc.gov/teachers/classroommaterials/presentationsandactivities/presentations/immigration/italian2.html.
23. Christopher Woolf, "A Brief History of America's Hostility to a Previous Generation of Mediterranean Migrants—Italians," *The World*, November 26, 2015, https://www.pri.org/stories/2015-11-26/brief-history-america-s-hostility-previous-generation-mediterranean-migrants; Tomchuk, *Transnational Radicals*, 109.
24. Woolf, "A Brief History"; Erin Blakemore, "The Grisly Story of America's Largest Lynching," History.com, October 25, 2017, https://www.history.com/news/the-grisly-story-of-americas-largest-lynching; Justin A. Nystrom, "Sicilian Lynchings in New Orleans," *64 Parishes*, https://64parishes.org/entry/sicilian-lynchings-in-new-orleans; "Immigration," Library of Congress.
25. Woolf, "A Brief History"; "The New-Orleans Affair," *New York Times*, March 16, 1891. More than a century later, in April 2019, the City of New Orleans issued an official apology to Italian Americans for the lynching. See Ryan Prior, "128 Years Later, New Orleans Is Apologizing for Lynching 11 Italians," CNN.com, April 1, 2019, https://www.cnn.com/2019/04/01/us/new-orleans-mayor-apologizes-italian-americans-trnd/index.html.
26. James M. O'Neill, "How Bomb Blasts a Century Ago Launched the Red Scare and a Raid against Paterson Anarchists," NorthJersey.com, May 31, 2019, https://www.northjersey.com/story/news/2019/05/31/1919-anarchist-bombings-paterson-nj/3741015002/.
27. O'Neill, "How Bomb Blasts"; "Bresci, Gaetano, 1869–1901," Libcom.org, May 9, 2007, https://libcom.org/history/bresci-gaetano-1869-1901; Jensen, *Battle against Anarchist Terrorism*, 188; Pernicone and Ottanelli, *Assassins against the Old Order*, 135–36.
28. Pernicone and Ottanelli, *Assassins against the Old Order*, 133–34.
29. Pernicone and Ottanelli, *Assassins against the Old Order*, 134–35; Kemp, *Bombs, Bullets and Bread*, 60.
30. Pernicone and Ottanelli, *Assassins against the Old Order*, 135, 140–41.
31. Pernicone and Ottanelli, *Assassins against the Old Order*, 128, 142; "1900: The Assassination of King Umberto I of Italy," Libcom.org, May 9, 2007, https://libcom.org/history/1900-assassination-king-umberto-i-italy; "Bresci, Gaetano, 1869–1901"; Kemp, *Bombs, Bullets and Bread*, 59–60; Carey, "Vessel," 50.
32. Carey, "Vessel," 46–47; Kemp, *Bombs, Bullets and Bread*, 61–62; Pernicone and Ottanelli, *Assassins against the Old Order*, 147–53.
33. Kemp, *Bombs, Bullets and Bread*, 61–62; Carey, "Vessel," 46–47.
34. Carey, "Vessel," 53; Pernicone and Ottanelli, *Assassins against the Old Order*, 164.
35. Pernicone and Ottanelli, *Assassins against the Old Order*, 164–66; Kemp, *Bombs, Bullets and Bread*, 62; Carey, "Vessel," 53.

36. Carey, "Vessel," 47, 50. Umberto's name is sometimes translated in English as "Humbert." See Shone, *American Anarchism*, 200–201.
37. Pernicone and Ottanelli, *Assassins against the Old Order*, 141, 145; Carey, "Vessel," 52–54.
38. Carey, "Vessel," 52–54.
39. Carey, "Vessel," 52.
40. Shone, *American Anarchism*, 201.
41. Galleani, *End of Anarchism?*, 94.
42. Jensen, *Battle against Anarchist Terrorism*, 188.
43. Carey, "Vessel," 54; "Paterson: History," City-Data.com, no date, http://www.city-data.com/us-cities/The-Northeast/Paterson-History.html.
44. Jensen, *Battle against Anarchist Terrorism*, 188; Hunt, *Wrongly Executed?*, 25–26; Shone, *American Anarchism*, 196; Colby, *International Year Book*, 489. There was another strike in 1913.
45. Carey, "Vessel," 55; Tomchuk, *Transnational Radicals*, 132.
46. Carey, "Vessel," 55; Shone, *American Anarchism*, 196; "Mad Riot in the Streets of Paterson," *New York Times*, June 19, 1902.
47. Carey, "Vessel," 55. An Italian-speaking eyewitness to Galleani's speech provided the English translation.
48. Carey, "Vessel," 55.
49. "Mad Riot in the Streets"; Shone, *American Anarchism*, 196; Tomchuk, *Transnational Radicals*, 132; Carey, "Vessel," 55.
50. "Mad Riot in the Streets"; Hunt, *Wrongly Executed?*, 26.
51. "Mad Riot in the Streets."
52. Shone, *American Anarchism*, 196–97; "Mad Riot in the Streets"; "Troops Called Upon to Protect Paterson," *New York Times*, June 20, 1902.
53. Colby, *International Year Book*, 489; "Mad Riot in the Streets"; Carey, "Vessel," 55. There have been different accounts of the casualties that day. Tomchuk (*Transnational Radicals*, 132) writes that eight strikers and one policeman were killed, but no other accounts of the riot corroborate this. There was, however, a policeman wounded by a revolver that may have been fired by Galleani. See Senta, *Luigi Galleani*, 129.
54. Carey, "Vessel," 55. Grossmann escaped to England before he had to serve his sentence.
55. Tomchuk, *Transnational Radicals*, 133; Senta, *Luigi Galleani*, 36, 50, 98–99.
56. "Grossman May Come Back," *Paterson Evening News*, July 8, 1903.
57. Senta, *Luigi Galleani*, 112, 114; Tomchuk, *Transnational Radicals*, 133.

2. GREEN MOUNTAIN BOYS

The Green Mountain Boys were a militia led by Ethan Allen. They were active both before and during the Revolutionary War in an area that is today the state of Vermont.

1. Morgan and Morgan, *Stamp Act Crisis*, 129.
2. "History," BarreCity.org, no date, https://www.barrecity.org/history.html.
3. Hoyt, "And They Called Them 'Galleanisti,'" 4–5; Avrich, *Sacco and Vanzetti*, 49–50; Ray, "No License to Serve," 13; Senta, *Luigi Galleani*, 115–17; "Bianco Narciso Detailed Description," *World of Stones*, http://www.worldofstones.com/blog/bianco-narciso-detailed-description/ (site discontinued); Richardson, "'Curse of Our Trade,'" 7. There was also a large Scottish immigrant community in Barre, most of them quarriers from Aberdeenshire. See United States Department of the Interior, Socialist Labor Party Hall, National Historic Landmark Nomination, May 16, 2000, 12, https://npgallery.nps.gov/NRHP/GetAsset/NHLS/98001267_text.
4. Seager, "Barre, Vermont Granite Workers," 61; Richardson, "'Curse of Our Trade,'" 7; Ray, "No License to Serve," 13–15.
5. Senta, *Luigi Galleani*, 116; Guglielmo, *Living the Revolution*, 142; Hoyt, "And They Called Them 'Galleanisti,'" 49.
6. Paul Heller, "Trouble at the Anarchists' Ball," *Barre-Montpelier Times Argus*, December 5, 2019, https://www.timesargus.com/trouble-at-the-anarchists-ball/article_296043af-32bc-5f32-87d0-3f66717213cd.html; "In Pious Old Vermont: Even in That Sterile Country a Breed of Redhanded Anarchists Show Themselves; Shoot Down an Officer," *Austin Daily Statesman*, December 28, 1900; "Shoot a Chief of Police. Italian Anarchists in Barre, Vt., Probably Fatally Wound Their Victim—Six under Arrest," *New York Times*, December 28, 1900.
7. "Anarchy," *Enterprise and Vermonter* (Vergennes VT), January 3, 1901.
8. Senta, *Luigi Galleani*, 115–17; Hoyt, "And They Called Them 'Galleanisti,'" 44, 70.
9. Senta, *Luigi Galleani*, 116–17.
10. Hoyt, "And They Called Them 'Galleanisti,'" 44–45; Senta, *Luigi Galleani*, 119; Avrich, *Sacco and Vanzetti*, 50.
11. Senta, *Luigi Galleani*, 117–18.
12. Quinn, "Chronicling Subversion," 6, 11; Hoyt, "And They Called Them 'Galleanisti,'" 45–46; Senta, *Luigi Galleani*, 117, 122.
13. Quinn, "Chronicling Subversion," 6; Leah Weinryb Grohsgal, "The Anarchist's Chronicle," *National Endowment for the Humanities* (blog), January 13, 2016, https://www.neh.gov/divisions/preservation/featured-project/the-anarchist%E2%80%99s-chronicle. The image of a woman flying with a torch and axe over an industrial city ready to obliterate it was used in a different but very effective way by Apple in one of the most famous commercials ever aired on television. The 1984 Super Bowl spot showed a woman running into a large meeting with a sledgehammer and hurling it at a Big Brother–type image on a screen. The ad announced Apple's new product, the Macintosh, one of the first-ever personal computers. For more on how the commercial was made, see Paige Leskin, "11 Things You Probably Didn't Know about Apple's Famous '1984' Super Bowl Ad That Almost

Didn't Air," *Business Insider*, February 7, 2019, https://www.businessinsider.com/apple-1984-super-bowl-ad-history-2019-2#the-director-of-the-1984-commercial-was-ridley-scott-who-has-a-history-of-directing-dystopian-like-movies-such-as-blade-runner-gladiator-and-alien-3.

14. Senta, *Luigi Galleani*, 117, 122; Hoyt, "And They Called Them 'Galleanisti,'" 46; Al Compagni (column), *Cronaca Sovversiva*, June 6, 1903, Chronicling America, https://chroniclingamerica.loc.gov/lccn/2012271201/1903-06-06/ed-1/seq-1/ocr/; Programma? (column), *Cronaca Sovversiva*, June 6, 1903, Chronicling America, https://chroniclingamerica.loc.gov/lccn/2012271201/1903-06-06/ed-1/seq-1/ocr/. All quotes from *Cronaca Sovversiva* accessed through Chronicling America have been translated from the original Italian.
15. "Emma Goldman alla 'Cronaca Sovversiva,'" *Cronaca Sovversiva*, June 6, 1903, Chronicling America, https://chroniclingamerica.loc.gov/lccn/2012271201/1903-06-06/ed-1/seq-1/ocr/.
16. Quinn, "Chronicling Subversion," 5–7, 10, 17.
17. Hoyt, "And They Called Them 'Galleanisti,'" 39, 82, 87–88; Senta, *Luigi Galleani*, 119–20. As Hoyt notes, Galleani's newspaper "habitually labeled its enemies: bandits, pirates, mercenaries, mobsters, above-the-law bigshots, systematic scammers, hypocrites, charlatans, thieves, criminals, blackmailers, murderers, sewer trash, Pharisees, bible thumpers, shameless conmen, spies, imposters, thugs, fetid carcasses, assassins, butchers, slave drivers, scabs, pigs, crows, pygmies, sheep, fools, idlers, vultures, shrews, proselytizing neophytes, tyrants, and on and on." See Hoyt, "And They Called Them 'Galleanisti,'" 129.
18. Editorial, *Chicago Tribune*, November 23, 1896.
19. Hoyt, "And They Called Them 'Galleanisti,'" 121–22.
20. Senta, *Luigi Galleani*, 120–21.
21. Paul Heller, "Luigi Galleani and the Anarchists of Barre," *Barre-Montpelier Times Argus*, April 30, 2010, https://www.timesargus.com/news/luigi-galleani-and-the-anarchists-of-barre/article_72ad097d-c841-5c41-9f27-51a377df63a2.html; Hoyt, "And They Called Them 'Galleanisti,'" 102, 106, 107, 109–20, 121, 124.
22. Hoyt, "And They Called Them 'Galleanisti,'" 28–29; James C. Mancuso, "Italy's Art in the United States: Tracing the Immigrants' Influence in the Upstate New York Region," Albany (NY) Area Lodge of the Sons of Italy, 1997, last modified August 2002, http://www.sersale.org/mancuso/itamarts.html.
23. Talk of the Town, *Barre Daily Times*, June 6, 1903; Editorial, *Orwell Citizen* (Vergennes VT), June 25, 1903.
24. Alvey A. Adee to J. G. McCullough, August 20, 1903, John G. McCullough Papers, A156, Item 6a, Vermont State Archives and Records Administration, Middlesex VT; J. G. McCullough to Frank A. Bailey, John G. McCullough Papers, A156, Item 49a, Vermont State Archives and Records Administration, Middlesex VT; "Barre

Anarchist Paper Thought Dangerous," *Montpelier (VT) Evening Argus*, August 25, 1903.

25. "Gov. McCullough, at Instance of State Department, Proceeds against Barre, Vt, Publication," *Boston Globe*, August 26, 1903; "Cronaca Sovversiva Not Dangerous," *Enterprise and Vermonter* (Vergennes VT), September 10, 1903; Editorial, *Barre Daily Times*, August 31, 1903.
26. Senta, *Luigi Galleani*, 103, 128; Hoyt, "And They Called Them 'Galleanisti,'" 136; Heller, "Luigi Galleani and the Anarchists"; Topp, *Those without a Country*, 45–46.
27. Zimmer, "'Whole World Is Our Country,'" 190–91; Hoyt, "And They Called Them 'Galleanisti,'" 136; Galleani, *End of Anarchism?*, 30, 32.
28. Hoyt, "And They Called Them 'Galleanisti,'" 136, 138; Senta, *Luigi Galleani*, 128.
29. Senta, *Luigi Galleani*, 128; Ben Collins, "Green Mountain Chronicles," interview by Mark Greenberg, Vermont Historical Society, July 9, 1981, https://vermonthistory.org/documents/GrnMtnChronTranscripts/199-17CollinsBen.pdf.
30. Hoyt, "And They Called Them 'Galleanisti,'" 136; Topp, *Those without a Country*, 46; Heller, "Luigi Galleani and the Anarchists"; Robin Ray, "The Italian Job: Recalling a Bloody Chapter in Barre's Radical Past," *Seven Days*, October 29, 2003, https://www.sevendaysvt.com/vermont/the-italian-job/Content?oid=2129099.
31. Mark Bushnell, "Then Again: Sculptor's Death Stunned Barre Immigrant Community," *VTDigger*, April 2, 2017, https://vtdigger.org/2017/04/02/then-again-sculptors-death-stunned-barre-immigrant-community/; "State News," *United Opinion* (VT), June 19, 1908; "Pardon for Garretto, Too," *Rutland (VT) Daily Herald*, August 5, 1909; Hoyt, "And They Called Them 'Galleanisti,'" 135; Topp, *Those without a Country*, 46. One newspaper account reported that Serrati had been at the hall that evening and was being detained as a witness on a charge of breach of the peace. See "Meeting Ends in a Battle," *San Francisco Chronicle*, October 5, 1903.
32. Avrich, *Sacco and Vanzetti*, 46; Galleani, *End of Anarchism?*, 17.
33. Avrich, *Sacco and Vanzetti*, 50; Senta, *Luigi Galleani*, 131; Galleani, *End of Anarchism?*, 18–19.
34. Senta, *Luigi Galleani*, 131; Galleani, *End of Anarchism?*, 18–19.
35. Galleani, *End of Anarchism?*, 22–23; Senta, *Luigi Galleani*, 131; Avrich, *Sacco and Vanzetti*, 50–51.
36. Avrich, *Sacco and Vanzetti*, 51; Galleani, *End of Anarchism?*, 22, 29.
37. Zicree, *Twilight Zone Companion*, 235–37.
38. Avrich, *Sacco and Vanzetti*, 98–99, 229n17; Senta, *Luigi Galleani*, 32, 139–43. There was a popular counterculture book published in the early 1970s by William Powell titled *The Anarchist Cookbook*, "a collection of recipes for drugs, weapons, bombs and other forms of mayhem." Powell later said that he regretted writing the book. See "'Power Must Be Taken': Excerpts from 'The Anarchist Cookbook,'" *New York Times*, March 29, 2017.

39. Robert D'Attilio, "La Salute è in Voi: The Anarchist Dimension," Sacco and Vanzetti Commemoration Society, no date, https://saccoandvanzetti.org/sn_display1.php?row_ID=14; Topp, *Sacco and Vanzetti Case*, 63.
40. Avrich, *Sacco and Vanzetti*, 99; Pernicone, "Luigi Galleani," 482; Quinn, "Chronicling Subversion," 12; "Correggete!" *Cronaca Sovversiva*, July 18, 1908, and December 26, 1908, Chronicling America, https://chroniclingamerica.loc.gov/lccn/2012271201/1908-07-18/ed-1/seq-4/ocr/ and https://chroniclingamerica.loc.gov/lccn/2012271201/1908-12-26/ed-1/seq-4/ocr/.
41. Senta, *Luigi Galleani*, 140, 238n6; Simon, *Lone Wolf Terrorism*, 114; David, excerpt from *Terrorism Reader*, 111. One of the earliest advocates of using dynamite as a terrorist weapon was Johann Most, the German anarchist holding a square dance in 1896 whom the *Chicago Tribune* wrote sarcastically about. (See the *Chicago Tribune* quote earlier in this chapter.) Most, who came to the United States in 1882 and died in 1906, urged his fellow anarchists to use dynamite "to strike fatal blows against capitalism and the state. . . . He helped to transform the neutral substance of dynamite into a great political symbol, shorthand for the vengeance of an aggrieved immigrant working class." See Gage, *The Day Wall Street Exploded*, 41–42.
42. Hoyt, "And They Called Them 'Galleanisti,'" 154–55; "L. Galleani Arrested," *Barre Daily Times*, December 31, 1906.
43. "May Suspend Anarchist Paper," *Enterprise and Vermonter* (Vergennes VT), August 3, 1905; "State of Vermont," *Herald and News* (Randolph VT), August 3, 1905; "Cronaca Locale," *Cronaca Sovversiva*, August 5, 1905, Chronicling America, https://chroniclingamerica.loc.gov/lccn/2012271201/1905-08-05/ed-1/seq-4/ocr/.
44. The fire also gutted a reading room that contained a valuable collection of Italian books and other writings. The printing press was located in a building across the street and was not damaged. Although some believed the fire had been deliberately set, the chief of the fire department did not find any evidence of arson. See Hoyt, "And They Called Them 'Galleanisti,'" 137; "Newspaper Burned Out," *Barre Daily Times*, January 14, 1905; (No headline), *Brattleboro (VT) Reformer*, January 20, 1905.
45. Ray, "No License to Serve," 16.
46. Ray, "No License to Serve," 16–18. It wasn't always easy for the authorities to jail widows selling liquor. As the state attorney for Washington County (which includes Barre) indicated years later, witnesses were reluctant to testify against the women. "It is difficult to enforce the liquor law in this County," J. Ward Carver wrote in a letter to the Vermont attorney general in July 1912. "The difficulty I have in enforcing is the tendency of the witnesses to commit perjury, while the same witnesses in most any other prosecution would undoubtedly tell the truth. The liquor sold in this County is mostly sold by Italians and in many cases by women who are

dependent upon the municipality, more or less, for support. My experience has been that in the County, with one or two exceptions, it has been impossible to get a town grand juror to sign a complaint for any offence and this necessitates the State's Attorney going to these small towns and looking after these small matters which take a great deal of time and is of some expense to the State." See J. Ward Carver to John G. Sargent, July 17, 1912, Series PRA-084, Box PRA-00422, Folder 19, Vermont State Archives and Records Administration, Middlesex VT.

47. Hoyt, "And They Called Them 'Galleanisti,'" 151n244; "L. Galleani Arrested."
48. "L. Galleani Arrested"; Senta, *Luigi Galleani*, 129; "Cheers and Tears for Him," *Barre Daily Times*, January 2, 1907; "Implicated in the Paterson Riot," *Brattleboro (VT) Reformer*, January 4, 1907.
49. "Sorprese di capo d'anno," *Cronaca Sovversiva*, January 26, 1907, Chronicling America, https://chroniclingamerica.loc.gov/lccn/2012271201/1907-01-26/ed-1/seq-1/ocr/; Hoyt, "And They Called Them 'Galleanisti,'" 151, 199–200. The "license only" side won the 1907 election but lost again in yet another referendum held the following year. See Ray, "No License to Serve," 19; Hoyt, "And They Called Them 'Galleanisti,'" 151. Galleani and the Italian anarchists had also angered the business interests in Barre by confronting local shopkeepers who raised prices on imported food from Italy. An article in *Cronaca Sovversiva* in February 1906 criticized "the powerful elite who have a monopoly over local industry and trade and thus hold the town by the writs, by the throat, and by the belly." Further alienating the local business interests, the anarchists organized imports of food from Boston in order to bypass the shopkeepers' inflated prices. See Hoyt, "And They Called Them 'Galleanisti,'" 147.
50. "Implicated in the Paterson Riot"; "Cheers and Tears for Him"; Senta, *Luigi Galleani*, 129; "Anarchy's Black Flag in a New Camp," *Ogden Standard* (Ogden City UT), July 30, 1910.
51. "Anarchist Galleani Arrives Here and Is Placed in a Cell," *Morning Call* (Paterson NJ), January 3, 1907.
52. "Anarchist Galleani Arrives."
53. "Anarchist Editor in Jail," *New York Times*, January 3, 1907; "Galleani Out on $8000 Bail," *Boston Globe*, January 18, 1907; "Anarchist Leader Out on Bail," *Washington Herald*, January 18, 1907; Senta, *Luigi Galleani*, 129. Some newspapers erroneously stated the amount of the bail. It was $6,000.
54. "Paterson Anarchist Free," *New York Times*, January 18, 1907; "Galleani Gets Bail," *Passaic (NJ) Daily News*, January 18, 1907.
55. Ray, "No License to Serve," 5; (No headline), *Cronaca Sovversiva*, January 26, 1907, Chronicling America, https://chroniclingamerica.loc.gov/lccn/2012271201/1907-01-26/ed-1/seq-2/ocr/. The opera house meeting was held to address the upcoming referendum on liquor licenses in Barre. It was advertised as being

"against license and the pirates." See "Emma Goldman's Speech Tame," *St. Albans (VT) Daily Messenger*, February 28, 1907.

56. Hoyt, "And They Called Them 'Galleanisti,'" 196, 201.
57. Senta, *Luigi Galleani*, 129; "Try Galleani This Week," *Passaic (NJ) Daily Herald*, April 22, 1907; "Galleani's Trial," *Montpelier (VT) Evening Argus*, April 26, 1907.
58. "Accused of Leading Riot," *Baltimore Sun*, April 25, 1907; "Galleani's Trial."
59. "Luigi Galleani on Trial in NJ," *Montpelier (VT) Daily Journal*, April 26, 1907; "Paterson," *Cronaca Sovversiva*, May 18, 1907, Chronicling America, https://chroniclingamerica.loc.gov/lccn/2012271201/1907-05-18/ed-1/seq-3/ocr/.
60. "Luigi Galleani on Trial in NJ"; "Two 'Doubles' Shown Witness in Riot Trial," *Buffalo Evening News*, April 26, 1907; "Mistaken Identity Galleani's Defense," *Barre Daily Times*, April 27, 1907.
61. "Two 'Doubles' Shown Witness"; "Defense Brings in Two Doubles," *Rochester (NY) Democrat and Chronicle*, April 26, 1907; "Galleani, Hero-Infidel," *Montpelier (VT) Daily Journal*, April 29, 1907; "Disagreement for Galleani," *Morning Call* (Paterson NJ), April 27, 1907.
62. "Jury Fails to Agree," *Passaic (NJ) Daily News*, April 27, 1907; "Anarchist Not Convicted," *York (PA) Dispatch*, April 27, 1907; "Disagreement for Galleani." Newspaper accounts described Maria as Galleani's wife, although as noted in chapter 1 (endnote 13), it appears that Galleani did not marry her until 1919.
63. "Disagreement for Galleani."
64. "Disagreement for Galleani."
65. "Disagreement for Galleani."
66. "Disagreement for Galleani"; Talk of the Town, *Barre Daily Times*, May 2, 1907; "Anarchy's Black Flag in a New Camp."
67. Hoyt, "And They Called Them 'Galleanisti,'" 38, 207, 216.
68. "The Anarchists," *Montpelier Daily Journal*, reprinted in the *Middlebury (VT) Record*, November 21, 1907. The word *outrage* was sometimes used interchangeably with *bombing* and words for other acts of violence.
69. Editorial, *Rutland (VT) Daily Herald*, September 3, 1909. One newspaper, however, suggested that the game of baseball might be an antidote to the danger of anarchism: "Sinister as are the influences of anarchy, there are two forces in Barre which counteract them. One is the spread of knowledge of American ideals of government, the other baseball. . . . [When] the younger [immigrant] element mingle with the native Vermonters of their own age and take up the great national game . . . dark and dangerous misgivings are often scattered." See "Anarchy's Black Flag in a New Camp."
70. Hoyt, "And They Called Them 'Galleanisti,'" 218–19, 222–23, 226.
71. Hoyt, "And They Called Them 'Galleanisti,'" 219, 238; "One Pleaded Guilty," *Barre Daily Times*, February 17, 1910.

72. "Sues for $5,000," *Barre Daily Times*, December 29, 1910; "Barre. Principal News from the Booming Granite City," *Northfield (VT) News*, January 24, 1911; Hoyt, "And They Called Them 'Galleanisti,'" 252–54. It was not determined where Galleani went to avoid the police. One report stated that "in the middle of the night . . . [he] took a train for parts unknown." Historian Andrew Hoyt suggests that he might have simply gone on one of his nationwide speaking tours or settled in Lynn, Massachusetts, where *Cronaca Sovversiva* would begin publishing in February 1912. See Hoyt, "And They Called Them 'Galleanisti,'" 253–54; "Barre. Principal News."
73. Senta, *Luigi Galleani*, 154; Hoyt, "And They Called Them 'Galleanisti,'" 262–63.
74. Hoyt, "And They Called Them 'Galleanisti,'" 283–85; *Cronaca Sovversiva*, February 10, 1912, Chronicling America, https://chroniclingamerica.loc.gov/lccn/2012271201/1912-02-10/ed-1/seq-1/.

3. TARGETING THE GALLEANISTS

1. "The Ludlow Massacre," *American Experience*, no date, https://www.pbs.org/wgbh/americanexperience/features/rockefellers-ludlow/; Senta, *Luigi Galleani*, 159; Lance Benzel, "Colorado's Ludlow Massacre: Death, Impact, and Legacy," *OutThere Colorado*, December 7, 2018, https://www.outtherecolorado.com/colorados-ludlow-massacre-death-impact-and-legacy/; Ben Mauk, "The Ludlow Massacre Still Matters," *New Yorker*, April 18, 2014, https://www.newyorker.com/business/currency/the-ludlow-massacre-still-matters.
2. "Ludlow Massacre," *American Experience*.
3. "Ludlow Massacre," *American Experience*; "Militia Slaughters Strikers at Ludlow, Colorado," History.com, November 16, 2009, https://www.history.com/this-day-in-history/militia-slaughters-strikers-at-ludlow-colorado; Mauk, "Ludlow Massacre Still Matters"; Benzel, "Colorado's Ludlow Massacre"; "45 Dead, 20 Hurt, Score Missing, in Strike War," *New York Times*, April 22, 1914.
4. Senta, *Luigi Galleani*, 160; "Non Disarmate!" *Cronaca Sovversiva*, May 16, 1914, Chronicling America, https://chroniclingamerica.loc.gov/lccn/2012271201/1914-05-16/ed-1/seq-1/ocr/.
5. This discussion of the bombing of the *Los Angeles Times* building is drawn from Simon, *Terrorist Trap*, 40–42. See also Burns, *Masked War*; Foner, *AFL in Progressive Era*, 13, 31; Smith, *America Enters the World*, 252–60; Cowan, *People v. Clarence Darrow*.
6. Foner, *AFL in Progressive Era*, 31.
7. Benzel, "Colorado's Ludlow Massacre."
8. "Rockefeller, Jr., Answers Critics," *New York Times*, May 1, 1914; "J. D. Rockefeller, Jr., Explains Why He Rejected Overtures for Peace," *New York Times*, April 29, 1914.
9. "Rockefeller Balks Sinclair Mourners," *New York Times*, April 30, 1914; "Pickets to Haunt J. D. Rockefeller, Jr.," *New York Times*, April 29, 1914.

10. Pernicone, *Carlo Tresca*, 79; Edmund, "Protests, Pageants, and Publications," 95–97; "Rockefeller 50-Ton Stone," *New York Times*, June 6, 1914; "Rockefeller Not Worried," *New York Times*, June 26, 1914.
11. "IWW Invades Tarrytown," *New York Times*, May 31, 1914.
12. "Anarchists Egged in Tarrytown Riot," *New York Times*, June 23, 1914.
13. "Rockefeller Guard Captures Intruder," *New York Times*, June 11, 1914; "More Rockefeller Guards," *New York Times*, June 25, 1914; "Rockefeller Not Worried."
14. "Take Pity on Rockefeller," *New York Times*, July 2, 1914.
15. Avrich, *Sacco and Vanzetti*, 100; "More Rockefeller Guards." In a story about the bombing, the *New York Times* reported, "The agitators understood that the home was empty, as Mr. Rockefeller had gone to Maine for the Summer." See "IWW Bomb Meant for Rockefeller Kills Four of Its Makers, Wrecks Tenement and Injures Many Tenants," *New York Times*, July 5, 1914.
16. Avrich, *Sacco and Vanzetti*, 100; Sam Roberts, "100 Years Later, Scar Remains from a Strike's Fatal Legacy in Manhattan," *New York Times*, July 3, 2014; "IWW Bomb."
17. Avrich, *Sacco and Vanzetti*, 99.
18. "'Reds' Eulogize Dead," *Washington Post*, July 12, 1914.
19. Gage, *The Day Wall Street Exploded*, 103; Pernicone, *Carlo Tresca*, 85.
20. Pernicone, *Carlo Tresca*, 85; Gage, *The Day Wall Street Exploded*, 103–4, 352n22; Avrich, *Sacco and Vanzetti*, 100; Tejada, *In Search of Sacco and Vanzetti*, 103; "Bomb in Tombs Court Part of Conspiracy by Anarchist Group," *Evening World* (New York), November 14, 1914.
21. "Bomb in Tombs Court."
22. "Bomb in Tombs Court."
23. "Bomb in Tombs Court."
24. "Bomb in Tombs Court."
25. "Bomb in Tombs Court"; Pernicone, *Carlo Tresca*, 85; Tejada, *In Search of Sacco and Vanzetti*, 103; Avrich, *Sacco and Vanzetti*, 100.
26. The People of the State of New York, Respondent, v. Frank Abarno and Carmine Carbone, Defendants-Appellants, Supreme Court App., First Department, Respondent's Brief, Statement, at 4 (April 19, 1915); Pernicone, *Carlo Tresca*, 85; Gage, *The Day Wall Street Exploded*, 103–4; Tunney, *Throttled!*, 44.
27. *People of the State of New York*, at 6; Pernicone, *Carlo Tresca*, 85; Tunney, *Throttled!*, 41.
28. *People of the State of New York*, at 9–10. According to Polignani, it was Abarno who said that St. Patrick's Cathedral was a rich church and that the millionaires would take notice of the bombing.
29. Larabee, *Wrong Hands*, 42. During the trial of Carbone and Abarno, the prosecution claimed that Carbone had in fact followed the directions described in *La Salute è in Voi!* for making bombs. Abarno told police after he was arrested

that Carbone "made the bomb according to directions in a book printed in Italian and circulated by the anarchists. This book tells how to make bombs, how to get chemicals, how to place them and how to get away." See Hunt, *Wrongly Executed?*, 34; *People of the State of New York*, at 2, 11.

30. Larabee, *Wrong Hands*, 42; Pernicone, *Carlo Tresca*, 85; *People of the State of New York*, at 3, 24.
31. *People of the State of New York*, at 24. When the plan to have one of the bomb's fuses lit by one of the anarchists became public after the arrests of Abarno and Carbone, rather than receiving criticism for endangering the lives of the people at the church, the police were praised in newspapers for their crafty detective work in catching the anarchists. "So carefully had the police worked out their plan," wrote the *Boston Globe*, "that the anarchist was even allowed to light the fuse of one of the bombs which he carried into the cathedral, despite the fact that the explosives were powerful enough to have badly damaged the edifice and possibly killed many of those in it." See "Anarchist Confession in Reign of Terror Plot," *Boston Globe*, March 3, 1915. At the trial, Abarno and Carbone's lawyer argued that the bomb was about as powerful as a big firecracker. See "No Danger in Bomb, New Defense Plea," *New York Times*, April 1, 1915.
32. *People of the State of New York*, at 25–29; "No Danger in Bomb."
33. Avrich, *Sacco and Vanzetti*, 101; "Trap Bomb Layer as He Lights Fuse in the Cathedral," *New York Times*, March 3, 1915; Hunt, *Wrongly Executed?*, 33–34.
34. "Charge Police Plot," *Washington Post*, March 4, 1915; "Assert Police Spy Made Their Bombs," *New York Times*, March 4, 1915; Hunt, *Wrongly Executed?*, 34–35; Pernicone, *Carlo Tresca*, 86; Avrich, *Sacco and Vanzetti*, 101; Gage, *The Day Wall Street Exploded*, 105. The jury was bothered by Polignani's role in the affair, and when they returned their verdict, they recommended mercy for the defendants. The judge agreed and instead of sentencing them to the maximum of twenty-five years in prison gave them the reduced sentence of six to twelve years. See Pernicone, *Carlo Tresca*, 86; Hunt, *Wrongly Executed?*, 36; "Detective Lit Bomb, Abarno Tells Court," *New York Times*, April 3, 1915; "Convict Bomb Men in Cathedral Plot," *New York Times*, April 13, 1915; "Bomb Plotters Get 6 to 12 Years," *New York Times*, April 20, 1915.
35. Avrich, *Sacco and Vanzetti*, 101; "Il Trionfo di Mardocheo," *Cronaca Sovversiva*, March 13, 1915, Chronicling America, https://chroniclingamerica.loc.gov/lccn/2012271201/1915-03-13/ed-1/seq-1/ocr/. Battery Park is in the lower end of Manhattan, and Harlem is in the northern end of the borough. The "two rivers" referred to by Galleani are the Hudson River and the East River. In some translations of his article, the word *reds* appears instead of *rebels*. See Senta, *Luigi Galleani*, 161.
36. The concept of a grand event ushering in a period of terrorism was first introduced by pioneering terrorism scholar David Rapoport. In his classic article

"The Four Waves of Modern Terrorism," Rapoport argues that the history of modern terrorism (terrorism since the late nineteenth century) can be divided into four basic periods or waves: the Anarchist Wave (1880s–1920s), the Anticolonial Wave (1920s–60s), the New Left Wave (1960s–90s), and the Religious Wave (1979–present). There can be overlap in the waves as one ebbs and another emerges, but each generally lasts for approximately forty years. While the waves have multiple properties and characteristics, Rapoport notes that they share one important feature—namely, some type of grand event or incident helping to galvanize and launch the global movement.

For example, the wounding in 1878 by Vera Zasulich of a Russian police commander who had mistreated political prisoners inspired the Anarchist Wave, particularly her proclamation that she was a "terrorist, not a killer" after throwing her weapon to the floor. She was acquitted at her trial and treated as a heroine after she was freed. German newspapers reported that pro-Zasulich demonstrations meant that a revolution was imminent in Russia. The Treaty of Versailles ending World War I precipitated the Anticolonial Wave, according to Rapoport, as the "victors applied the principle of national self-determination to break up the empires of the defeated states." The third wave, the New Left Wave, found its inspiration in the Vietnam War and the effective role of the Viet Cong in its battles with American and South Vietnamese troops. The war led to the formation of radical groups in the Third World and the West, where they saw themselves as vanguards for the Third World masses. The Soviet Union offered training and weapons to these groups, including the West German Red Army Faction, the Italian Red Brigades, and the Japanese Red Army. The fourth wave, the Religious Wave, was launched after the 1979 Iranian revolution. This, along with the Soviet invasion of Afghanistan that same year, led to religious extremism in many parts of the world. The Iranian revolution, as Rapoport points out, "was clear evidence to believers that religion now had more political appeal than did the prevailing third-wave ethos because Iranian Marxists could only muster meager support against the Shah." The Ayatollah Khomeini regime in Iran influenced Shiite extremist movements beyond Iran's borders, such as those in Iraq, Saudi Arabia, Kuwait, and Lebanon. See Rapoport, "The Four Waves of Modern Terrorism."

37. "Dynamite Hall of Bronx Borough," *New York Times*, May 4, 1915; "Bomb Rocks Police Headquarters, Shattering the Doors and Offices," *New York Times*, July 6, 1915; Gage, *The Day Wall Street Exploded*, 105–6, 209; Avrich, *Sacco and Vanzetti*, 55, 99, 101. Nobody was injured in the bombings at the Bronx Borough Hall and the NYPD headquarters.

There was also an attempt in June 1915 to dynamite the New York City home of industrialist Andrew Carnegie, but the fuse was put out by a patrolman working for a security company. See "Plot to Dynamite Andrew Carnegie's Home; Patrolman Snuffs Out Lighted Fuse of Bomb," *New York Times*, June 24, 1915.

In another incident during this period, a mentally unstable man named Erich Muenter placed a bomb underneath the switchboard of a public phone at the U.S. Capitol in Washington DC on July 2 and then traveled to New York in a failed attempt the next day to assassinate the powerful and famous banker J. P. Morgan at his home in Long Island. His motive was to protest World War I and the role the Morgan family was playing in financing it. He claimed that he had not intended to kill Morgan but rather hold his wife and children hostage until "the Morgan leadership went about calling off the war." The bomb he'd planted at the Capitol exploded, destroying the Senate Reception Room but not injuring anybody. Muenter wound up hanging himself while in jail. See Gage, *The Day Wall Street Exploded*, 22–23, 25, 106.

38. Pernicone, *Carlo Tresca*, 49–50; Senta, *Luigi Galleani*, 157–58.
39. Senta, *Luigi Galleani*, 158; Pernicone, *Carlo Tresca*, 54; "January 12, 1912: Bread and Roses Strike Begins," Massmoments.org, no date, https://www.massmoments.org/moment-details/bread-and-roses-strike-begins.html.
40. "January 12, 1912: Bread and Roses"; Pernicone, *Carlo Tresca*, 50; Senta, *Luigi Galleani*, 158;
41. Senta, *Luigi Galleani*, 158–59; Pernicone, *Carlo Tresca*, 54; Avrich, *Sacco and Vanzetti*, 26.
42. Pernicone, *Carlo Tresca*, 55; Senta, *Luigi Galleani*, 159.
43. Senta, *Luigi Galleani*, 138, 159; Pernicone, *Carlo Tresca*, 58; Avrich, *Sacco and Vanzetti*, 52.
44. Senta, *Luigi Galleani*, 138; Pernicone, *Carlo Tresca*, 58.
45. Avrich, *Sacco and Vanzetti*, 97; Gage, *The Day Wall Street Exploded*, 209; Senta, *Luigi Galleani*, 145; Robert D'Attilio, "La Salute è in Voi: The Anarchist Dimension," Sacco and Vanzetti Commemoration Society, no date, https://saccoandvanzetti.org/sn_display1.php?row_ID=14.
46. Avrich, *Sacco and Vanzetti*, 58.
47. Senta, *Luigi Galleani*, 163, 167–68.
48. Gage, *The Day Wall Street Exploded*, 108; Johnson, *1916 Preparedness Day Bombing*, 64.
49. "Preparedness Day Arranged for DC," *Evening Star* (Washington DC), May 27, 1916; John DeFerrari, "A Demonstration for 'Everyone': The Preparedness Day Parade 100 Years Ago," *Streets of Washington* (blog), October 17, 2016, http://www.streetsofwashington.com/2016/10/a-demonstration-for-everyone.html.
50. "135,683 Paraded for Preparedness by Actual Count of Times Reporters," *New York Times*, May 14, 1916; "Chicago Host to Parade for Preparedness," *Chicago Tribune*, May 15, 1916. The actual quote by the letter writer to the *Chicago Tribune* was "I have always felt in my heart that Chicago cannot do better," which is the opposite of what she apparently intended to convey. The *Chicago Tribune* claimed that the total number of people in the crowd for the New York parade was 125,683,

shaving off ten thousand from the *New York Times* figure of 135,683. The number of people who marched in the Chicago parade was reported to be 130,214. The *Tribune* boasted not only that Chicago beat New York in the numbers game but also that their parade was the "largest in the history of America." See Henry M. Hyde, "Detail [*sic*] Story of Greatest Parade in Chicago's History," *Chicago Sunday Tribune*, June 4, 1916.

51. "Preparedness Day Bombing in San Francisco," History.com, November 5, 2009, https://www.history.com/this-day-in-history/preparedness-day-bombing-in-san-francisco; Jonah Owen Lamb, "Preparedness Day Bombing Tore Through Cultural Fabric of SF," *San Francisco Examiner*, June 12, 2015, https://www.sfexaminer.com/uncategorised/preparedness-day-bombing-tore-through-cultural-fabric-of-sf/; Johnson, *1916 Preparedness Day Bombing*, 71–72, 79. Johnson describes the bomb as "a 6-8-in. diameter iron pipe" on p. 79 in his book, but on p. 72 writes that it "was a 4-inch pipe."
52. Lamb, "Preparedness Day Bombing Tore Through"; "Preparedness Day Bombing in San Francisco"; Gage, *The Day Wall Street Exploded*, 108; Johnson, *1916 Preparedness Day Bombing*, 76–78.
53. Gary Kamiya, "Miscarriage of Justice Sends 2 Innocent Men to Prison," *SFGATE*, May 16, 2014, https://www.sfgate.com/bayarea/article/Miscarriage-of-justice-sends-2-innocent-men-to-5484853.php; Johnson, *1916 Preparedness Day Bombing*, 151. Mooney's wife, Rena, and two other men were also arrested and tried for the crime, but they were eventually acquitted. See Paul Drexler, "The Mooney-Billings Case Pt. 2," *San Francisco Examiner*, September 18, 2016, https://www.sfexaminer.com/news/the-mooney-billings-case-pt-2/. Mooney claimed he and his wife were on a rooftop watching the parade when the bomb went off. A photo depicts the pair doing exactly that on the day of the bombing. See photo number 15 in this book.
54. Johnson, *1916 Preparedness Day Bombing*, 151–52; William J. Flynn, "On the Trail of the Anarchist Band—Chief Flynn," *New York Herald*, March 5, 1922.
55. Johnson, *1916 Preparedness Day Bombing*, 32; "Comunicati," *Cronaca Sovversiva*, January 29, 1916, Chronicling America, https://chroniclingamerica.loc.gov/lccn/2012271201/1916-01-29/ed-1/seq-4/ocr/; Avrich and Avrich, *Sasha and Emma*, 254; Raney, "Group That Does Things," 125–27.
56. Avrich, *Sacco and Vanzetti*, 138; McCormick, *Hopeless Cases*, 24–25; Affidavit of John A. Ryder, February 12, 1919, RG 85, INS 54,235/33, NARA. It is possible that when Galleani told the inspector that the perpetrator of the bombing had come to him for advice, he meant *after* the bombing and not before. The advice the bomber was seeking could have been how to avoid being identified as the bomber. If so, then Galleani, by saying he "wished not to learn of it," was protecting himself from future accusations of involvement in the bombing.

57. Johnson, *1916 Preparedness Day Bombing*, 70; "Nation-Wide Plot Behind Bomb Outrage," *Evening News* (Wilkes-Barre PA), July 25, 1916. See the introduction in this book for a discussion of the Dondoglio/Crones poison-soup case.
58. "Think Outrage Work of Jean Crones Gang," *Los Angeles Daily Times*, July 25, 1916; "Nation-Wide Plot Behind Bomb." The *Los Angeles Times* was known as the *Los Angeles Daily Times* in 1916.
59. Johnson, *1916 Preparedness Day Bombing*, 152; Avrich and Avrich, *Sasha and Emma*, 265.
60. Avrich, *Sacco and Vanzetti*, 63, 101–2, 135. During this period, Galleani was active in a wildcat coal miners' strike in Dupont, Pennsylvania. He was arrested in September 1916 and charged with inciting rebellion. He was released on bail, but there was never a trial. See Senta, *Luigi Galleani*, 172–73; *Report of Hearing in the Case of Galleani, Luigi, 56, m. Italian*, June 27, 1917, RG 85, INS 54,235/33, NARA; "State Troopers Get Five Leaders of IWW in Big Raid at Dupont," *Scranton (PA) Republican*, September 13, 1916.
61. Simon, *Terrorists and Potential Use*, 16.
62. Avrich, *Sacco and Vanzetti*, 58; Senta, *Luigi Galleani*, 175.
63. "Matricolati!" *Cronaca Sovversiva*, May 26, 1917, Chronicling America, https://chroniclingamerica.loc.gov/lccn/2012271201/1917-05-26/ed-1/seq-1/ocr/; Avrich, *Sacco and Vanzetti*, 59; Pernicone, "Luigi Galleani," 483; Senta, *Luigi Galleani*, 175.
64. Avrich, *Sacco and Vanzetti*, 59, 93; Senta, *Luigi Galleani*, 175–76; Simon, "Forgotten Terrorists," 198.
65. Avrich, *Sacco and Vanzetti*, 95–96; Senta, *Luigi Galleani*, 176–78; McCormick, *Hopeless Cases*, 13; Simon, "Forgotten Terrorists," 198; Pernicone, "Luigi Galleani," 484. The following Bureau of Investigation report describes the scene at the Galleani home when the agents came to arrest him at midnight: "We rapped on the door of Galerini's [*sic*] residence several times, without an answer. Finally we heard 'Hello' as if quite a way off, and after asking Mr. Gallerini [*sic*] to come to the door to talk to the officers he did open the door. He was dressed only in night robe, and refused to let us enter. He slammed the door and attempted to bolt it but we forced the door open against the efforts of Gallerini [*sic*] and his wife to keep it closed. After strong protest against our action in serving the Federal warrant at midnight he finally dressed and we took him, in the automobile, to Police Station 19, on Morton Street, Dorchester District, Boston, Mass., arriving here at 2.30 a.m." See Henry M. Bowen, "In re: Louis [*sic*] Gallerini [*sic*] and John Eramo: European Neutrality Matter," June 15, 1917, Case Number 20713, RG 65, OG, M1085, Fold3, NARA.
66. "Warrant-Arrest of Alien," June 27, 1917, RG 85, INS 54,235/33, NARA; Pettine & De Pasquale to Secretary of Commerce & Labor, Bureau of Immigration, "Application for Warrant for the Deportation of Luigi Galliani of Wrentham, Mass. and

John Eramo of Lynn, Mass," June 25, 1917, RG 85, INS 54,235/33, NARA; Avrich, *Sacco and Vanzetti*, 95. The Bureau of Immigration was part of the Department of Labor at this time. In 1940 it was transferred to the Department of Justice. See Avrich, *Sacco and Vanzetti*, 128.

67. *Report of Hearing in the Case of Galleani.*
68. *Report of Hearing in the Case of Galleani.*
69. *Report of Hearing in the Case of Galleani.*
70. *Report of Hearing in the Case of Galleani.* Maria had two children from two previous marriages and four children with Galleani, one born in Egypt and three born in the United States. See Senta, *Luigi Galleani*, 79.
71. Commissioner-General to Commissioner of Immigration, August 25, 1917, RG 85, INS 54,235/33, NARA.
72. *Report of Hearing in the Case of Giovanni Eramo, 35, m. Italian*, June 27, 1917, RG 85, INS 54,235/33, NARA.
73. *Report of Hearing in the Case of Giovanni Eramo.*
74. Avrich, *Sacco and Vanzetti*, 95, 122; McCormick, *Hopeless Cases*, 13.
75. Avrich, *Sacco and Vanzetti*, 65.
76. Avrich, *Sacco and Vanzetti*, 62–65.
77. Pernicone, "Luigi Galleani," 484; Tejada, *In Search of Sacco and Vanzetti*, 67–68.
78. Avrich, *Sacco and Vanzetti*, 104; Tejada, *In Search of Sacco and Vanzetti*, 104.
79. Gordon, "'To Make a Clean Sweep,'" 22; Doug Moe, "A Riveting Look at the Unsolved Milwaukee Police Station Bombing of 1917," *Milwaukee*, October 29, 2017, https://www.milwaukeemag.com/unsolved-milwaukee-police-station-bombing-1917/; Avrich, *Sacco and Vanzetti*, 104–5. Nobody was ever charged in the case, but Avrich believes that Buda and Valdinoci were responsible for the bombing.
80. Avrich, *Sacco and Vanzetti*, 105–6.
81. "Dynamite Girl Throws Light on IWW Plot," *Chicago Tribune*, January 20, 1918; Avrich, *Sacco and Vanzetti*, 108, 112.
82. Avrich, *Sacco and Vanzetti*, 108; Tomchuk, *Transnational Radicals*, 126; Gordon, "'To Make a Clean Sweep,'" 17.
83. Gordon, "'To Make a Clean Sweep,'" 17, 23–24; Tejada, *In Search of Sacco and Vanzetti*, 104–5; McCormick, *Hopeless Cases*, 14; Avrich, *Sacco and Vanzetti*, 107, 109, 207.
84. Gordon, "'To Make a Clean Sweep,'" 17; Avrich, *Sacco and Vanzetti*, 110–11, 120; Tejada, *In Search of Sacco and Vanzetti*, 105.
85. Gordon, "'To Make a Clean Sweep,'" 17.
86. Gordon, "'To Make a Clean Sweep,'" 24–25; Avrich, *Sacco and Vanzetti*, 114–18.
87. Avrich, *Sacco and Vanzetti*, 112–13; Gordon, "'To Make a Clean Sweep,'" 24. The bomb with the sulfuric acid malfunctioned, while the one with the fuse failed to detonate due to rainfall that night that dampened the fuse.

4. YOU HAVE SHOWN NO PITY TO US!

1. "Administrator's Sale," advertisement, *Sun* (Baltimore MD), January 17, 1961.
2. McCormick, *Hopeless Cases*, 15.
3. McCormick, *Hopeless Cases*, 15–16.
4. McCormick, *Hopeless Cases*, 16; Avrich, *Sacco and Vanzetti*, 118.
5. Avrich, *Sacco and Vanzetti*, 118–20.
6. Avrich, *Sacco and Vanzetti*, 61, 119–21.
7. Avrich, *Sacco and Vanzetti*, 122; McCormick, *Hopeless Cases*, 13, 22.
8. Avrich, *Sacco and Vanzetti*, 123; McCormick, *Hopeless Cases*, 22.
9. Special Employe [*sic*] Finch, "In re Luigi Galleani, Rafael Schiavina, John Eramo, and A. Bottonelli," March 27, 1918, Case Number 8000-20713, RG 65, OG, M1085, Fold3, NARA. "Matricolati!" ("Registrants!") is the article written by Galleani in the May 26, 1917, issue of *Cronaca Sovversiva* regarding registering for the military draft. See chapter 3.
10. Sp. Employe [*sic*] Finch, "In re: Luigi Galleani," March 28, 1918, RG 85, INS 54,235/33, NARA.
11. Sp. Employe [*sic*] Finch, "In re: Luigi Galleani."
12. Sp. Employe [*sic*] Finch, "In re: Luigi Galleani"; Avrich, *Sacco and Vanzetti*, 125–26. The Bureau of Immigration, not the Bureau of Investigation, had the authority to issue such warrants.
13. R. W. Finch, "In re: Italian Anarchists, 'Cronaca Sovversiva,'" May 22, 1918, Case Number 8000-20713, RG 65, OG, M1085, Fold3, NARA.
14. *Report of Hearing in the Case of Galleani, Luigi, 56, m. Italian*, June 27, 1917, RG 85, INS 54,235/33, NARA; *Report of Hearing in the Case of Luigi Galleani, Italian*, May 16, 1918, RG 85, INS 54,235/33, NARA.
15. *Report of Hearing in the Case of Luigi Galleani, Italian.*
16. *Report of Hearing in the Case of Luigi Galleani, Italian.*
17. *Report of Hearing in the Case of Luigi Galleani, Italian.*
18. *Report of Hearing in the Case of Luigi Galleani, Italian.*
19. *Report of Hearing in the Case of Giovanni Eramo, Italian*, May 16, 1918, RG 85, INS 54,235/33, NARA.
20. Avrich, *Sacco and Vanzetti*, 93–94; Tejada, *In Search of Sacco and Vanzetti*, 106; Simon, "Forgotten Terrorists," 198.
21. Avrich, *Sacco and Vanzetti*, 127–28.
22. Avrich, *Sacco and Vanzetti*, 128–29; McCormick, *Hopeless Cases*, 24.
23. Avrich, *Sacco and Vanzetti*, 130–31.
24. McCormick, *Hopeless Cases*, 32; Avrich, *Sacco and Vanzetti*, 132–34; Tejada, *In Search of Sacco and Vanzetti*, 107.
25. Avrich, *Sacco and Vanzetti*, 132.
26. McCormick, *Hopeless Cases*, 15–16, 27.

27. McCormick, *Hopeless Cases*, 27–28.
28. McCormick, *Hopeless Cases*, 28, 38; R. W. Finch, "In re: IWW Situation, Confidential Informant B-10," November 20, 1918, Case Number 8000-208369, RG 65, OG, M1085, Fold3, NARA.
29. R. W. Finch, "In re: IWW Situation."
30. McCormick, *Hopeless Cases*, 29–30, 38–41; Avrich, *Sacco and Vanzetti*, 147; Memorandum by J. Edgar Hoover, "British Espionage in the United States: A Secret Memorandum Prepared by the United States Dept. of Justice," February 15, 1921, MID Document 9944-A-178, NARA Declassification NND740058, declassified October 26, 1988, https://www.marxists.org/history/usa/government/dept-justice/1921/0215-doj-britespionage.pdf.
31. George J. Starr, "In re: Raymond Finch—Alleged British Agent," July 6, 1921, Case Number 216551, RG 65, BS, M1085, Fold3, NARA.
32. McCormick, *Hopeless Cases*, 16, 165n18; *Our Journal: Official Organ of the MPIU [Metal Polishers International Union]*, vol. 29 (Cincinnati, 1920), 25; *Hearings before a [Senate] Subcommittee of the Committee on Education and Labor*, 75th Cong., 2nd Sess., November 18, 1937. In *Hopeless Cases* McCormick writes that, for the detective agency, Finch tracked down an embezzler believed to have fled the United States for Mexico (165n18).
33. McCormick, *Hopeless Cases*, 24–25; Affidavit of John A. Ryder, February 12, 1919, RG 85, INS 54,235/33, NARA.
34. Anthony Caminetti to John Abercrombie, "In re John Eramo, Supplemental Memorandum for the Acting Secretary," March 17, 1919, RG 85, INS 54,235/33, NARA. In April 1920 Caminetti wrote to the assistant secretary of labor, Louis Post, that Eramo had complied with the terms of his parole and that the Bureau of Immigration was recommending that the warrant for his arrest for deportation be canceled. See Anthony Caminetti to Louis Post, "In re Giovanni Eramo, 2nd Supplemental Memorandum for the Acting Secretary," April 30, 1920, RG 85, INS 54,235/33, NARA.
35. Avrich, *Sacco and Vanzetti*, 135.
36. Avrich, *Sacco and Vanzetti*, 137. More leaflets, believed to have been the work of anarchists, although not necessarily Galleanists, were left in a series of bombings at the homes of the president of the chamber of commerce, the acting superintendent of police, and a judge in Philadelphia on December 30, 1918. The circular claimed that the rule of priests, judges, police, soldiers, and others was coming to an end. No one was seriously injured in the blasts. A fourth bomb was discovered at the office of a U.S. attorney. See Avrich, *Sacco and Vanzetti*, 138–39.
37. Avrich, *Sacco and Vanzetti*, 137, 139; McCormick, *Hopeless Cases*, 35.
38. Simon, "Forgotten Terrorists," 199.

39. McCormick, *Hopeless Cases*, 35; Avrich, *Sacco and Vanzetti*, 140, 145; Barry, *Great Influenza*, 396–97; Gage, *The Day Wall Street Exploded*, 26–27. The worldwide death total from the influenza pandemic has been estimated to be at least 50 million. See Barry, *Great Influenza*, 397.
40. Avrich, *Sacco and Vanzetti*, 134.
41. Avrich, *Sacco and Vanzetti*, 56, 147–48.
42. Schmidt, *Red Scare*, 28; Simon, "Forgotten Terrorists," 199.
43. "22 Bombs Are Found in Mails for Nation's Public Men; 16 Here," *New York Tribune*, May 1, 1919; "36 Dynamite Bombs, Made Here, Mailed to Prominent Men of U.S.; 16 Are Found in NY Post Office," *Sun* (New York), May 1, 1919; Avrich, *Sacco and Vanzetti*, 140; McCormick, *Hopeless Cases*, 36; Simon, "Forgotten Terrorists," 199.
44. "Leniency towards Anarchist to End," *Fall River (MA) Daily Evening News*, May 1, 1919; "22 Bombs Are Found in Mails"; "Here're Infernal Machines," *Knoxville (TN) Sentinel*, May 13, 1919; Avrich, *Sacco and Vanzetti*, 141; McCormick, *Hopeless Cases*, 37–38; Simon, "Forgotten Terrorists," 199–200.
45. Avrich, *Sacco and Vanzetti*, 143.
46. Avrich, *Sacco and Vanzetti*, 144–45.
47. Avrich, *Sacco and Vanzetti*, 97, 145.
48. Avrich, *Sacco and Vanzetti*, 145–46; "The Alien Agitators," *Jackson (MS) Daily News*, March 15, 1919.
49. Avrich, *Sacco and Vanzetti*, 145–46.
50. Avrich, *Sacco and Vanzetti*, 147. Ciofalo was a member of the Bresci Group in New York and had been part of the group of Galleanists who went to Mexico during the summer of 1917. He was arrested in March 1919 and faced likely deportation. See Avrich, *Sacco and Vanzetti*, 99, 102, 134.
51. Avrich, *Sacco and Vanzetti*, 62–64, 107, 109, 146, 207; Simon, "Forgotten Terrorists," 201.
52. Avrich, *Sacco and Vanzetti*, 142; "Leniency towards Anarchist to End"; "22 Bombs Are Found in Mails." Some newspaper and other accounts reported a total of thirty-six bombs, but Avrich believes this was erroneous. See Avrich, *Sacco and Vanzetti*, 235n19. There were also reports that the first package bombs had been put in the mails on April 23, not April 22 as Avrich states. See "Leniency towards Anarchist to End."
53. Phil Dougherty, "Seattle Mayor Ole Hanson Gets a Bomb in His Mail on April 28, 1919," HistoryLink.org, September 4, 2015, https://www.historylink.org/File/11106; "Bomb for Ole Hanson Sent from East Stirs Home of Seattle's Fighting Mayor," *New York Times*, April 29, 1919; "Bomb Sent to Mayor," *Seattle Star*, April 28, 1919; Simon, "Forgotten Terrorists," 199–200. Different explanations have been given for why the package bomb did not explode. According to one account, the acid had leaked through the package, preventing the explosion from occurring.

Another explanation was that the glass vial dropped out intact onto the table in the mayor's office. See Avrich, *Sacco and Vanzetti*, 140–41, 235n10.

54. "Bomb from NY Is Sent to Hardwick," *New York Tribune*, April 30, 1919; "Bomb for Ole Hanson Sent from East"; Gage, *The Day Wall Street Exploded*, 27. The package was originally sent to Hardwick's former home in Sandersville, Georgia, and then forwarded to his Atlanta apartment.
55. "22 Bombs Are Found in Mails"; "36 Dynamite Bombs"; Avrich, *Sacco and Vanzetti*, 141.
56. "How the Unselfish Devotion to Duty, Intelligence and Ready Wit of a Post Office Clerk Saved Many Lives," *Post Office Clerk* 17, no. 6 (June 1919): 6, 27.
57. "22 Bombs Are Found in Mails"; "36 Dynamite Bombs." The package bombs that got through either had enough postage or the insufficient postage had not been noticed by the other postal clerks who'd handled them. Some reports indicate the short-payment department (where the package bombs remained for several days) was located in the basement of the post office and not on the main floor. See Post, *Deportations Delirium*, 37.
58. "22 Bombs Are Found in Mails"; "36 Dynamite Bombs." The first notification to Gimbels about the packages needing more postage was made on the same morning that the Hanson bomb in Seattle was discovered. The second notification was made the next day. By that time the Hanson bomb had been reported in some New York newspapers. Whoever was contacted at Gimbels and whoever called the store from the post office most likely did not know about the Hanson bomb or they would have realized that the sixteen packages at the post office might also contain bombs. Louis Gimbel, who'd commented on the Hanson bomb, was almost certainly not the person contacted by the post office, since the caller would not bother an executive with such a trivial matter as insufficient postage. Had the caller done so, though, Gimbel at least would likely have made the connection between the packages at the post office and the one that had been sent to Hanson.
59. "How the Unselfish Devotion to Duty"; "36 Dynamite Bombs"; "Finder of Mail Bombs Promoted as Reward," *Evening World* (New York), May 31, 1919.
60. "36 Dynamite Bombs"; "22 Bombs Are Found in Mails"; "Eagan, Bomb Wizard Dies Going to Duty," *New York Times*, March 3, 1920; "Bomb Expert Eagan: Special Interview to the Electrical Experimenter," *Electrical Experimenter*, August 1919, 296, 343, https://www.americanradiohistory.com/Archive-Electrical-Experimenter/EE-1919-08.pdf. The *New York Times* article states that Eagan lost his finger when he placed his right hand on the earlier bomb, but other accounts state that his left finger was missing. See "Bomb Expert Eagan." The quote by Eagan about bombs being made by all types of men was originally in italics in the *Electrical Experimenter* article.

61. "36 Dynamite Bombs"; "22 Bombs Are Found in Mails."
62. "36 Dynamite Bombs."
63. "Infernal Machine for Sen. Overman," *Salisbury (NC) Evening Post*, May 1, 1919; "Overman Bomb Blown to Bits," *Messenger and Intelligencer* (Wadesboro NC), May 8, 1919; "Would Have Been Opened Promptly If Delivered," *Fall River (MA) Daily Evening News*, May 1, 1919; "Salisbury the Scene of a Double Wedding," *Greensboro (NC) Daily News*, May 1, 1919; "Find More Bombs Sent in the Mails; One to Overman," *New York Times*, May 2, 1919.
64. "Nation-Wide Bomb Plot Aims at U.S. Notables and SF Men," *San Francisco Chronicle*, May 1, 1919; "Bomb in Mails Show National Terrorist Plot," *Pittsburgh Gazette Times*, May 1, 1919; "Widespread Conspiracy of Terrorists to Assassinate Highly Placed Persons Is Unearthed in New York City," *Miami Herald*, May 1, 1919; "Hanson Warns America," *New York Times*, May 2, 1919; "Senator King Introduces Bill," *Ogden (UT) Standard*, May 23, 1919.
65. Simon, "Forgotten Terrorists," 200.
66. Simon, "Forgotten Terrorists," 200; "The Bomb Plot," *New York Times*, May 2, 1919.
67. "Practical Jokers Send 'Some' Bombs," *Times and Democrat* (Orangeburg SC), May 8, 1919; "Bomb for J. L. Burnett," *New York Times*, May 1, 1919; Editorial, *Guntersville (AL) Democrat*, May 7, 1919.
68. Simon, "Forgotten Terrorists," 200–201; Avrich, *Sacco and Vanzetti*, 144; "Bomb Injures Ex-Senator's Wife, Maims a Servant," *New York Times*, April 30, 1919. Federal and state agencies actually got involved before the sixteen package bombs were discovered in the New York post office. The package bomb sent to former senator Hardwick led many agencies, including military intelligence, to begin their investigations that day, hours before postal clerk Charles Kaplan read about the incident and told his superiors about the similar packages at the post office. The discovery of those packages revealed the enormity of the nationwide plot and intensified the investigations.
69. "36 Dynamite Bombs"; McCormick, *Hopeless Cases*, 38; "Find First Clue in Police Search for Bomb Maker," *New York Times*, May 3, 1919; Avrich, *Sacco and Vanzetti*, 144.
70. "Radicals Watched in Bomb Plot Hunt," *New York Times*, May 4, 1919; "Federal Investigators Complain of Police," *Washington Herald*, May 6, 1919; McCormick, *Hopeless Cases*, 38.
71. "36 Dynamite Bombs."
72. "Bombs Made Like Mines," *Pittsburgh Post*, May 2, 1919; "Lawyer's Home Is Wrecked by Bomb," *Brooklyn Daily Eagle*, May 5, 1919.
73. "22 Bombs Are Found in Mails."
74. "Metal Experts to Work on Bomb Plot," *New York Times*, May 5, 1919; "Radicals Watched in Bomb Plot."

75. "Police Ask Help to Find Bomb Senders," *New York Times*, May 13, 1919; "Arnoldo Sopelano," August 26, 1919, Case Number 341792, RG 65, OG, M1085, Fold3, NARA; "In re: Sending of Package Bombs through the Mails to Prominent Persons," May 13, 1919, Case Number 341792, RG 65, OG, M1085, Fold3, NARA; "In re: Jose Grau, Alias A. Sapelano, Alias Jose Grado, Alias Adolfe Apells," July 17, 1919, Case Number 341792, RG 65, OG, M1085, Fold3, NARA. Grau's alias was sometimes spelled "Arnoldo Sopelano" in Bureau of Investigation reports.
76. "Treat Them Rough," *Cronaca Sovversiva*, May 1, 1919, Chronicling America, https://chroniclingamerica.loc.gov/lccn/2012271201/1919-05-01/ed-1/seq-4/ocr/. Despite the government shutting down *Cronaca Sovversiva* in July 1918 after previously banning it from the mails, the Galleanists still managed to put out two more issues, with the May 1, 1919, edition being its very last one. Interestingly, another editorial with a different viewpoint was published in North Carolina's *Salisbury Evening Post* on May 1: "Deal With Them Rough." In this piece the writer argues, "The efforts of the anarchists to terrorize the nation by sending bombs to prominent governmental officials and others, ought to be met with a strong hand, and dealt with vigorously. . . . It is certainly time for Uncle Sam to take his coat off and go after the nest of disloyals and anarchist [*sic*] with the determination to root them out and live up to a policy of America for Americans, with the doors sealed tight against the overstocked anarchists of other lands." See "Deal With Them Rough," *Salisbury (NC) Evening Post*, May 1, 1919.
77. Simon, *Terrorist Trap*, 5; Parry, *Terrorism*, 87–88.
78. Simon, "Forgotten Terrorists," 201.
79. Simon, "Forgotten Terrorists," 200, 202; "Bomb Plot"; Avrich, *Sacco and Vanzetti*, 159; Depaolis, *1978: A New Stage?*, 91–92. The Red Brigades issued many communiqués during the 1970s and 1980s. See Pluchinsky, *Reagan and George H. W. Bush Administrations*, 13–16.
80. "Find More Bombs Sent"; Simon, "Forgotten Terrorists," 202–3.
81. "Senator Has Great Praise for Veterans," *Dayton Herald*, May 31, 1919.

5. ROUNDUP

1. "Boston Red Sox at Washington Senators Box Score, June 2, 1919," Baseball-Reference.com, https://www.baseball-reference.com/boxes/WS1/WS1191906020.shtml.
2. DeMichael, *Baseball FAQ*, 41; Matthew Feeney, "Fear Beats Civil Liberties, Every Time," CATO Institute, April 7, 2017, https://www.cato.org/publications/commentary/fear-beats-civil-liberties-every-time; Reppetto, *Battleground New York City*, 96; Jeffrey Rosen, "Palmer Raids Redux: The NSA v. Civil Liberties," Reuters, June 12, 2013, https://www.reuters.com/article/us-rosen-nsa/palmer-raids-redux-the

-nsa-v-civil-liberties-idUSBRE95B0QQ20130612; "Maj. Pullman Tells How Police Handled Case," *Evening Star* (Washington DC), June 3, 1919.

3. "Bombs in 8 Cities Kill 5," *Chicago Daily Tribune*, June 3, 1919.
4. Reppetto, *Battleground New York City*, 96; "Bombs in 8 Cities Kill 5"; Hagedorn, *Savage Peace*, 219; Avrich, *Sacco and Vanzetti*, 153.
5. "Maj. Pullman Tells How"; Avrich, *Sacco and Vanzetti*, 153–56; McCormick, *Hopeless Cases*, 50–51; McCann, *Terrorism on American Soil*, 60; "Bombs in 8 Cities Kill 5."
6. Avrich, *Sacco and Vanzetti*, 149–50; "Text of 'Plain Words,' Anarchists' Circular," *Evening Star* (Washington DC), June 3, 1919.
7. Avrich, *Sacco and Vanzetti*, 149–50; "Text of 'Plain Words.'"
8. Avrich, *Sacco and Vanzetti*, 149–50; "Text of 'Plain Words.'"
9. Avrich, *Sacco and Vanzetti*, 152.
10. "Squirrel Hill and Sheraden Homes Are Struck by Shrapnel," *Pittsburgh Post-Gazette*, June 3, 1919; "Pittsburgh Homes Damaged by Bombs," *New York Times*, June 3, 1919; Avrich, *Sacco and Vanzetti*, 152.
11. "Squirrel Hill and Sheraden Homes"; "Pittsburgh Homes Damaged"; Avrich, *Sacco and Vanzetti*, 152.
12. Avrich, *Sacco and Vanzetti*, 148, 150.
13. "Maj. Pullman Tells How"; Tejada, *In Search of Sacco and Vanzetti*, 111; Avrich, *Sacco and Vanzetti*, 149; McCann, *Terrorism on American Soil*, 57; McCormick, *Hopeless Cases*, 39; "Bombs in 8 Cities Kill 5"; Kathy Weiser, "1919 Anarchist Bombings," Legends of America, last modified September 2019, https://www.legendsofamerica.com/ah-1919bombings/; "20 Pounds of Dynamite Used in New York," *Washington Post*, June 4, 1919.
14. Avrich, *Sacco and Vanzetti*, 151–52, 236n11.
15. Avrich, *Sacco and Vanzetti*, 150–51; Tejada, *In Search of Sacco and Vanzetti*, 111; "Police Here Start 'Red' Still Hunt," *Sun* (New York), June 4, 1919.
16. "Bombing Brigade Very Busy: Effort to Kill Att'y-General Palmer: Terror Reign in Many Cities," *Atlanta Constitution*, June 3, 1919; "Reign of Terror Starts," *Topeka (KS) Daily Capital*, June 3, 1919; Albert W. Fox, "Terrorism Must End," *Washington Post*, June 4, 1919. Fox mistakenly wrote that eight, not seven, cities were the sites of the bombings. Along with some others who listed eight and not seven cities attacked, he might have counted Newtonville, Massachusetts (a village in Newton where the bombing of State Representative Leland W. Powers's home occurred), as a separate city rather than a suburb of Boston, where there were two bombings that night.
17. "Brings Data on 'Red,'" *Washington Post*, June 8, 1919.
18. Avrich, *Sacco and Vanzetti*, 152; "Judge Hayden Says, 'I Can Not Be Intimidated,'" *Boston Globe*, June 3, 1919.

19. *Hearings before a [Senate] Subcommittee of the Committee on the Judiciary*, 66th Cong. 3rd Sess., January 19–March 3, 1921, 580 ("Charges of Illegal Practices of the Department of Justice"); "Clear and Present Danger: A. Mitchell Palmer Goes Hunting for Bolsheviks," *Lapham's Quarterly*, Spring 2014, https://www.laphamsquarterly.org/revolutions/clear-and-present-danger; Avrich, *Sacco and Vanzetti*, 166.
20. "Flynn, Here, Bares Workings of Vast German Spy System in United States," *Los Angeles Times*, April 7, 1918; Gage, *The Day Wall Street Exploded*, 126; "Clear and Present Danger." For an excellent account of Flynn's pursuit of counterfeiters and mobsters, see Dash, *First Family*.
21. McCormick, *Hopeless Cases*, 46; Gage, *The Day Wall Street Exploded*, 125–26; Weiner, *Enemies*, 21; "Flynn, Here, Bares Workings"; "W. J. Flynn, Noted Detective, Dead," *New York Times*, October 15, 1928.
22. "W. J. Flynn, Noted Detective"; Dash, *First Family*; Thomas P. Hunt, "The Barrel Mystery (1919) by William J. Flynn," MafiaHistory.us, no date, http://mafiahistory.us/a027/f_flynn.html#:~:text=The%20Barrel%20Mystery%22%20describes%20his,barrel%20on%20a%20Manhattan%20sidewalk.&text=The%20Barrel%20Mystery%22%20by%20William%20J; Flynn, *Barrel Mystery*; Gage, *The Day Wall Street Exploded*, 126; McCormick, *Hopeless Cases*, 79.
23. McCormick, *Hopeless Cases*, 44–45; Flynn, *Eagle's Eye*; "W. J. Flynn, Noted Detective"; "Chief Flynn Quits Secret Service; May Head Police," *New York Times*, December 23, 1917; "Directors, Then and Now: William J. Flynn, July 1, 1919–August 21, 1921," FBI.gov, no date, https://www.fbi.gov/history/directors/william-j-flynn; Frederic J. Haskin, "A New National Police Force," *Star Press* (Muncie IN), May 4, 1919.
24. "Flynn, Here, Bares Workings"; Flynn, *Eagle's Eye*; "Uncle Sam's Master Sleuth Rounds Up Traitors and Spies," *Ogden (UT) Standard*, March 19, 1917; "The U.S. Secret Service during the First World War," Department of Homeland Security World War I Centennial Poster Series, vol. 4, 2017, https://www.uscis.gov/sites/default/files/USCIS/History%20and%20Genealogy/Our%20History/WWI/WWI_18x24_USSS.pdf.
25. Gage, *The Day Wall Street Exploded*, 126; McCormick, *Hopeless Cases*, 45; Schmidt, *Red Scare*, 148, 150–51; Avrich, *Sacco and Vanzetti*, 168.
26. Brigadier General M. Churchill to W. E. Allen, June 5, 1919, Case Number 8000-364028, RG 65, OG, M1085, Fold3, NARA. In another analysis of the circular conducted almost a year later, the New Jersey branch of the Bureau of Investigation compared the style of writing in *Plain Words* with letters that Galleani had written in the past and found enough similarities to conclude that Galleani was the author of the leaflet. See "Summary Report in re Bomb Explosions of June 2, 1919. New Jersey Investigation," May 25, 1920, File Number 211205-X, BI, FOIA.

27. *Hearings before the [House] Committee on Rules*, 66th Cong., 2nd Sess., June 1, 1920, pt. 1, 159 ("Attorney General A. Mitchell Palmer on Charges Made against Department of Justice by Louis F. Post and Others"); "Bomb Plotters Sought on Ships by NY Officials," *Evening World* (New York), June 6, 1919; "Trail Reds in Secret," *Washington Post*, June 7, 1919.
28. *Hearings before Committee on Rules* (June 1, 1920), 159.
29. Gage, *The Day Wall Street Exploded*, 211; *Hearings before Committee on Rules* (June 1, 1920), 159; Avrich, *Sacco and Vanzetti*, 168. Another person convinced that the bombings were the work of the Galleanists was Rayme Finch, the former BI agent who'd spent many years investigating Galleani and his followers. He visited the New York branch of the bureau in August 1919 to offer his views on the case. "It is Mr. Finch's opinion," wrote an agent in his report, "that the bombs were exploded by friends of Luigi Galleani. The reason given by Mr. Finch is that Galleani's friends are bitter towards the government for having had Galleani deported, together with a number of other anarchists, also Galleani's friends." See P. Pigniuolo, "In re: Anarchist Activities, Bomb Explosions in the Cities of June 2nd," August 22, 1919, Case Number 360086, RG 65, BS, M1085, Fold3, NARA.
30. Avrich, *Sacco and Vanzetti*, 168; Gage, *The Day Wall Street Exploded*, 211.
31. "Summary Report in re Bomb Explosions of June 2, 1919." Galleani was deported on June 24, not June 2 as stated in the BI report.
32. Avrich, *Sacco and Vanzetti*, 135–36; Senta, *Luigi Galleani*, 184–86; McCormick, *Hopeless Cases*, 42.
33. Sayers, foreword, 6.
34. *Hearings before Committee on Rules* (June 1, 1920), 160; Gage, *The Day Wall Street Exploded*, 212; Avrich, *Sacco and Vanzetti*, 155. There is no record that investigators learned the name of the customer. It may be that the only information the laundry had was the street the customer lived on and not his name or exact address.
35. *Hearings before Committee on Rules* (June 1, 1920), 160; Memorandum, May 25, 1920, File Number 211205-X, BI, FOIA.
36. Memorandum, May 25, 1920; *Hearings before Committee on Rules* (June 1, 1920), 160.
37. Schmidt, *Red Scare*, 148; J. F. McDevitt, "Re: Bomb Explosions—June 2nd—Pro Prensa Society—Genaro Pazos—E. Paredes: Lugio [*sic*] Galleni [*sic*]," October 3, 1919, Case Number 360086, RG 65, BS, M1085, Fold3, NARA.
38. M. R. Valkenburgh, "In re: Bomb outrages in Washington DC, Cleveland, Boston, etc.; (Anarchistic Activities)," July 8, 1919, Case Number 360086, RG 65, BS, M1085, Fold3, NARA; Avrich, *Sacco and Vanzetti*, 62, 95, 156, 171–73.
39. "Conversation of Informant with Mario," January 14, 1920, Case Number 360086, RG 65, BS, M1085, Fold3, NARA; Weiner, *Enemies*, 44; *Hearings before Committee on Rules* (June 1, 1920), 163; Avrich, *Sacco and Vanzetti*, 171–73.

40. Avrich, *Sacco and Vanzetti*, 178–79; Gage, *The Day Wall Street Exploded*, 221–22; McCormick, *Hopeless Cases*, 54.
41. Avrich, *Sacco and Vanzetti*, 179–80.
42. Gage, *The Day Wall Street Exploded*, 213; Avrich, *Sacco and Vanzetti*, 181; McCormick, *Hopeless Cases*, 54; Memorandum by J. Edgar Hoover to Mr. Flynn, March 8, 1920, Case Number 360086, RG 65, BS, M1085, Fold3, NARA. Hoover, who met with Caminita on Ellis Island, believed he was telling the truth when he said that his group, L'Era Nuova, was not involved in the June 2 bombings. But Hoover shrewdly got Caminita to cooperate by initially telling him that some Italians had claimed he was the leader of the bomb plot. "This seemed to anger Caminetta [*sic*] exceedingly," Hoover wrote in another memo to Flynn on March 8, "and I told him that unless he came across with all the information he had that I thought the evidence was sufficient to send him to the penitentiary for twenty years, and that further if he told all that he knew I would more likely be able to arrange for the cancellation of his deportation, thus enabling him to return to his wife and child." See Memorandum by J. Edgar Hoover to Chief Flynn, March 8, 1920, Case Number 360086, RG 65, BS, M1085, Fold3, NARA.

    In the other memo to Flynn on March 8 (cited at the beginning of this note), Hoover wrote, "It is believed that the bombs were made at Gallinani's [*sic*] home in Massachusetts. While Gallianni [*sic*] himself has been deported, Caminetta [*sic*] claims that his children are carrying out the work of the father. There is living in Gallineani's [*sic*] house a man who is supposed to be the bomb maker. This individual has all of his fingers of his lefthand [*sic*] blown off." The man with all the fingers missing was Recchi.

    In the first memo listed here, Hoover's statement that Caminita "can not be handled in any third degree manner" refers to "the use of interrogation methods that inflict physical or mental pain on suspects in order to get the suspect to make a confession." See "The Third Degree of Coerced Confessions, before 1930," Coerced Confessions CRJA 3400, no date, https://sites.google.com/site/coercedconfessionscrja3400/home/third-degree-technique.
43. Avrich, *Sacco and Vanzetti*, 184–85; *Hearings before Committee on Rules* (June 1, 1920), 162; Gage, *The Day Wall Street Exploded*, 213.
44. Gage, *The Day Wall Street Exploded*, 214; Pernicone, *Carlo Tresca*, 116; Avrich, *Sacco and Vanzetti*, 196–97; *Hearings before Committee on Rules* (June 1, 1920), 163.
45. Avrich, *Sacco and Vanzetti*, 185, 192–94; Gage, *The Day Wall Street Exploded*, 214; McCormick, *Hopeless Cases*, 60; *Hearings before Committee on Rules* (June 1, 1920), 162.
46. Avrich, *Sacco and Vanzetti*, 195; "Red's Death Plunge, 14 Stories, Bares Long Bomb Trail," *New York Times*, May 4, 1920; "Witness in Bomb Plot Jumps 14 Stories to Death," *St. Louis Post-Dispatch*, May 3, 1920.

47. Zimmer, *Immigrants against the State*, 155; Bennett Muraskin, "Constructing Liberty: An Immigration Anthology," *Jewish Currents*, February 14, 2017, https://jewishcurrents.org/constructing-liberty-an-immigration-anthology/; Caminita, excerpt from *Becoming Americans*, 170–77. I would like to thank Kenyon Zimmer for the information regarding Ludovico Caminita's several arrests and subsequent releases from Ellis Island.
48. M. J. Davis, "In re: Bomb Outrage of June 2nd, 1919. 'Confidential Informant D-5,'" March 29, 1920, Case Number 360086, RG 65, BS, M1085, Fold3, NARA; Pernicone, *Carlo Tresca*, 115; McCormick, *Hopeless Cases*, 54; Avrich, *Sacco and Vanzetti*, 179–80.
49. *Hearings before Committee on Rules* (June 1, 1920), 163.
50. Avrich, *Sacco and Vanzetti*, 157–58.
51. Avrich, *Sacco and Vanzetti*, 157–58, 237n33; Gage, *The Day Wall Street Exploded*, 216; "Summary Report in re Bomb Explosions of June 2, 1919."
52. Avrich, *Sacco and Vanzetti*, 62, 157–58. One of the BI agents in Pittsburgh had some fun with his superiors in Washington when he was requested the day after the bombings to file a report about the progress of the investigation there. He wrote that, despite detaining and questioning about fifteen of the "dangerous radicals" in the area, "we have no definite clues as to the perpetrators of the outrages." The agent explained that their most valuable informant had been out of town for a few days, and they were working hard to get him back to learn more about the bombings that took place in Pittsburgh. Not afraid to use a little humor regarding the *Plain Words* leaflets found at the bomb sites, the agent wrote, "To speak in *plain words*, we are now working the dark. [Emphasis added.]" See "In re: Anarchist Bomb Explosion. Pittsburgh, Penn'a," June 3, 1919, Case Number 360086, RG 65, BS, M1085, Fold3, NARA.
53. Avrich, *Sacco and Vanzetti*, 158; William J. Flynn, "On the Trail of the Anarchist Band—Chief Flynn," *New York Herald*, March 5, 1922.
54. Avrich, *Sacco and Vanzetti*, 158.
55. McCormick, *Hopeless Cases*, 47.
56. Mark Kessler, "A. Mitchell Palmer," *First Amendment Encyclopedia*, 2009, https://www.mtsu.edu/first-amendment/article/1273/a-mitchell-palmer; Rosen, "Palmer Raids Redux"; Asinof, *1919: America's Loss*, 204–5; Hagedorn, *Savage Peace*, 226.
57. McCormick, *Hopeless Cases*, 44.
58. Weiner, *Enemies*, 3–5, 44–45; Hagedorn, *Savage Peace*, 327; McCormick, *Hopeless Cases*, 43; Avrich, *Sacco and Vanzetti*, 167; Schmidt, *Red Scare*, 158. The Radical Division was also known as the General Intelligence Division.
59. Gage, *The Day Wall Street Exploded*, 128; Hagedorn, *Savage Peace*, 328; McCormick, *Hopeless Cases*, 43; Adam Hochschild, "When America Tried to Deport Its Radicals,"

New Yorker, November 4, 2019, https://www.newyorker.com/magazine/2019/11/11/when-america-tried-to-deport-its-radicals; Avrich, *Sacco and Vanzetti*, 168.

60. Feeney, "Fear Beats Civil Liberties"; Schmidt, *Red Scare*, 162–64; Avrich, *Sacco and Vanzetti*, 167; Hagedorn, *Savage Peace*, 328–30; Gage, *The Day Wall Street Exploded*, 128.
61. Hagedorn, *Savage Peace*, 329–30, 382–83; Hochschild, "When America Tried"; Gage, *The Day Wall Street Exploded*, 28, 128–29; Asinof, *1919: America's Loss*, 208–9; Avrich, *Sacco and Vanzetti*, 175.
62. Hagedorn, *Savage Peace*, 412–13; Avrich, *Sacco and Vanzetti*, 175; Schmidt, *Red Scare*, 275.
63. Post, *Deportations Delirium*, 5–6.
64. Weiner, *Enemies*, 35; Hagedorn, *Savage Peace*, 420–22; Topp, *Sacco and Vanzetti Case*, 17, 83; Avrich, *Sacco and Vanzetti*, 175; Post, *Deportations Delirium*, 98, 100, 121, 209. Following the January raids, Simon Wolf, a prominent Washington lawyer who represented the B'nai B'rith, an international Jewish organization, and the Union of American Hebrew Congregations, wrote to Attorney General Palmer inquiring whether "any men of the Jewish faith" were arrested in the raids. Wolf was worried that if there were Jewish radicals among those arrested, it could tarnish the image of the Jewish organizations, both of which "are in full accord with the United States Government in its effort to crush and destroy the enemies of law and order." Palmer wrote back that "there were a large number of Russian Jews among those arrested." But he tried to put Wolf at ease, pointing out that those radicals arrested may no longer be Jewish. "It is impossible to state at the present," Palmer wrote, "whether or not these persons still adhere to the Jewish faith, for previous investigations by the department have shown that many of the persons arrested as alien anarchists are atheists in belief and while previously members of the Jewish faith have renounced that faith and are at the present time in no way connected with any religion." See Simon Wolf to Hon. A. M. Palmer, January 3, 1920, RG 60, DJ Central Files, Straight Numerical Files 202600-117, NARA; A. Mitchell Palmer to Honorable Simon Wolf, January 9, 1920, RG 60, DJ Central Files, Straight Numerical Files 202600-117, NARA.
65. "Red Backbone Broken by Raid Says Official," *Los Angeles Evening Express*, January 3, 1920; Hochschild, "When America Tried"; Post, *Deportations Delirium*, 161.
66. Weiner, *Enemies*, 40; Hochschild, "When America Tried"; Post, *Deportations Delirium*, 148–49.
67. Avrich, *Sacco and Vanzetti*, 176; Hochschild, "When America Tried"; Gage, *The Day Wall Street Exploded*, 181; Weiner, *Enemies*, 40. Post writes that he canceled thousands of deportation warrants. "I decided as consistently as I could, the 3,700 to 4,000 'red' cases which it became my official duty to decide, ordering about

700 aliens to be deported and cancelling (in addition to the 300 Communist Labor Party warrants that were cancelled by instructions from Secretary Wilson), about 2,700 of the warrants under which the regular hearings in the 'red' cases had been held." See Post, *Deportations Delirium*, 187.

68. Post, *Deportations Delirium*, 147.
69. Post, *Deportations Delirium*, 209.
70. Thomas J. Callaghan to Frank Burke, Esq., March 20, 1920, Case Number 385499, RG 65, OG, M1085, Fold3, NARA; Weiner, *Enemies*, 40–45; Hochschild, "When America Tried"; Post, *Deportations Delirium*, 245.
71. Hochschild, "When America Tried"; Schmidt, *Red Scare*, 236; *To the American People: Report Upon the Illegal Practices of the United States Department of Justice* (Washington DC: National Popular Government League, 1920), 4.
72. *To the American People*, 3.
73. Hochschild, "When America Tried"; Weiner, *Enemies*, 44–45.
74. "Third International," *Encyclopedia Britannica*, last modified April 28, 2017, https://www.britannica.com/topic/Third-International; McCormick, *Hopeless Cases*, 47.

6. FINAL BLOW

1. James, "Story of Mario Buda," 4.
2. Avrich, *Sacco and Vanzetti*, 9–10, 15, 19–21, 26, 62; James, "Story of Mario Buda," 12; Robert D'Attilio, "La Salute è in Voi: The Anarchist Dimension," Sacco and Vanzetti Commemoration Society, no date, https://saccoandvanzetti.org/sn_display1.php?row_ID=14; Presutto, "'Man Who Blew Up Wall Street,'" 83, 86; Topp, *Sacco and Vanzetti Case*, 9, 11.
3. Avrich, *Sacco and Vanzetti*, 25–26, 31–37.
4. James, "Story of Mario Buda," 12–13; Avrich, *Sacco and Vanzetti*, 60, 62–63, 65–67.
5. Avrich, *Sacco and Vanzetti*, 157, 201–2.
6. Tejada, *In Search of Sacco and Vanzetti*, 4; Watson, *Sacco and Vanzetti*, 35; Dorothy G. Wayman, "Sacco-Vanzetti: The Unfinished Debate," *American Heritage*, December 1959, https://www.americanheritage.com/sacco-vanzetti-unfinished-debate#2.
7. Tejada, *In Search of Sacco and Vanzetti*, 4–5; Rick Collins, "Sacco-Vanzetti Case Still Poses Mystery," *Patriot Ledger*, May 4, 2005, http://www.southofboston.net/specialreports/saccovanzetti/pages/050405.shtml.
8. Tejada, *In Search of Sacco and Vanzetti*, 5, 315n16.
9. Avrich, *Sacco and Vanzetti*, 199–201; Topp, *Sacco and Vanzetti Case*, 20.
10. Felix Frankfurter, "Case of Sacco and Vanzetti," *Atlantic*, March 1927, https://www.theatlantic.com/magazine/archive/1927/03/the-case-of-sacco-and-vanzetti/306625/; Pernicone, *Carlo Tresca*, 117–18; Tejada, *In Search of Sacco and Vanzetti*, 6, 22–26; McCormick, *Hopeless Cases*, 97–98.

11. Tejada, *In Search of Sacco and Vanzetti*, 26; Avrich, *Sacco and Vanzetti*, 203–4; "Red's Death Plunge, 14 Stories, Bares Long Bomb Trail," *New York Times*, May 4, 1920; "Suicide Betrayed Lynn Anarchists," *Boston Globe*, May 4, 1920. The *New York Times* story identifies both Salsedo and Elia as cooperating; the *Boston Globe* story only mentions Salsedo and states that unidentified others were cooperating.

    The Galleanists had actually been advised earlier to get rid of any incriminating materials related to their anarchist activities that could result in deportation. Carlo Tresca, the prominent Italian anarchist who had disagreements with Galleanists in the past but who "was a tolerant and forgiving man," told Vanzetti to get rid of the materials when Vanzetti went to New York in April to learn about the holding of Roberto Elia and Andrea Salsedo incommunicado by federal agents. He warned Vanzetti that the government might be planning new raids against anarchists. See Pernicone, *Carlo Tresca*, 116–17.
12. Tejeda, *In Search of Sacco and Vanzetti*, 27–28; Avrich, *Sacco and Vanzetti*, 199, 201–2. Orciani was arrested and released, but Buda was never found. See Avrich, *Sacco and Vanzetti*, 204–7.
13. Tejeda, *In Search of Sacco and Vanzetti*, 28–29; Pernicone, *Carlo Tresca*, 117; Topp, *Sacco and Vanzetti Case*, 18–19; Avrich, *Sacco and Vanzetti*, 199, 202–3.
14. Topp, *Sacco and Vanzetti Case*, 19–21; Tejeda, *In Search of Sacco and Vanzetti*, 75–85; Avrich, *Sacco and Vanzetti*, 203–5.
15. Avrich, *Sacco and Vanzetti*, 3–4.
16. Topp, *Sacco and Vanzetti Case*, 2–3, 39, 43–44; Tejeda, *In Search of Sacco and Vanzetti*, 260; "Sacco and Vanzetti Followed by 7,000 in Boston Funeral," *New York Times*, August 29, 1927; Avrich, *Sacco and Vanzetti*, 5–6.
17. Avrich, *Sacco and Vanzetti*, 207, 210; "Mike Boda Still in Prison in Italy," *Boston Globe*, September 29, 1932; James, "Story of Mario Buda," 1, 14.
18. "Blueblood Crusades for Sacco and Vanzetti, Says Men Represent a Cause," *Dayton (OH) Daily News*, June 1, 1927; James, "Story of Mario Buda," 1, 15.
19. Avrich, *Sacco and Vanzetti*, 210; "Seeks to Clear Names of Sacco, Vanzetti," *St. Louis Post-Dispatch*, April 30, 1932.
20. "May Shed Light on Sacco Case," *Boston Globe*, September 27, 1932; "The Return of Mario Buda," *St. Louis Post-Dispatch*, November 26, 1932.
21. "See Hard Time for Boda," *Boston Globe*, April 30, 1932.
22. "Boda Disappeared after Braintree Slaying," *Boston Globe*, April 29, 1932; "See Hard Time for Boda"; "Seeks to Clear Names"; "Sacco & Vanzetti. New Facts Supporting Plea of Innocence," *Manchester Guardian* (UK), December 3, 1928; Topp, *Sacco and Vanzetti Case*, 20. Sacco and Vanzetti's defense team contended during the trial that if Buda could be brought to testify, he could produce evidence that a bandit group known as the Morelli gang was responsible for the

South Braintree attack. See "Seeks to Clear Names"; Avrich, *Sacco and Vanzetti*, 4; Tejeda, *In Search of Sacco and Vanzetti*, 212–13.

23. "Two Romances of Brooklynites Ended by Blast," *Brooklyn Daily Times*, September 17, 1920; "34 Dead in Blast, 16 from Bklyn-LI, 53 in Hospitals," *Brooklyn Daily Eagle*, September 18, 1920; "Victim of Blast Wounded in War," *Evening World* (New York), September 18, 1920; "Victory Day Plans Ready," *Brooklyn Daily Times*, December 26, 1918.
24. "Laugh at Death in France Only to Find It in Wall St.," *Chicago Tribune*, September 17, 1920; Gage, *The Day Wall Street Exploded*, 1, 329–30. All but $20,000 of the securities were recovered. See "Laugh at Death."
25. Simon, "Forgotten Terrorists," 205; "Wall Street Explosion Kills 30, Injures 300; Morgan Office Hit, Bomb Pieces Found; Toronto Fugitive Sent Warnings Here," *New York Times*, September 17, 1920; "Hospital Forces Taxed to Limit by Wounded Scores," *New York Daily News*, September 17, 1920; Avrich, *Sacco and Vanzetti*, 205–6; Bill Torpy, "Echoes of a Blast: Before There Was a September 11, There Was a September 16, 1920," *Atlanta Journal-Constitution*, December 14, 2001; "Boy's Rescue Work," *Gazette* (Montreal), September 17, 1920.
26. Avrich, *Sacco and Vanzetti*, 205–6; Torpy, "Echoes of a Blast"; Simon, "Forgotten Terrorists," 205; "Wall Street Explosion Kills 30."
27. Simon, "Forgotten Terrorists," 205–6; Simon, *Terrorist Trap*, 5; Parry, *Terrorism*, 87–88; Gage, *The Day Wall Street Exploded*, 171; Avrich, *Sacco and Vanzetti*, 206.
28. Avrich, *Sacco and Vanzetti*, 206; Simon, "Forgotten Terrorists," 206; "Red Bomb in NY," *Chicago Daily Tribune*, September 17, 1920; "30 Die in Wall St. Blast; Traced to Red Bomb," *Washington Herald*, September 17, 1920; "Blame Reds in Wall St. Horror," *Los Angeles Times*, September 17, 1920; "To Put Down Terrorists," *New York Times*, September 18, 1920.
29. Simon, "Forgotten Terrorists," 206; "To Put Down Terrorists."
30. Avrich, *Sacco and Vanzetti*, 206; Simon, "Forgotten Terrorists," 206; "Bomb Plot, Says Palmer," *New York Times*, September 18, 1920; "Flynn Hastens to Scene," *Los Angeles Times*, September 17, 1920.
31. "Flynn Hastens to Scene"; Avrich, *Sacco and Vanzetti*, 206; Simon, "Forgotten Terrorists," 206; William J. Flynn, "On the Trail of the Anarchist Band—Chief Flynn," *New York Herald*, March 5, 1922.
32. McCormick, *Hopeless Cases*, 125–26; Gage, *The Day Wall Street Exploded*, 136–38, 141.
33. Gage, *The Day Wall Street Exploded*, 137; "Detective Burns Says Police Have Enough Evidence to Find Bombers in Ten Days," *Washington Times*, September 17, 1920.
34. Gage, *The Day Wall Street Exploded*, 141–42, 150–53, 168; McCormick, *Hopeless Cases*, 69–70, 75; "Wall Street Bombing 1920," FBI, no date, https://www.fbi.gov/history/famous-cases/wall-street-bombing-1920.

35. G. O. Holdridge to William J. Flynn, October 15, 1920, File Number 61-5, BI, FOIA.
36. J. S. Johnson, "Statement of J. J. Dobbyn, Manager Hollister Lynn & Walton, 7 Wall Street, NY City," September 21, 1920, File Number 61-5, BI, FOIA; Gage, *The Day Wall Street Exploded*, 133; "Review and Outlook: Dynamite for Wall Street," *Wall Street Journal*, September 17, 1920.
37. C. J. Scully to Director W. J. Flynn, memorandum, "In re: Wall Street Explosion," October 18, 1920, File Number 61-5, BI, FOIA; Gage, *The Day Wall Street Exploded*, 325.
38. Gage, *The Day Wall Street Exploded*, 215.
39. Gage, *The Day Wall Street Exploded*, 175–77; McCormick, *Hopeless Cases*, 77; "Bomb Plot Day Set in Warning," *Sun and New York Herald*, September 18, 1920.
40. "Calls Psychic 'Tip' of Fischer Feasible," *New York Times*, September 19, 1920.
41. "Question Zelenko Closely," *Citizen* (Ottawa), October 4, 1920; Gage, *The Day Wall Street Exploded*, 204; McCormick, *Hopeless Cases*, 77–79. It was also reported that Zelenko did not intend to stay in Pittsburgh and instead had a layover there before he was to take a train to New York City. See "Arrest May Lead to a Solution of Wall St. Disaster," *Citizen* (Ottawa), October 4, 1920.
42. McCormick, *Hopeless Cases*, 77–79; Gage, *The Day Wall Street Exploded*, 204; "Zelenska Accused under Commerce Act," *New York Times*, October 6, 1920; "Considers Zelenko Innocent of Bomb," *Los Angeles Evening Express*, October 5, 1920; "Zelenko Stole the Dynamite," *Kansas City (MO) Star*, October 5, 1920; "Zelenko Examined about Dynamite," *Lancaster (PA) New Era*, October 5, 1920. There are different spellings of Zelenko's name in various newspapers, but "Zelenko" is the version that appears most frequently in government documents. See Gage, *The Day Wall Street Exploded*, 365n43. There are also two different variations of his first name. Some newspapers and scholarly sources used "Florean," while others went with "Florian."
43. Scully to Director Flynn, memorandum, October 18, 1920. George Lamb, the BI's New York division superintendent, assigned his entire force of fifteen thousand men to canvass all the Italian stables in New York City "on the theory that the Galliani [*sic*] group may be connected with the outrage." See Mr. Lamb to Mr. Neal, "Memorandum of Telephone Information," September 17, 1920, 4:30 p.m., File Number 61-5-211205-2X, BI, FOIA.
44. Special Assistant to the Attorney General to Mr. Hatrick, General Manager, International Film Service, December 30, 1920, File Number 211205-412, BI, FOIA; Special Assistant to the Attorney General to H. E. Hancock, Esq., Editor, Fox Film News, December 30, 1920, File Number 211205-413, BI, FOIA; Memorandum to Mr. Hoover, December 16, 1920, File Number 61-5-0, BI, FOIA; The Associated Screen News to Mr. W. W. Grimes, January 6, 1921, File Number 211205-420X, BI,

FOIA; McCormick, *Hopeless Cases*, 89–90. The sign at the site of the bombing read, "Albert A. Volk Co. House Wreckers, New York, 20th St. & 11th Ave." The firm did excavating as well as wrecking. See "Skyscrapers Torn Down," *Popular Science*, January 1936, 14.

45. "Wall Street Explosion Solved; Bomb in Building Trade Graft. Set in Revenge upon Brindell. Not Anarchists, but Men Blackjacked Out of Jobs," *Evening World* (New York), November 11, 1920; McCormick, *Hopeless Cases*, 89–91.
46. Nathan Ward, "The Fire Last Time," *American Heritage*, November/December 2001, https://www.americanheritage.com/fire-last-time; Avrich, *Sacco and Vanzetti*, 207; Capo, Zuckerman, and Zuckerman, *It Happened in New York City*, 61; Martinez, *Terrorist Attacks on American Soil*, 139–40; McCormick, *Hopeless Cases*, 110–18; Gage, *The Day Wall Street Exploded*, 242–53.
47. McCormick, *Hopeless Cases*, 109, 118; Gage, *The Day Wall Street Exploded*, 261.
48. McCormick, *Hopeless Cases*, 131–33; Gage, *The Day Wall Street Exploded*, 281–90; "Third International," *Encyclopedia Britannica*, last modified April 28, 2017, https://www.britannica.com/topic/Third-International. Burns also became embroiled in a scandal when he used BI agents to try to gather evidence of criminal activity on the part of Senator Burton K. Wheeler from Montana, who had called for Congress to investigate abuses in the Justice Department. See McCormick, *Hopeless Cases*, 140–41; and Gage, *The Day Wall Street Exploded*, 321.
49. Gage, *The Day Wall Street Exploded*, 322, 324.
50. Scully to Director Flynn, memorandum, October 18, 1920; Gage, *The Day Wall Street Exploded*, 324–25; Flynn, "On the Trail."
51. Avrich, *Sacco and Vanzetti*, 64, 103, 207; James, "Story of Mario Buda," 15; Basso, "Italian in America," 193–208.
52. Avrich, *Sacco and Vanzetti*, 199–202.
53. James, "Story of Mario Buda," 5.
54. Avrich, *Sacco and Vanzetti*, 204–7.
55. Avrich, *Sacco and Vanzetti*, 245n32, 159; Davis, *Buda's Wagon*, 2; Gage, *The Day Wall Street Exploded*, 325–26; Simon, "Forgotten Terrorists," 202; Zimmer, *Immigrants against the State*, 152; Watson, *Sacco and Vanzetti*, 77; Watson, "Prime Suspect," *New York Times*, March 18, 2009; Tejada, *In Search of Sacco and Vanzetti*, 278–79; Pernicone, "Luigi Galleani," 469–70, 487.
56. Avrich, *Sacco and Vanzetti*, 212–13.

7. THE LEGACY OF THE GALLEANISTS

1. James Barron, "After 1920 Blast, the Opposite of 'Never Forget': No Memorials on Wall St. for Attack That Killed 30," *New York Times*, September 17, 2003; Gage, *The Day Wall Street Exploded*, 1; Simon, "Forgotten Terrorists," 208–9.
2. Simon, "Forgotten Terrorists," 208–9.

3. Gage, *The Day Wall Street Exploded*, 165; Barron, "After 1920 Blast."
4. Gage, "Explosion on Wall Street," 11; Simon, "Forgotten Terrorists," 208.
5. Simon, "Forgotten Terrorists," 195, 209.
6. Simon, "Forgotten Terrorists," 209.
7. Simon, "Forgotten Terrorists," 209.
8. Simon, *Alphabet Bomber*, 172–74.
9. Simon, *Alphabet Bomber*, 174.
10. Mary Elizabeth Dean, "Defining Closure Psychology," BetterHelp.com, May 11, 2020, last modified January 26, 2021, https://www.betterhelp.com/advice/relations/defining-closure-psychology/; Abigail Brenner, "5 Ways to Find Closure from the Past," *Psychology Today*, April 6, 2011, https://www.psychologytoday.com/us/blog/in-flux/201104/5-ways-find-closure-the-past.
11. See Simon, *Lone Wolf Terrorism*, 78–79, for the discussion of Epstein.
12. Gary Brown, "Monday After: Remembering the Wall Street Bombing 100 Years Ago," *Canton (OH) Repository*, September 21, 2020, https://www.cantonrep.com/story/news/local/canton/2020/09/21/monday-after-remembering-wall-street-bombing-100-years-ago/42673125/.
13. Emily Bazelon, "Why Some Terrorist Attacks Go Unsolved," *Slate*, April 18, 2013, https://slate.com/news-and-politics/2013/04/boston-marathon-bombing-why-some-terrorist-attacks-go-unsolved-and-what-clues-they-offer-for-the-attack-in-boston.html; Don Babwin, "25 Years Later, Tylenol Tampering Case Remains Unsolved," *Orange County Register*, September 29, 2007, https://www.ocregister.com/2007/09/29/25-years-later-tylenol-tampering-case-remains-unsolved/; Simon, *Alphabet Bomber*, 180; Andy Rose and Hollie Silverman, "A Judge Has Approved an $800 Million Settlement for Victims of the Las Vegas Shooting," CNN.com, last modified September 30, 2020, https://www.cnn.com/2020/09/30/us/las-vegas-shooting-settlement-approved/index.html; Ryan Gaydos, "Las Vegas Shooting Still a Mystery as FBI Closes Investigation," FoxNews.com, January 29, 2019, https://www.foxnews.com/us/las-vegas-shooting-still-a-mystery-as-fbi-closes-investigation.
14. Simon, "Forgotten Terrorists," 196–97, 209; Avrich, *Sacco and Vanzetti*, 51–52; Galleani, *End of Anarchism?*, 61.
15. Davis, *Buda's Wagon*, 1–2; Avrich, *Sacco and Vanzetti*, 65, 99, 158; McCormick, *Hopeless Cases*, 36; Simon, "Forgotten Terrorists," 197, 209, 214n60.
16. Simon, *Lone Wolf Terrorism*, 34; Kevin Grisham, "Far-Right Groups Move to Messaging Apps as Tech Companies Crack Down on Extremist Social Media," *Conversation*, January 22, 2021, https://theconversation.com/far-right-groups-move-to-messaging-apps-as-tech-companies-crack-down-on-extremist-social-media-153181.
17. Simon, *Lone Wolf Terrorism*, 237–39; Simon, "Forgotten Terrorists," 210.
18. Simon, "Forgotten Terrorists," 210; Simon, *Lone Wolf Terrorism*, 237–39.

19. Simon, "Forgotten Terrorists," 210; Simon, *Terrorist Trap*, 216.
20. Rapoport, "Four Waves of Modern Terrorism"; Simon, "Forgotten Terrorists," 196; Avrich, *Sacco and Vanzetti*, 174–75; Post, *Deportations Delirium*, 308–9. For a discussion of Rapoport's wave theory, see note 36 in chapter 3.
21. Avrich, *Sacco and Vanzetti*, 184–85, 192–94, 196–97; Gage, *The Day Wall Street Exploded*, 213–14; McCormick, *Hopeless Cases*, 58, 60; *Hearings before the [House] Committee on Rules*, 66th Cong., 2nd Sess., June 1, 1920, pt. 1, 162–63 ("Attorney General A. Mitchell Palmer on Charges Made Against Department of Justice by Louis F. Post and Others").
22. Gage, *The Day Wall Street Exploded*, 310–11.
23. "Civil Liberties," Gallup, no date, https://news.gallup.com/poll/5263/civil-liberties.aspx. In a nationwide survey conducted by Michigan State University between November 14, 2001, and January 15, 2002, respondents specified which civil liberties they were willing to give up in the aftermath of the 9/11 attacks. Sixty percent favored censoring school teachers, restricting their freedom to say anything critical of U.S. counterterrorism policy. More than half the respondents (54 percent) favored everybody having to carry national ID cards. Almost half the respondents (47 percent) supported detaining suspected terrorists indefinitely. And 23 percent were in favor of allowing searches without court warrants. See Davis and Silver, "Civil Liberties vs. Security."
24. Simon, "Forgotten Terrorists," 211.
25. Crenshaw, "Causes of Terrorism," 123; Simon, *Terrorist Trap*, 24. Personal grievance and moral outrage have been found by researchers to be among the factors explaining lone-wolf terrorist behavior. See Meloy and Genzman, "Clinical Threat Assessment," 655.
26. Simon, *Terrorist Trap*, 23–24; Price, "Revenge."
27. The Ludlow Massacre was cited by Nestor Dondoglio, a.k.a. "Jean Crones" (the Galleanist discussed in the introduction who poisoned the soup at the banquet dinner held in honor of the newly appointed archbishop of Chicago in February 1916), as the reason why he became an anarchist in the first place. See "Crones Now Gives 2 Days to Get Him," *New York Times*, February 19, 1916.
28. Lizzie Dearden, "Osama bin Laden's Son Calls for Terrorists to Avenge His Father's Death," *Independent*, November 8, 2017, https://www.independent.co.uk/news/world/middle-east/osama-bin-laden-son-revenge-terror-attacks-calls-hamza-avenge-fathers-dead-al-qaeda-resurgence-strength-syria-a8044571.html; Bridget Johnson, "6 Terrorism Trends to Watch in 2020," *Homeland Security Today*, January 11, 2020, https://www.hstoday.us/subject-matter-areas/infrastructure-security/6-terrorism-trends-to-watch-in-2020/; "How IS Leader Abu Bakr al-Baghdadi Was Cornered by the US," BBC News, October 27, 2019, https://www.bbc.com/news/av/world-middle-east-50203917.

29. Simon, *Alphabet Bomber*, 156–57.
30. Avrich, *Sacco and Vanzetti*, 52, 64; Sayers, foreword, 6.
31. Sayers, foreword, 11.

8. BACK HOME AGAIN

1. L. Galleani to Joe Russo, November 12, 1920, Case Number 202600-2159, RG 65, BS, M1085, Fold3, NARA.
2. Avrich, *Sacco and Vanzetti*, 208, 245n4; Senta, *Luigi Galleani*, 188–89; L. Galleani to Joe Russo, April 11, 1921, Case Number 202600-2159, RG 65, BS, M1085, Fold3, NARA; M. Bombino to Joe Russo, December 14, 1920, Case Number 202600-2159, RG 65, BS, M1085, Fold3, NARA.
3. Senta, *Luigi Galleani*, 197–98; Raffaele Schiavina, "A Fragment of Luigi Galleani's Life," Kate Sharpley Library, no date, https://www.katesharpleylibrary.net/d51cvp; Gage, *The Day Wall Street Exploded*, 228; Avrich, *Sacco and Vanzetti*, 209, 213. It is not known why Galleani decided to turn himself in. Senta writes that he did this "against the advice of his closest comrades." See Senta, *Luigi Galleani*, 198.
4. Gage, *The Day Wall Street Exploded*, 226–28; Senta, *Luigi Galleani*, 198.
5. Gage, *The Day Wall Street Exploded*, 227–28; Senta, *Luigi Galleani*, 188, 198.
6. Avrich, *Sacco and Vanzetti*, 209; Senta, *Luigi Galleani*, 198–99.
7. Senta, *Luigi Galleani*, 199–200; Avrich, *Sacco and Vanzetti*, 209; Sartin [pseudonym], introduction, 14–15. The introduction in *The End of Anarchism?* (for the first English-language edition published in 1982) is attributed to "Max Sartin," who was really Raffaele Schiavina. Schiavina writes that in early 1924, Galleani was released from prison, whereas Senta claims it was late 1923.
8. Avrich, *Sacco and Vanzetti*, 209; Galleani, *End of Anarchism?*, 60; Senta, *Luigi Galleani*, 199, 201.
9. Senta, *Luigi Galleani*, 199–200, 205; Galleani to Joe Russo, September 1, 1920, Case Number 202600-2159, RG 65, BS, M1085, Fold3, NARA.
10. Senta, *Luigi Galleani*, 202–3.
11. Senta, *Luigi Galleani*, 202–3; Avrich, *Sacco and Vanzetti*, 212; Watson, *Sacco and Vanzetti*, 264; Robert D'Attilio, "La Salute è in Voi: The Anarchist Dimension," Sacco and Vanzetti Commemoration Society, no date, https://saccoandvanzetti.org/sn_display1.php?row_ID=14.
12. Senta, *Luigi Galleani*, 201–2.
13. Senta, *Luigi Galleani*, 203–4; Avrich, *Sacco and Vanzetti*, 208–11; Basso, "Italian in America," 193–208.
14. Senta, *Luigi Galleani*, 204–5; Avrich, *Sacco and Vanzetti*, 209.
15. Senta, *Luigi Galleani*, 207–8.
16. Senta, *Luigi Galleani*, 208–9; Avrich, *Sacco and Vanzetti*, 209.
17. Avrich, *Anarchist Voices*, 111, 120, 157.

BIBLIOGRAPHY

Asinof, Eliot. *1919: America's Loss of Innocence*. New York: Donald I. Fine, 1990.

Avrich, Paul. *Anarchist Voices: An Oral History of Anarchism in America*. Oakland CA: AK Press, 2005. First published 1995 by Princeton University Press (Princeton NJ).

———. *Sacco and Vanzetti: The Anarchist Background*. Princeton NJ: Princeton University Press, 1991.

Avrich, Paul, and Karen Avrich. *Sasha and Emma: The Anarchist Odyssey of Alexander Berkman and Emma Goldman*. Cambridge MA: Belknap Press of Harvard University Press, 2012.

Barry, John M. *The Great Influenza: The Story of the Deadliest Pandemic in History*. New York: Penguin Books, 2004.

Basso, Chiara. "An Italian in America: Mario Buda, the Man Who Blew Up Wall Street." *Italies* 5 (2001): 193–208. https://translate.google.com/translate?hl=en&sl=it&u=https://journals.openedition.org/italies/2048&prev=search&pto=aue.

Burns, William. *The Masked War*. Mass Violence in America, edited by Robert M. Fogelson and Richard E. Rubenstein. Reprint, New York: Arno Press and *New York Times*, 1969.

Caminita, Ludovico. Excerpt from *On the Island of Tears: Ellis Island*. In *Becoming Americans: Immigrants Tell Their Stories from Jamestown to Today*, edited by Ilan Stavans, 170–77. New York: Library of America, 2009.

Capo, Frank, Art Zuckerman, and Susan Zuckerman. *It Happened in New York City: Remarkable Events That Shaped History*. Guilford CT: Morris Book Publishing, 2010.

Carey, George W. "The Vessel, the Deed, and the Idea: Anarchists in Paterson, 1895–1908." *Antipode* 10–11, no. 3–1 (December 1978): 46–58.

Colby, Frank Moore, ed. *The International Year Book: A Compendium of the World's Progress during the Year 1902*. New York: Dodd, Mead and Company, 1903.

Cowan, Geoffrey. *The People v. Clarence Darrow: The Bribery Trial of America's Greatest Lawyer*. New York: Times Books/Random House, 1993.

Crenshaw, Martha. "The Causes of Terrorism." In *International Terrorism: Characteristics, Causes, Controls*, edited by Charles W. Kegley Jr., 113–26. New York: St. Martin's Press, 1990.

Dash, Mike. *The First Family: Terror, Extortion and the Birth of the American Mafia*. New York: Random House, 2009.

David, Henry. Excerpt from *The History of the Haymarket Affair: A Study in the American Social-Revolutionary and Labor Movements*. In *The Terrorism Reader: The Essential Source Book on Political Violence Both Past and Present*, rev. ed., edited by Walter Laqueur and Yonah Alexander, 111. New York: Meridian, 1987.

Davis, Darren W., and Brian D. Silver. "Civil Liberties vs. Security: Public Opinion in the Context of the Terrorist Attacks on America." *American Journal of Political Science* 48, no. 1 (January 2004): 28–46. https://doi.org/10.2307/1519895.

Davis, Mike. *Buda's Wagon: A Brief History of the Car Bomb*. London: Verso, 2007.

DeMichael, Tom. *Baseball FAQ: All That's Left to Know About America's Pastime*. Montclair NJ: Backbeat Theatre & Cinema Books, 2015.

Depaolis, Joshua, trans. and ed. *1978: A New Stage in the Class War? Selected Documents on the Spring Campaign of the Red Brigades*. Montreal: Kersplebedeb, 2019.

Edmund, Jayme. "Protests, Pageants, and Publications: Narratives of Labor Agitators, 1913–1914." Master's thesis, University of Northern Iowa, 2017. https://scholarworks.uni.edu/cgi/viewcontent.cgi?article=1362&context=etd.

Flynn, William J. *The Barrel Mystery*. New York: James A. McCann Company, 1919.

———. *The Eagle's Eye: A True Story of the Imperial German Government's Spies and Intrigues in America from Facts Furnished by William J. Flynn, Recently Retired, Chief of the U.S. Secret Service, Novelized by Courtney Ryley Cooper*. New York: McCann Company, 1919.

Foner, Philip S. *The AFL in the Progressive Era: 1910–1915*. Vol. 5 of *History of the Labor Movement in the United States*. New York: McGraw-Hill, 1985.

Gage, Beverly. *The Day Wall Street Exploded: A Story of America in Its First Age of Terror*. New York: Oxford University Press, 2009.

———. "Explosion on Wall Street." *New York Archives* 2, no. 2 (Fall 2002).

Galleani, Luigi. *The End of Anarchism?* Translated by Max Sartin [pseudonym] and Robert D'Attilio. London: Elephant Editions, 2012. First published in English in 1982 by Cienfuegos Press (Orkney, Scotland). First published in Italian in 1925 by *L'Adunata dei Refrattari* editors (Newark NJ).

Gordon, Michael A. "'To Make a Clean Sweep': Milwaukee Confronts an Anarchist Scare in 1917." *Wisconsin Magazine of History* 93, no. 2 (Winter 2009–10): 16–27.

Guglielmo, Jennifer. *Living the Revolution: Italian Women's Resistance and Radicalism in New York City, 1880–1945*. Chapel Hill: University of North Carolina Press, 2012.

Hagedorn, Ann. *Savage Peace: Hope and Fear in America, 1919*. New York: Simon & Schuster, 2007.

Hoyt, Andrew Douglas. "And They Called Them 'Galleanisti': The Rise of the *Cronaca Sovversiva* and the Formation of America's Most Infamous Anarchist Faction (1895–1912)." PhD diss., University of Minnesota, 2018. https://conservancy.umn

.edu/bitstream/handle/11299/200170/Hoyt_umn_0130E_19406.pdf?sequence=1&isAllowed=y.

Hunt, Thomas. *Wrongly Executed? The Long-Forgotten Context of Charles Sberna's 1939 Electrocution*. Whiting VT: Seven-Seven-Eight, 2016.

James, Edward Houlton. "The Story of Mario Buda Before the Jury of the World." Typescript, Rome, February 21, 1928. Sandor Teszler Library Archives and Special Collections, Wofford College, Spartanburg SC.

Jensen, Richard Bach. *The Battle against Anarchist Terrorism: An International History, 1878–1934*. New York: Cambridge University Press, 2014.

Johnson, Jeffrey A. *The 1916 Preparedness Day Bombing: Anarchy and Terrorism in Progressive Era America*. New York: Routledge, 2018.

Kemp, Michael. *Bombs, Bullets and Bread: The Politics of Anarchist Terrorism Worldwide, 1866–1926*. Jefferson NC: McFarland & Company, 2018.

Larabee, Ann. *The Wrong Hands: Popular Weapons Manuals and Their Historic Challenges to a Democratic Society*. New York: Oxford University Press, 2015.

Martinez, J. Michael. *Terrorist Attacks on American Soil: From the Civil War Era to the Present*. Lanham MD: Rowman & Littlefield, 2012.

McCann, Joseph T. *Terrorism on American Soil: A Concise History of Plots and Perpetrators from the Famous to the Forgotten*. Boulder CO: Sentient Publications, 2006.

McCormick, Charles H. *Hopeless Cases: The Hunt for the Red Scare Terrorist Bombers*. Lanham MD: University Press of America, 2005.

Meloy, J. Reid, and Jacqueline Genzman. "The Clinical Threat Assessment of the Lone-Actor Terrorist." *Psychiatric Clinics of North America* 39, no. 4 (August 27, 2016): 649–62.

Morgan, Edmund S., and Helen M. Morgan. *The Stamp Act Crisis: Prologue to Revolution*. 3rd ed. Chapel Hill: University of North Carolina Press, 1995.

Parry, Albert. *Terrorism: From Robespierre to Arafat*. New York: Vanguard Press, 1976.

Pernicone, Nunzio. *Carlo Tresca: Portrait of a Rebel*. Oakland CA: AK Press, 2010.

———. "Luigi Galleani and Italian Anarchist Terrorism in the United States." *Studi Emigrazione/Etudes Migrations* 30, no. III (1993): 469–89.

Pernicone, Nunzio, and Fraser M. Ottanelli. *Assassins against the Old Order: Italian Anarchist Violence in Fin de Siècle Europe*. Urbana: University of Illinois Press, 2018.

Pluchinsky, Dennis A. *The Reagan and George H. W. Bush Administrations*. Vol. 2 of *Anti-American Terrorism: From Eisenhower to Trump—A Chronicle of Threat and Response*. London: World Scientific Publishing Europe, 2020.

Post, Louis F. *The Deportations Delirium of Nineteen-Twenty: A Personal Narrative of an Historic Official Experience*. Chicago: Charles H. Kerr & Company, 1923.

Presutto, Michele. "'The Man Who Blew Up Wall Street': The Story of Mario Buda." *Altreitalie: International Journal of Studies on Italian Migrations in the World* (January/June 2010): 83–107.

Price, Michael. "Revenge and the People Who Seek It." *Monitor on Psychology* 40, no. 6 (June 2009). https://www.apa.org/monitor/2009/06/revenge.

Quinn, Adam. "Chronicling Subversion: The *Cronaca Sovversiva* as Both Seditious Rag and Community Paper." *Radical Americas* 3, no. 1 (2018): 1–22.

Raney, Reb. "A Group That Does Things." In *Life of an Anarchist: The Alexander Berkman Reader*, edited by Gene Fellner, 125–27. New York: Seven Stories Press, 1992.

Rapoport, David C. "The Four Waves of Modern Terrorism." In *Attacking Terrorism: Elements of a Grand Strategy*, edited by Audrey Kurth Cronin and James M. Ludes, 46–73. Washington DC: Georgetown University Press, 2004.

Ray, Robin Hazard. "No License to Serve: Prohibition, Anarchists, and the Italian-American Widows of Barre, Vermont, 1900–1920." *Italian Americana* 29, no. 1 (Winter 2011): 5–22.

Reppetto, Thomas A. *Battleground New York City: Countering Spies, Saboteurs, and Terrorists Since 1861*. Washington DC: Potomac Books, 2012.

Richardson, Wendy. "'The Curse of Our Trade': Occupational Disease in a Vermont Granite Town." *Vermont History: The Proceedings of the Vermont Historical Society* 60, no. 1 (Winter 1992): 5–28.

Sartin, Max [pseudonym]. Introduction to *The End of Anarchism?*, by Luigi Galleani, 9–16. Translated by Max Sartin [pseudonym] and Robert D'Attilo. London: Elephant Editions, 2012. First published in English in 1982 by Cienfuegos Press (Orkney, Scotland).

Sayers, Sean. Foreword to *Luigi Galleani: The Most Dangerous Anarchist in America*, by Antonio Senta, 1–11. Translated by Andrea Asali and Sean Sayers. Edinburgh: AK Press, 2019. First published 2018 by Nova Delphi (Rome).

Schmidt, Regin. *Red Scare: FBI and the Origins of Anticommunism in the United States, 1919–1943*. Copenhagen, Denmark: Museum Tusculanum Press, 2000.

Seager, David R. "Barre, Vermont Granite Workers and the Struggle Against Silicosis, 1890–1960." *Labor History* 42, no. 1 (2001): 61–79.

Senta, Antonio. *Luigi Galleani: The Most Dangerous Anarchist in America*. Translated by Andrea Asali and Sean Sayers. Edinburgh: AK Press, 2019. First published 2018 by Nova Delphi (Rome).

Shone, Steve J. *American Anarchism*. Leiden, Netherlands: Brill Academic Publishers, 2013.

Simon, Jeffrey D. *The Alphabet Bomber: A Lone Wolf Terrorist Ahead of His Time*. Lincoln NE: Potomac Books, 2019.

———. "The Forgotten Terrorists: Lessons from the History of Terrorism." *Terrorism and Political Violence* 20, no. 2 (April–June 2008): 195–214.

———. *Lone Wolf Terrorism: Understanding the Growing Threat*. Amherst NY: Prometheus Books, 2013.

———. *Terrorists and the Potential Use of Biological Weapons: A Discussion of Possibilities*. Document no. R-3771-AFMIC. Santa Monica CA: RAND Corporation, December 1989.

———. *The Terrorist Trap: America's Experience with Terrorism*. Bloomington: Indiana University Press, 1994.

Smith, Page. *America Enters the World: A People's History of the Progressive Era and World War I*. Vol. 7 of *A People's History of the United States*. New York: McGraw-Hill, 1985.

Tejada, Susan. *In Search of Sacco and Vanzetti: Double Lives, Troubled Times, and the Massachusetts Murder Case That Shook the World*. Boston: Northeastern University Press, 2012.

Tomchuk, Travis. *Transnational Radicals: Italian Anarchists in Canada and the U.S., 1915–1940*. Winnipeg: University of Manitoba Press, 2015.

Topp, Michael M. *The Sacco and Vanzetti Case: A Brief History with Documents*. Boston: Bedford/St. Martin's, 2005.

———. *Those without a Country: The Political Culture of Italian American Syndicalists*. Minneapolis: University of Minnesota Press, 2001.

Tunney, Thomas J. *Throttled! The Detection of the German and Anarchist Bomb Plotters*. Boston: Small, Maynard & Company, 1919.

Watson, Bruce. *Sacco and Vanzetti: The Men, the Murders, and the Judgment of Mankind*. New York: Viking, 2007.

Weiner, Tim. *Enemies: A History of the FBI*. New York: Random House, 2012.

Zicree, Marc Scott. *The Twilight Zone Companion*. New York: Bantam Books, 1982.

Zimmer, Kenyon. *Immigrants against the State: Yiddish and Italian Anarchism in America*. Urbana: University of Illinois Press, 2015.

———. "'The Whole World Is Our Country': Immigration and Anarchism in the United States, 1885–1940." PhD diss., University of Pittsburgh, 2010. http://d-scholarship.pitt.edu/7910/1/Zimmer_dissertation.pdf.

INDEX